THE
100 BEST
MUTUAL FUNDS
YOU CAN BUY
2001

Gordon K. Williamson

Adams Media Corporation
Holbrook, Massachusetts

Also by Gordon K. Williamson
Big Decisions, Small Investor
Low Risk Investing
Making the Most of Your 401(k)

• • •

Dedication
This book is dedicated to all of my clients.
I would be nowhere without their trust and support.

Acknowledgments
Special thanks to Cynthia Shaffer for her computer skills.
This is a truly thankless job, and I appreciate everything she has done.

Published by Adams Media Corporation
260 Center Street, Holbrook, MA 02343
www.adamsmedia.com

ISBN: 1-58062-424-3

Printed in Canada.

J I H G F E D C B

This publication is designed to provide accurate and authoritative information with regard to the subject matter covered. It is sold with the understanding that the publisher is not engaged in rendering legal, accounting, or other professional advice. If legal advice or other expert assistance is required, the services of a competent professional person should be sought.
—From a *Declaration of Principles* jointly adopted by a Committee of the American Bar Association and a Committee of Publishers and Associations

While due care has been taken to ensure accurate and current data, the ideas, principles, conclusions, and general suggestions contained in this volume are subject to the laws and regulations of local, state, and federal authorities, as well as to court cases and any revisions of court cases. Due to the magnitude of the database and the complexity of the subject matter, occasional errors are possible; the publisher assumes no liability direct or incidental for any actions or investments made by readers of this book, and strongly suggests that readers seek consultation with legal, financial, or accounting professionals before making any investment.

The data used to analyze the funds is current through June 30, 2000.

This book is available at quantity discounts for bulk purchases.
For information, call 1-800-872-5627.

Visit our exciting small business Web site at businesstown.com

Contents

I.
About This Book

There are roughly 6 million business entities operating in the United States; close to 15,000 of these businesses are publicly held (meaning they have issued stock to the public). Of the 15,000 publicly traded companies, fewer than 4,000 are listed on the New York Stock Exchange (NYSE). The world's total stock market capitalization is approximately $20 trillion, one-half of which is represented by domestic equities.

There are over 13,000 mutual funds. There are well over three times as many mutual funds as there are stocks listed on the NYSE! The mutual fund industry is now the second largest financial institution in the nation, with assets exceeding $7 trillion, up from $1 trillion in 1991. By the beginning of the year 2000, U.S. households held 81 percent of mutual fund assets, up from 74 percent in 1990. Individual stocks and mutual funds accounted for 38 percent of U.S. households' financial assets, surpassing the previous all-time high of 34 percent in 1968. Just under 49 million households own shares of one or more mutual funds, up from 4.6 million in 1980.

Mutual funds are the *best* investment vehicle that has been developed in the 20th century. When properly selected, these vehicles combine professional management, ease of purchase and redemption, simple record keeping, risk reduction, and superb performance, all in one type of investment. There are dozens of other types of investments, but none match the overall versatility of mutual funds.

A mutual fund is simply one method of investing. When you invest in a fund, your money is pooled with thousands of other investors' monies. This large pool of money is overseen by the fund's management. These managers invest this pool of money in one or more types of investments. The universe of investments includes common stocks, preferred stocks, corporate bonds, tax-free municipal bonds, U.S. government obligations, zero-coupon bonds, convertible securities, gold, silver, foreign securities, and even real estate. The amount of money invested in one or more of these categories depends upon the fund's objectives and restrictions and on the management's perception of the economy.

The beauty of mutual funds is that once the investor decides upon the *type* of investment desired there are several funds that fulfill that criterion. As an example, someone who needs current income would be attracted to bond funds (or a series of equity-oriented funds coupled with what is known as a "systematic withdrawal plan"—a monthly income program described in Appendix D). A person interested in appreciation would focus on an aggressive growth, growth and income, and/or international stock fund. A person who wanted some current income plus some growth to offset the effects of inflation should consider a balanced fund.

The track records of these funds can easily be obtained, as contrasted to the track records of stockbrokers, who are not ranked at all. A few mutual fund sources even look at a fund's risk-adjusted return, a standard of measurement that has not been sufficiently emphasized in the past.

This book was written to fill a void. There are already several mutual fund books and directories, but none deal exclusively with the very best funds. More important, *none of these publications measure risk properly*.

This is the 11th edition of this book. If you have read one or more of the previous editions, you will notice that this edition includes many funds not previously listed and that several of the *previous* "100 Best" are not included here. This does not mean that you should sell or transfer from a previous recommendation to one that appears in this edition. For the most part, mutual funds described in past editions are still excellent choices and should not be moved. There are a number of reasons why a fund no longer appears in this, or previous, editions. These reasons will be detailed in Chapter 10.

Moving from one fund to another can often spell trouble. Consider a Morningstar study that compared the performance of its growth fund index with the average investor's return during the five-year period ending May 31, 1994. While the overall market gained, on average, 12.5 percent a year, the average investor *lost* 2.5 percent a year. Volatility can make it easy for investors to forget about the long-term case for stocks. In the third quarter of 1999, when the market suffered, the possibility of choosing a stock that dropped 20 percent or more in value was one in four, versus one in a 1,000 for a mutual fund.

Speaking of performance, unusually high stock returns during the 1990s has caused investor expectations to soar. Recent chart-toppers have threatened to raise expectations even higher: 177 funds posted 1999 returns of more than 100 percent. From 1989 to 1998, only 10 funds could claim an annual return that high.

Other sources give almost endless numbers and performance statistics for hundreds and hundreds of mutual funds, leaving readers to draw their own conclusions as to what are the best funds. This book will save you a great deal of time because it has taken the over 13,000 existing funds and narrowed them down to the best 100, ranked by specific category and risk level. Even money market funds are included, a category rarely covered by any other publication.

Investors and financial advisors are not concerned with mediocre or poor performers; they simply want the best funds, *given certain parameters*. Personal investment considerations should include (in order of priority) your time horizon, risk tolerance, financial goals, existing portfolio, and tax bracket. Parameters within a given fund category include risk, performance, and consistency.

Current books and periodicals that cover funds focus on how a fund has performed in the past. Studies clearly point out that a fund whose performance is in the top half one year has a 50–50 chance of being in the bottom half the next year, or the year after that. Since there is little correlation between the past and the future when it comes to market returns, this book concentrates on consistency in management and the amount of risk assumed.

The model used to rank the 100 best is fully described in a later chapter. It is a logical, common-sense approach that cuts through the statistical jargon; it is also easy to understand. As my dad used to say, "There is nothing as uncommon as common sense."

II.
What Is a Mutual Fund?

A mutual fund is an investment company—an entity that makes investments on behalf of individuals and institutions who share common financial goals. The fund pools the money of many people, each with a different amount to invest. Professional money managers then use the pool of money to buy a variety of stocks, bonds, or money market instruments that, in their judgment, will help the fund's shareholders achieve their financial objectives.

Each fund has an investment objective, described in the fund's prospectus, that is important to both the manager and the potential investor. The fund manager uses it as a guide when choosing investments for the fund's portfolio. Prospective investors use it to determine which funds are suitable for their own needs. Mutual funds' investment objectives cover a wide range. Some follow aggressive investment policies, involving greater risk, in search of higher returns; others seek current income from more conservative investments.

When the fund earns money, it distributes the earnings to its shareholders. Earnings come from stock dividends, interest paid by bonds or money market instruments, and gains from the sale of securities in the fund's portfolio. Dividends and capital gains produced are paid out in proportion to the number of fund shares owned. Thus, shareholders who invest a few hundred dollars get the same investment return per dollar as those who invest hundreds of thousands.

Mutual funds remain popular because they are convenient and efficient investment vehicles that give all individuals—even those with small sums to invest—access to a splendid array of opportunities. Mutual funds are uniquely democratic institutions. They can take a portfolio of giant blue-chip companies like IBM, General Electric, and General Motors and slice it into small enough pieces so that almost anyone can buy.

Mutual funds allow you to participate in foreign stock and bond markets that might otherwise demand too much time, expertise, or expense to be worthwhile. International funds make investing across national borders no more difficult than investing across state lines. Over the next decade, as securities markets develop in the former Iron Curtain countries, mutual funds will no doubt give investors many opportunities to participate in those markets as well.

Mutual funds have opened up a world of fixed-income investing to people who, until recently, had few choices apart from passbook accounts and savings bonds. Through bond funds, shareholders can tap into the interest payments from any kind of fixed-income security you can imagine—and many you have never heard of. The range goes from U.S. Treasury bonds (T-bonds) to collateralized mortgage obligations

(CMOs), adjustable-rate preferred stock, floating-rate notes, and even to other countries' debts—denominated both in U.S. dollars and in other currencies.

What is heavily marketed is not necessarily what is appropriate for you to invest in. A global biotechnology fund may be a great investment, but it may not be the right mutual fund for you. Buying what is "hot" rather than what is appropriate is one of the most common mistakes made by investors and an issue that is addressed throughout this book.

A reason to invest is to offset the effects of inflation. Over time, inflation can erode individuals' purchasing power. Mutual funds that invest primarily in common stocks may help keep you ahead of inflation over the long term.

	year	amount
a gallon of milk	2018	$5.16
	1998	$2.88
	1978	$1.42
a new car	2018	$33,271
	1998	$18,565
	1978	$6,478
a gallon of gasoline	2018	$1.90
	1998	$1.06
	1978	$0.67

Source: Economic and Statistic Administration, U.S. Bureau of Economic Analysis.

III.
How to Invest in a Mutual Fund

Investing in a mutual fund means buying shares of the fund. An investor becomes an owner of shares in the fund just as he or she might be an owner of shares of stock in a large corporation. The difference is that a fund's only business is investing in securities, and the price of its shares is directly related to the value of the securities held by the fund.

Mutual funds continually issue new shares for purchase by the public. The price per share for existing fund investors is not decreased by the ongoing issuance of new shares because each share created is offset by the amount of new money coming in. Phrased another way, new money that comes into the fund is used to purchase additional securities in order not to dilute the income or value for existing shareholders.

A fund's share price can change from day to day, depending on the daily value of the securities held by the fund. The share price is called the net asset value (NAV), which is calculated as follows. The total value of the fund's investments at the end of the day, after expenses, is divided by the number of shares outstanding.

Newspapers report mutual fund activity every day. An example from the *Wall Street Journal* is shown below.

Everett Funds:

Evrt r	12.38	NL	−.01
MaxRtn	18.39	NL	+.06
ValTr	12.33	NL	−.01
LtdSl	17.71	NL	−.14
ExtrMid	2.82	2.95	−.02
ExJY p	7.24	7.60	+.01
FBK Gth t	11.06	11.06	..

FJA Funds:

Capit f	14.67	15.69	−.02
NwHrz	9.65	10.10	..
Permt	12.91	13.81	..
Perrin	20.96	22.42	−.02

The first column in the table is the fund's abbreviated name. Several funds under a single heading indicate a family of funds.

The second column is the net asset value (NAV) per share as of the close of the preceding business day. In some newspapers, the NAV is identified as the sell or the bid price—the amount per share you would receive if you sold your shares.

Each mutual fund determines its net asset value every business day by dividing the market value of its total assets, less liabilities, by the number of shares outstanding. On any given day, you can determine the value of your holdings by multiplying the NAV by the number of shares you own.

The third column is usually the offering price or, in some papers, the buy or the asked price—the price you would pay if you purchased shares. The buy price is the NAV plus any sales charges. If there are no sales charges, an NL for no load appears in this column. In such a case, the buy price would be the same as the NAV.

The next column shows the change, if any, in the net asset value (NAV) from the preceding quotation—in other words, the change over the most recent one-day trading period. Thus, if you see a "+.06" in the newspaper next to your fund, *each* of your shares in the fund went up in value by six cents during the previous day.

A *p* following the abbreviated name of the fund denotes a fund that charges a fee that is subtracted from assets for marketing and distribution costs, also known as a 12b-1 plan (named after the federal government rule that permits such an expense). If the fund name is followed by an *r*, the fund has a contingent deferred sales load (CDSL) or a redemption fee. A CDSL is a charge incurred if shares are sold within a certain period; a redemption fee is a cost you would pay *whenever* shares are sold. An *f* indicates a fund that habitually enters the previous day's prices, instead of the current day's. A *t* designates a fund that has both a CDSL or a redemption fee and a 12b-1 plan.

IV.
How a Mutual Fund Operates

A mutual fund is owned by all of its shareholders, the people who purchased shares of the fund. The day-to-day operation of a fund is delegated to a management company.

The management company, often the organization that created the fund, may offer other mutual funds, financial products, and financial services as well. The management company usually serves as the fund's investment advisor.

The investment advisor manages the fund's portfolio of securities. The advisor is paid for its services in the form of a fee that is based on the total value of the fund's assets; fees average 0.5 percent. The advisor employs professional portfolio managers who invest the fund's money by purchasing a number of stocks or bonds or money market instruments, depending on what type of fund it is.

These fund professionals decide where to invest the fund's assets. The money managers make their investment decisions based on extensive, ongoing research into the financial performance of individual companies, taking into account general economic and market trends. In addition, they are backed up by economic and statistical resources. On the basis of their research, money managers decide what and when to buy, sell, or hold for the fund's portfolio, in light of the fund's specific investment objective.

In addition to the investment advisor, the fund may also contract with an underwriter that arranges for the distribution of the fund's shares to the investing public. The underwriter may act as a wholesaler, selling fund shares to security dealers, or it may retail directly to the public.

V.
Different Categories of Mutual Funds

Aggressive Growth. The investment objective of aggressive growth funds is maximum capital gains, with little or no concern for dividends or income of any kind. What makes this category of mutual funds unique is that fund managers often have the ability to use borrowed money (leverage) to increase positions. Sometimes they deal in stock options and futures contracts (commodities). These trading techniques sound, and can be, scary, but such activities represent only a minor portion of the funds' holdings.

Because of their bullish dispositions, these funds will usually stay fully invested in the stock market. For investors, this means better-than-expected results during good (bull) markets and worse-than-average losses during bad (bear) market periods. Fortunately, the average bull market is almost four times as long as the typical bear market.

Do not be confused by economic conditions and stock market performance. There have been eight recessions since World War II. During seven of those eight recessions, U.S. stocks went up. During all eight recessions, stocks posted impressive gains in the second half of every recession. By the same token, do not underestimate the impact of a loss. A 20 percent decline means that you must make 25 percent to break even. A loss of 20 percent does not happen very often to aggressive growth funds, particularly on a calendar year basis, but you should be aware that such extreme downward moves are possible. Often brokers like to focus on the +45 percent and +50 percent years, such as 1980 and 1991, while glossing over a bad year, such as 1984, when aggressive growth funds were down almost 13 percent on average.

One of the great wonders of the stock market is how volatility of returns is reduced when one's holding period is increased. Because of this, aggressive growth funds should only be owned by one of two kinds of investors: those who can live with high levels of daily, monthly, quarterly, and/or annual price per share fluctuations, and those who realize the importance of a diversified portfolio that cuts across several investment categories—the investor who looks at how the entire package is performing, not just one segment.

The typical price-earnings (p/e) ratio for stocks in this category is 46, a figure that is about 24 percent higher than the S & P 500 Index (which has an average p/e ratio of 37). This group of funds has an average beta of 1.0, making its *market-related* risk the same as that of the S & P 500 (which always has a beta of 1.0, no matter what market conditions or levels are).

The standard deviation for aggressive growth funds is 39 percent. This means that one's expected return for any given year may vary either way by 39 percent.

In other words, since aggressive growth funds have averaged 38.1 percent over the past three years, annual returns are expected to range from –0.9 percent (38.1–39) to 77.1 percent (38.1 + 39). This would represent *one* standard deviation (39 percent in the case of aggressive growth funds). A single standard deviation accounts for what you can expect every two out of three months (67 percent of the time or roughly two out of every three years). If you are looking for greater assurance, then two standard deviations must be used (multiply 39 percent times 2 in this case). This means that returns for about 95 percent of the months (two standard deviations) would be 38.1 percent plus or minus 78 percent. In other words, a range of –39.9 percent to +116.1 percent.

Small-company stocks have an average p/e ratio of 32. (The price-earnings ratio refers to the selling price of a stock in relation to its annual earnings. Thus a fund category that has a p/e ratio of, say, 10 is comprised of mutual funds whose typical stock in the portfolio is selling for 10 times what the corporation's earnings are for the year.) Small-company stock funds have a standard deviation of 33 percent and a beta of 0.8 percent, figures that support the view that this category is less volatile than aggressive growth funds.

Historical returns over the past 3, 5, 10, and 15 years for aggressive growth and small-company stock funds are shown below. All of the figures shown are average *annual* rates of return (all periods ending March 31, 2000).

category	3 years	5 years	10 years	15 years
aggressive growth	38%	28%	18%	16%
small company stocks	24%	20%	17%	15%
S & P 500	22%	25%	18%	17%
T-bills	5%	5%	5%	6%
CPI (rate of inflation)	2%	2%	3%	3%

The aggressive growth fund category is dominated by technology and service stocks. Technology alone represents close to 48 percent of the typical aggressive growth fund's portfolio, followed by 20 percent in service and 9 percent in health stocks. Small-company stocks are also dominated by technology (33 percent) and service issues (19 percent).

Balanced. This kind of fund invests in common stocks and corporate bonds. The weighting given to stocks depends upon the fund manager's perception of, or belief in, the market. The more bullish the manager is, the more likely the portfolio will be loaded up with equities. Yet no matter how strongly management feels about the stock market, it would be very rare to see stocks equal more than 67 percent of the portfolio. Similarly, no matter how bearish one becomes, it would be unlikely for a balanced fund to have more than 67 percent of its holdings represented by bonds. Often a fund's prospectus will outline the weighting ranges: The fund's managers must stay within these wide boundaries at all times. A small portion of these funds is made up of cash equivalents (T-bills, CDs, commercial paper, etc.) with a very small amount sometimes dedicated to preferred stocks and convertible securities.

Three other categories, "multi-asset global," "convertible," and "asset alloca-tion" have been combined with balanced funds for the purposes of this book. This grouping together is logical; because overall objectives are largely similar, general portfolio composition can be virtually identical in many cases, and the fund man-agers in each of these categories have the flexibility to load up heavily on stocks, bonds, preferreds, or convertible securities.

Multi-asset global funds typically emphasize bonds more than stocks or cash. It is not uncommon to see a multi-asset global fund that has 60 percent of its hold-ings in bonds, with 10 to 20 percent in stocks, and the remainder in foreign equi-ties, preferred stocks, and cash. For the *stock* portion of this category, the p/e ratio is 35 and the standard deviation is 14 percent. On the bond side, the average matu-rity of debt instruments in the portfolio is 10 years.

Convertible funds, as the name implies, are made up mostly of convertible preferred stocks and convertible bonds. The conversion feature allows the owner, the fund in this case, to convert or exchange securities for the corporation's common stock. Conversion and price appreciation take place during bull-market periods. Uncertain or down markets make conversion much less likely; instead, management falls back on the comparatively high dividend or interest payments that convertibles enjoy. The typical convertible fund has somewhere between two-thirds and three-quarters of its holdings in convertibles; the balance is in cash, stocks, and preferreds. For the stock portion of this category, the p/e ratio is 34 and the standard deviation is 17 percent. On the bond side, the average maturity of debt instruments in the portfolio is seven years.

Asset allocation funds, like other categories that fall under the broad defini-tion of "balanced," are hybrid in nature—part equity and part debt. These funds have a tendency to emphasize stocks over bonds. A fund manager who wants to take a defensive posture may stay on the sidelines by converting moderate or large parts of the portfolio into cash equivalents. The average asset allocation fund has somewhere between 50 and 65 percent of its portfolio in common stocks, with the remainder in bonds, foreign stocks, and cash. For the stock portion of this category, the p/e ratio is 34 and the standard deviation is 13 percent. On the bond side, the average maturity of debt instruments in the portfolio is nine years.

The typical price-earnings (p/e) ratio for stocks in this category is 33, a figure that is lower than that of the S & P 500. This group of funds has an average beta of 0.6, making its *market-related risk* 40 percent less than the S & P 500. Keep in mind that beta refers to a portfolio's *stock market-related* risk—it is not a mean-ingful way to measure bond or foreign security risk. The typical bond in these funds has an average maturity of nine years.

The standard deviation for balanced funds is 12 percent, approximately one-fourth the level of aggressive growth funds. This means that one's expected return for any given year will vary by 12 percent. (For example, if you were expecting an annualized return of 14 percent, your actual return would range from 2 percent to 26 percent most of the time.)

Historical returns over the past 3, 5, 10, and 15 years for balanced, multi-asset global, convertible, and asset allocation funds are shown below. All of the figures shown are average *annual* rates of return (all periods ending March 31, 2000).

category	3 years	5 years	10 years	15 years
balanced	14%	15%	12%	12%
multi-asset global	11%	12%	8%	10%
convertible	21%	18%	15%	14%
asset allocation	15%	15%	12%	10%
Corp./Gov't Bond Index	7%	7%	8%	9%

The equity portion of the balanced fund category is dominated by technology and service stocks. These two groups represent over one-third of the typical balanced fund's stock portfolio. The other three top equity sectors are financials, industrial cyclicals, and health stocks.

Like other hybrid funds, balanced funds provide an income stream. The average yield of balanced, multi-asset global, and asset allocation funds is under 2.5 percent. The typical yield for convertible securities funds is about 2.8 percent. High-tax-bracket investors who want to invest in these funds should consider using tax-sheltered money, if possible. Balanced, multi-asset global, asset allocation, and convertible bond funds are particularly attractive within an IRA, other qualified retirement plans, or variable annuities. (For more information about both fixed-rate and variable annuities, see two of my other books, *The 100 Best Annuities* and *Getting Started In Annuities*.)

Corporate Bonds. These funds invest in debt instruments (IOUs) issued by corporations, governments, and agencies of the U.S. government. Perhaps the typical corporate bond fund should be called a "government-corporate" fund. Bond funds have a wide range of maturities. The name of the fund will often indicate whether it is made up of short-term or medium-term obligations. If the name of the fund does not include the words "short-term" or "intermediate," then the fund most likely invests in bonds with average maturities over 10 years. The greater the maturity, the more the fund's share value can change. There is an inverse relationship between interest rates and the value of a bond; when one moves up, the other goes down.

The weighted maturity date of the bonds within this group averages eight years, with a typical coupon rate of 6.9 percent. (The coupon rate represents what the corporation or government pays out annually on a per-bond basis.) All bonds have a maturity date—a date when the issuer (the government, municipality, or corporation) pays back the *face value* of the bond (which is almost always $1,000 per bond) and stops paying interest. There are often hundreds of different securities in any given bond fund. Each one of these securities (bonds in this case) has a maturity date; these maturity dates can range anywhere from a few days to up to 30 years. "Weighted maturity" refers to the time left until the average bond in the portfolio comes due (matures).

The standard deviation for corporate bonds is 3 percent, less than one-third of that found with balanced funds. This means that one's expected return for any given month, quarter, or year will be more predictable than almost any other category of mutual funds.

Using a beta measurement for bonds is of little value, because beta defines *stock market* risk and has nothing to do with interest-rate or financial risk. Historical returns over the past 3, 5, 10, and 15 years for corporate bond funds are shown below. All of the figures shown are average *annual* rates of return (all periods ending March 31, 2000).

category	3 years	5 years	10 years	15 years
corporate bond funds	6%	6%	7%	9%
government bond funds	6%	6%	7%	8%
municipal bond funds	4%	5%	6%	8%
world bond funds	3%	7%	6%	10%
CPI (rate of inflation)	2%	2%	3%	3%

Like income funds, corporate funds provide a high yield that is fully taxable and should be sheltered whenever possible. The average yield of these bond funds is just over 6 percent.

Global Stock. This category of mutual funds invests in equities issued by domestic and foreign firms. Fifteen of the 20 largest corporations in the world are located outside of the United States. It makes sense to be able to invest in these and other corporations and industries—to be able to take advantage of opportunities wherever they appear. Global, also known as world, stock funds have the ability to invest in any country. The more countries a fund is able to invest in, the lower its overall risk level will be; often return potential will also increase.

For the purposes of this book, the global stock category includes foreign and international equity funds. When it comes to investing in mutual funds, the words "foreign" and "international" are interchangeable. A foreign, or international, fund invests in securities outside of the United States. Some foreign funds are broadly diversified, including stocks from European as well as Pacific Basin economies. Other international funds specialize in a particular region or country. A global fund invests in domestic as well as foreign securities. The portfolio manager of a global fund generally has more latitude in the securities selected, since either domestic or foreign securities can end up representing 50 percent or more of the portfolio, depending upon management's view of the different markets, whereas a foreign or international fund may not be allowed to invest in U.S. stocks or bonds.

The typical price-earnings (p/e) ratio for stocks in this category is 36, a figure that is virtually identical to that of the S & P 500. This group of funds has an average beta of 0.8, meaning that its *U.S. market-related* risk is about 20 percent less than that of the general market, as measured by the S & P 500. The standard deviation for global stock funds is 24 percent, versus 27 percent for growth funds.

Foreign stock funds, which are exclusive of U.S. investments, have a p/e ratio of 37. Their standard deviation over the past three years has been 24 percent. Pacific Basin funds, a more narrowly focused type of foreign fund, have an average p/e ratio of 36 and a standard deviation of 36 percent. European funds, another type of specialized international fund, have a price-earnings ratio of 35 and a standard deviation of 25 percent.

Historical returns over the past 3, 5, 10, and 15 years for global stocks are shown below. All of the figures shown are average *annual* rates of return (all periods ending March 31, 2000).

category	3 years	5 years	10 years	15 years
global stock funds	22%	20%	13%	15%
foreign stock funds	18%	15%	11%	16%
emerging markets funds	4%	8%	9%	11%
Pacific Basin funds	7%	6%	6%	12%
European funds	20%	21%	12%	n/a

The four areas that dominate world stock funds are the United States (36 percent of a typical fund's holdings), Europe (35 percent), Japan (10 percent), and the Pacific Rim (6 percent).

Government Bonds. These funds invest in securities issued by the U.S. government or one of its agencies (or former affiliates), such as GNMA, FHLMC, or FNMA. Investors are attracted to bond funds of all kinds for two reasons. First, bond funds have monthly distributions; individual bonds pay interest only semiannually. Second, effective management can control interest rate risk by varying the average maturity of the fund's portfolio. If management believes that interest rates are moving downward, the fund will load up heavily on long-term obligations. If rates do decline, long-term bonds will appreciate more than their short- and medium-term counterparts. Conversely, if the manager anticipates rate hikes, average portfolio maturity can be pared down so that there will be only modest principal deterioration if rates do go up.

Bond funds have portfolios with a wide range of maturities. Many funds use their names to characterize their maturity structure. Generally, "short term" means that the portfolio has a weighted average maturity of less than five years. "Intermediate" implies an average maturity of 5 to 10 years, and "long term" is over 10 years. The longer the maturity, the greater the change in the fund's price per share (your principal) when interest rates change. Longer-term bond funds are riskier than short-term funds but tend to offer higher yields. The top holdings of government bond funds are GNMAs and U.S. Treasury notes (T-notes) of varying maturities.

The weighted maturity date of the bonds within this group averages just under nine years, with a typical coupon rate of 7 percent (the coupon rate represents what is paid out annually on a per bond basis)—figures that are virtually identical to the corporate bond category. These funds have a standard deviation of 3 percent— again the figure is almost identical to that for corporate bonds. This means that corporate and government bonds have similar volatilities.

Historical returns over the past 3, 5, 10, and 15 years for government bond funds are shown below (all periods ending March 31, 2000).

category	3 years	5 years	10 years	15 years
government bond funds	6%	6%	7%	8%
high-yield bond funds	4%	8%	10%	9%
CPI (rate of inflation)	2%	2%	3%	3%
utility funds	22%	19%	14%	14%
convertible bond funds	21%	18%	15%	14%

Like corporate bond funds, government funds provide a high yield that is fully taxable on the federal level and should be sheltered whenever possible. Interest from direct obligations of the U.S. government—T-bonds, T-notes, T-bills, EE bonds, and HH bonds—are exempt from state and local income taxes. This means that a part of the income you receive from funds that include such securities is exempt from *state* taxes.

Corporate bonds are rated as to their safety. The two major rating services are Moody's and Standard and Poor's. By reading the fund's prospectus or by telephoning the mutual fund company, you can find out how safe a corporate bond fund is. The vast majority of these funds are extremely conservative and safety (default) is not really an issue. U.S. government bonds are not rated since it is believed that there is no chance of default—unlike a corporation, the federal government can print money.

Growth. These funds seek capital appreciation with dividend income as a distant secondary concern. Indeed, the average annual income stream from growth funds is just 1.3 percent. Investors who are attracted to growth funds are aiming to sell stock at a profit; they are not normally income oriented. If you are interested in current income you will want to look at Appendix D: Systematic Withdrawal Plan.

Growth funds are attracted to equities from large, well-established corporations. Unlike aggressive growth funds, growth funds may end up holding large cash positions during market declines or when investors are nervous about recent economic or market activities. The typical price-earnings (p/e) ratio for stocks in this category is 38, compared to 37 for the S & P 500. This group of funds has an average beta of 0.9, which is roughly 10 percent less than the S & P 500.

The standard deviation for growth funds is 27 percent. This means that one's expected return for any given year will vary by 27 percentage points. As an example, if you were expecting a 15 percent annual return, annual returns would probably range between negative 12 percent and positive 42 percent (15 percent plus or minus 27 percent).

Historical returns over the past 3, 5, 10, and 15 years for growth and small-company stock funds are shown below. All of the figures shown are average *annual* rates of return (all periods ending March 31, 2000).

category	3 years	5 years	10 years	15 years
growth funds	28%	25%	18%	17%
small-company stock funds	24%	20%	17%	15%
S & P 500	22%	25%	18%	17%
growth & income funds	19%	20%	15%	14%
global stock funds	22%	20%	13%	15%

Technology (33 percent of the typical portfolio), service (17 percent), financial (12 percent), and health stocks (10 percent) dominate growth funds.

Growth and Income. With a name like this, one would think that this category of mutual funds is almost equally as concerned with income as it is with growth. The fact is, growth and income funds have an average dividend yield of just 1.25 percent. This boost in income is due to the small holdings in bonds and convertibles possessed by most growth and income funds.

The typical price-earnings (p/e) ratio for stocks in this category is 32, versus 37 for the S & P 500. This group of funds has an average beta of 0.9, meaning that its *market-related risk* is 10 percent less than that of the general market, as measured by the S & P 500.

The standard deviation for growth and income funds is 21 percent, about 20 percent less than that found with the average growth fund. This means that, as a group, growth and income funds have slightly more predictable returns than growth funds.

For the purposes of this book, a second category, "equity-income funds," has been combined with growth and income. Equity-income funds have a lower standard deviation (18 percent compared to 21 percent for growth and income funds), a higher yield (1.6 percent compared to 1.2 percent), and a lower beta (0.8 percent compared to 0.9 percent for growth and income funds).

The typical growth and income fund is divided as follows: 90 percent in common stocks (4 percent of which is in foreign stock), 4 percent in cash, 2 percent in bonds, and 4 percent in other assets. The average equity-income fund is divided as follows: 84 percent in common stocks (5 percent of which is in foreign stock), 5 percent in bonds, 3 percent in cash, and 3 percent in other assets. The typical price-earnings (p/e) ratio for stocks in this category is 25.

Historical returns over the past 3, 5, 10, and 15 years for growth and income funds are shown below. All of the figures shown are average *annual* rates of return (all periods ending March 31, 2000).

category	3 years	5 years	10 years	15 years
growth and income funds	19%	20%	15%	14%
equity-income funds	13%	16%	13%	13%
growth funds	28%	25%	18%	17%
balanced funds	14%	15%	12%	12%
foreign stock funds	18%	15%	11%	16%

Technology, financial, and service stocks dominate growth and income funds, representing over half of the typical portfolio. Industrial cyclicals, health, and energy stocks represent the other major industry groups for this category.

High-Yield. These funds generally invest in lower-rated corporate debt instruments. Bonds are characterized as either "bank quality," also known as "investment grade," or "junk." Investment-grade bonds are bonds rated AAA, AA, A, or BAA; junk bonds are instruments rated less than BAA: BA, B, CCC, CC, C, and

D. High-yield bonds, also referred to as junk bonds, offer investors higher yields in exchange for the additional risk of default. High-yield bonds are subject to less *interest-rate risk* than regular corporate or government bonds. However, when the economy slows or people panic, these bonds can quickly drop in value.

The average weighted maturity date of the bonds within this group is seven years, a figure similar to that for high-quality corporate and government bond funds. The typical coupon rate is 9 percent. (The coupon rate represents what the corporation pays out annually on a per bond basis.) When it comes to high-yield bonds, investors would be wise to accept a lower yield in return for more stability of principal and appreciation potential. As with income funds, corporate funds provide a high yield that is fully taxable and should be sheltered whenever possible.

The standard deviation for high-yield bond funds is 8 percent, a figure that is more than twice the rate of corporate and government bond funds as a whole but 4 percent less than balanced and 5 percent less than global bond funds. Historical returns over the past 3, 5, 10, and 15 years for high-yield corporate bond funds are shown below. All of the figures shown are average *annual* rates of return (all periods ending March 31, 2000).

category	3 years	5 years	10 years	15 years
high-yield bond funds	4%	8%	10%	9%
corporate bond funds	6%	6%	7%	9%
government bond funds	6%	6%	7%	8%
world bond funds	3%	7%	6%	10%
balanced funds	14%	15%	12%	12%

Metals and Natural Resources. Metals funds invest in precious metals and mining stocks from around the world. The majority of these stocks are located in North America; South Africa and Australia are the only other major players. Most of these companies specialize in gold mining. Some funds own gold and silver bullion outright. Direct ownership of the metal is considered to be a more conservative posture than owning stocks of mining companies; these stocks are more volatile than the metal itself.

Metals funds, also known as gold funds, are the most speculative group represented in this book. They are considered to be a sector or specialty fund in that they are only able to invest in a single industry or country. Metals funds enjoy international diversification but are still narrowly focused; the limitations of the fund are what make it so unpredictable. Usually, fund management can invest in only three things: mining stocks, direct metal ownership (bullion or coins), and cash equivalents.

Despite their volatile nature, gold funds are included in the book because they can actually reduce portfolio risk. Why? Because gold and other investments often move in opposite directions. For example, when government bonds are moving down in value, gold funds often increase in value. What could otherwise be viewed as a wild investment becomes somewhat tame when included as part of a diversified portfolio.

The typical dividend for metal funds is 0.5 percent. The typical price-earnings (p/e) ratio for stocks in this category is 31, about 20 percent less than the p/e ratio for the S & P 500.

This group of funds has an average beta of 0.7, meaning that its stock market-related risk is modest—but do not let this fool you. We are only talking about *stock market risk*. Beta focuses on that portion of risk that investors cannot reduce by further diversification in U.S. stocks. Metals funds, as shown by their wild track record, are anything but conservative. A 0.7 beta indicates that movement in this category has a fair amount to do with the direction of the S & P 500, therefore, risk can be reduced by further diversification. The standard deviation for metals funds is 36 percent, versus a standard deviation of 63 percent for technology funds and 35 percent for emerging markets funds.

Another category, natural resources, has been combined with metals funds for this book. As the name implies, natural resources funds are commodity-driven, just as metals funds are heavily influenced by two commodities: gold and silver. In the case of natural resources funds, the prices of oil, gas, and timber are the driving force. Natural resources funds invest in companies that are involved with the discovery, exploration, development, refinement, storage, and transportation of one or more of these three natural resources. The standard deviation for this group is 30 percent, beta is 0.8, and the p/e ratio is 34.

Historical returns over the past 3, 5, 10, and 15 years for metals and natural resources funds are shown below. All of the figures shown are average *annual* rates of return (all periods ending March 31, 2000).

category	3 years	5 years	10 years	15 years
metals funds	–21%	–13%	–7%	–2%
aggressive growth funds	38%	28%	18%	16%
natural resources funds	2%	9%	8%	9%
emerging markets funds	4%	8%	9%	11%
CPI (rate of inflation)	2%	2%	3%	3%

Money Market. These funds invest in short-term money market instruments such as bank CDs, T-bills, and commercial paper. By maintaining a short average maturity and investing in high-quality instruments, money market funds are able to maintain a stable $1 net asset value. Since money market funds offer higher yields than a bank's insured money market deposit accounts, they are a very attractive haven for savings or temporary investment dollars. Like bond funds, money market funds come in both taxable and tax-free versions. Reflecting their tax-free status, municipal money market funds pay lower *before-tax* yields than taxable money market funds but can offer higher returns on an *after-tax* basis.

Since the price per share of taxable money market funds always stays at $1, interest is shown by the accumulation of additional shares. (For example, at the beginning of the year you may have 1,000 shares, and by the end of the year 1,050. The 50-share increase, or $50, represents interest.) There are no such things as capital gains or unrecognized gains in a money market fund. The entire return, or yield, is fully taxable (except in the case of a tax-free money market fund where your gain or return would always be exempt from federal taxes and possibly state income taxes as well).

These funds are designed as a place to park your money for a relatively short period of time, in anticipation of a major purchase such as a car or house, or until conditions appear more favorable for stocks, bonds, and/or real estate. There has only been one money market fund, now defunct, that has ever lost money for its investors (most of whom were bankers).

There are approximately 900 taxable money market funds and 450 tax-exempt money funds. By far the largest money market fund is the Merrill Lynch CMA Money Fund ($68 billion). As of March 31, 2000, the 10 largest money market funds controlled close to $350 billion and had an average maturity of 58 days. The five highest-yielding taxable money market funds as of the middle of 2000 were Strong Investors Money Fund (5.6 percent over the past 12 months), Scudder Premium Money Market Shares (5.5 percent), OLDE Premium Plus MM Series (5.4 percent), Zurich YieldWise Government Money Fund (5.4 percent), and Aon Money Market Fund (5.4 percent).

The standard deviation for money market funds is lower than any other category of mutual funds. Historical returns over the past 3, 5, 10, and 15 years for taxable and tax-free money market funds are shown below. All of the figures shown are average *annual* rates of return (all periods ending March 31, 2000).

category	3 years	5 years	10 years	15 years
money market funds	5%	5%	5%	6%
tax-free money market funds	3%	3%	3%	4%
gov't money market funds	5%	5%	5%	6%
government bond funds	6%	6%	7%	8%
CPI (rate of inflation)	2%	2%	3%	3%

Municipal Bonds. Also known as tax-free, these funds are made up of tax-free debt instruments issued by states, counties, districts, or political subdivisions. Interest from municipal bonds is normally exempt from federal income tax. In almost all states, interest is also exempt from state and local income taxes if the portfolio is made up of issues from the investor's state of residence, a U.S territory (Puerto Rico, the U.S. Virgin Islands, etc.), or the District of Columbia.

Until the early 1980s, municipal bonds were almost as sensitive to interest rate changes as corporate and government bonds. During the last several years, however, tax-free bonds have taken on a new personality. Now when interest rates change, municipal bonds exhibit only one-half to one-third the price change that occurs with similar funds comprised of corporate or government issues. This decreased volatility is due to a smaller supply of municipal bonds and the elimination of almost all tax shelters, which has increased the popularity of tax-free bonds.

Three kinds of events may result in tax liability for every mutual fund except money market funds. The first two events described below cannot be controlled by the investor. The final event is determined solely by you, the shareholder (investor).

First, when bonds or stocks are sold in the fund portfolio for a profit (or loss), a capital gain (or capital loss) occurs. These gains and losses are passed down to the shareholder. Tax-free bond funds are not immune from capital gains taxes (or capital losses).

Second, interest and/or dividends paid by the securities within the fund are also passed on to shareholders (investors). As already mentioned, interest from municipal bonds is free from federal income taxes and, depending on the fund, may also be exempt from state income taxes. Municipal bond funds do not own stocks or convertibles, so they never throw off dividends.

Third, a taxable event may occur when you sell or exchange shares of a fund for cash or to go into another fund. As an example, suppose you bought into the fund at X dollars and cents per share. If shares are sold (or exchanged) by you for X plus Y, then there will a taxable gain (on Y, in this example). If shares are sold or exchanged for a loss (X minus Y), then there will be a capital loss. Municipal bond funds are subject to such capital gains or losses. Fortunately, you are never required to sell off shares in any mutual fund; the decision as to when and how much is always yours.

The standard deviation for municipal bond funds is 3 percent, meaning that this category's volatility is virtually identical to corporate bonds and government securities. Historical returns over the past 3, 5, 10, and 15 years for municipal funds are shown below. All of the figures shown are average *annual* rates of return (all periods ending March 31, 2000).

category	3 years	5 years	10 years	15 years
municipal bond funds	4%	5%	6%	8%
CA municipal bond funds	4%	5%	6%	7%
NY municipal bond funds	4%	5%	6%	7%
government bond funds	6%	6%	7%	8%
muni bonds (single state)	4%	5%	6%	7%

Technology. It is difficult to identify a segment of the economy that has not been profoundly influenced by technology. From traditional manufacturers developing e-commerce strategies to emerging companies with revolutionary new products, technology is changing businesses and creating unprecedented opportunities for investors. Techology represents nearly half of all business equipment spending by U.S. companies. Consumer spending on information technology as a percentage of disposable income has nearly tripled in the past 12 years. Today, nearly one-third of the S & P 500 Index is made up of technology stocks, up from just 7 percent in 1990.

Because of this sector's volatility, most investors historically have considered the technology sector a "speculative sector play" and consequently either have limited their holdings in this area to a small portion of their overall portfolios or avoided them altogether. In light of the astonishing returns achieved by many technology fund managers in 1999, some investors may have forgotten that the technology market itself returned 116 percent. These funds invest in common stocks of all aspects of technology, including computer hardware and software, telecommunications, semiconductor, networking, data storage, data security, fiber optics, wireless, and the Internet.

Technology is changing the way we work, live, and think. As the computer revolution evolves into the Internet revolution and then the wireless revolution, technology continues to amaze and dazzle us. This is true for investors in technology stocks as well. The technology sector of the stock market, as measured by the S & P

500 Technology Index, has outperformed the general stock market, as measured by the S & P 500, over the past 1-, 3-, 5-, and 10-year periods—by a wide margin.

Annualized Returns: Technology Stocks vs. the S & P 500
(all periods ending June 30, 2000)

period	technology sector	S & P 500
1 year	44.5%	7.3%
3 years	47.4%	19.7%
5 years	42.1%	23.8%
10 years	28.1%	17.8%

The typical price-earnings (p/e) ratio for stocks in this category is 55, versus 37 for the S & P 500. This group of funds has an average beta of 1.1, meaning that its *market-related risk* is 10 percent greater than that of the general market, as measured by the S & P 500. This statement is misleading due to the category's extremely high standard deviation (see next paragraph).

The standard deviation for technology funds is 63 percent, a figure that is significantly higher than any other category in the book. The next closest category, aggressive growth funds, has a standard deviation of 39. This means that, as a group, technology funds are expected to have less predictable returns than any other fund or category in the book.

Historical returns over the past 3, 5, 10, and 15 years for technology funds are shown below. All of the figures shown are average *annual* rates of return (all periods ending March 31, 2000).

category	3 years	5 years	10 years	15 years
technology funds	69%	44%	31%	25%
aggressive growth funds	38%	28%	18%	16%
growth funds	28%	25%	18%	17%
S & P 500	22%	25%	18%	17%
utility funds	22%	19%	14%	14%

Utilities. These funds invest in common stocks of utility companies. A small percentage of the funds' assets are invested in bonds. Investors opposed to or in favor of nuclear power can seek out funds that avoid or buy into such utility companies by reviewing a fund's semiannual report or by telephoning the fund using its toll-free phone number.

If you like the usual stability of a bond fund but want more appreciation potential, then utility funds are for you. Since these funds are interest-rate sensitive, their performance somewhat parallels that of bonds but is also influenced by the stock market. The large dividend stream provided by utility funds makes them less risky than other categories of stock funds. Recession-resistant demand for electricity, gas, and other utilities translates into a comparatively steady stream of returns.

Since a healthy portion of the total return for utility funds (dividends) cannot be controlled by the investor, these funds are best suited for retirement plans or as part of some other tax-sheltered vehicle. But even if you do not have a qualified retirement plan such as an IRA, pension plan, or TSA, utility funds can be a wise choice to lower overall portfolio volatility. The average p/e (price/earnings) ratio for this category is 27. The standard deviation for utility funds is 17 percent, a figure that is about 20 percent lower than that of growth and income funds. Utility funds have a beta of 0.5.

Historical returns over the past 3, 5, 10, and 15 years for utilities funds are shown below. All of the figures shown are average *annual* rates of return (all periods ending March 31, 2000).

category	3 years	5 years	10 years	15 years
utility funds	22%	19%	14%	14%
convertible funds	21%	18%	15%	14%
multi-asset global funds	11%	12%	8%	10%
asset allocation funds	15%	15%	12%	10%
balanced funds	14%	15%	12%	12%

World Bonds. Although the United States leads the world in outstanding debt, other countries and foreign corporations also issue IOUs as a way of financing projects and operations. As high as our debt seems, it is not out of line when compared to our GNP (now called GDP—gross domestic product). The ratio of our debt to GDP is lower than any other member of the group of seven. (The other G-7 members are Germany, Japan, Canada, Italy, the United Kingdom, and France.)

International, also known as foreign, bond funds invest in fixed-income securities outside of the United States. Global, or world, bond funds invest around the world, including the United States. Foreign bond funds normally offer higher yields than their domestic counterparts but also provide additional risk. Global bonds, on the other hand, provide less risk than a pure U.S. bond portfolio and also enjoy greater rates of return.

Global diversification reduces risk because the major economies around the world do not move up and down at the same time. As we climb out of a recession, Japan may be just entering one, and Germany may still be in the middle of one. When Italy is trying to stimulate its economy by lowering interest rates, Canada may be raising its rates in order to curtail inflation. By investing in different world bond markets, you ensure that you will not be at the mercy of any one country's political environment or fiscal policy.

The weighted maturity date of the bonds within this group is eight years, about one year less than U.S. government bond funds. Global bond funds have an average coupon rate of 7 percent. As with any investment that throws off a high current income, global and foreign bond funds should be part of a qualified retirement plan or variable annuity whenever possible.

The standard deviation for world bond funds is 9 percent, a low figure but one that is still about three times as great as the typical U.S. government bond fund. Historical returns over the past 3, 5, 10, and 15 years for world bond funds are shown below. All of the figures shown are average *annual* rates of return (all periods ending March 31, 2000).

category	3 years	5 years	10 years	15 years
world bond funds	4%	7%	6%	10%
government bond funds	6%	6%	7%	8%
corporate bond funds	6%	6%	7%	9%
high-yield bond funds	4%	8%	10%	9%
CPI (rate of inflation)	2%	2%	3%	3%

All Categories. An inescapable conclusion drawn from these different tables is that patience usually pays off. The single-digit performers over the past 15 years have been corporate bonds, government bonds, high-yield bonds, metals (the only negative performer), money market, municipal bonds, and natural resources. The most important thing left out of all of these tables is risk. However, one could make the case that stocks are not much riskier than bonds when one's holding period is 10–15 years. The tables also do not take into account the tax advantages of certain investments. Government bonds are exempt from state and local income taxes. (Note: this is only true with direct obligations of the United States, it does not apply to GNMAs, FNMAs, or other government-agency issues.) Municipal bonds are exempt from federal income taxes and, depending upon the type of tax-free fund as well as your state of residency, may also be exempt from any state or local taxes.

Money market funds should never be considered an investment. Money market funds, T-bills, and bank CDs should be viewed as places to park your money temporarily. Such accounts are best used to earn interest before you make a major purchase, while you are becoming educated about investing in general, or until market conditions change. Metals funds should be avoided by almost all investors. The track record of this category is wild and usually negative. It is doubtful that a strong case can be made for metals. Diversification and risk reduction can be accomplished by owning other categories such as money market, one or more of the bond categories, and even possibly natural resources.

Average Annual Returns for the 15-Year Period Ending March 31, 2000

category	15 years	category	15 years
aggressive growth	16%	growth & income	14%
asset allocation	10%	high-yield	9%
balanced	12%	metals (only)	–2%
convertible bond	14%	money market	6%
corporate bond	9%	multi-asset global	10%
emerging markets	11%	municipal bond	8%
equity-income	13%	natural resources	9%
foreign	16%	small company	15%
global equity	15%	technology	25%
government bond	8%	utilities	14%
growth	17%	world bond	10%
		average for all categories	12%

A common theme throughout this book is that, given time, equity (the different stock categories) always outperforms debt (the different bond categories). This does not mean that all of your money should be in the equity categories. Not everyone has the same level of patience or time horizon. It does mean that the great majority of investors need to review their portfolios and perhaps begin to emphasize domestic and foreign stocks more.

VI.
Which Funds Are Best for You?

When asked what they are looking for, investors typically say "I want the best." This could mean that they are looking for the most safety and greatest current income or the highest total return. There is no single "best" fund. The top-performing fund may have incredible volatility, causing shareholders to redeem their shares at the first sign of trouble. The "safest" fund may be devastated by risks not previously thought of: inflation and taxes.

As you have already seen, there are several different categories of mutual funds, ranging from tax-free money market accounts to precious metals. During one period or another, each of these categories has dominated some periodical's "10 best funds" list. These impressive scores may only last a quarter, six months, or a year. The fact is that no one knows what will be the *next* best-performing category or individual fund.

For some fund groups, such as international stocks, growth, growth and income, and aggressive growth, the reign at the top may last for several years. For other categories, such as money market, government bond, and precious metals, the glory may last a year or even less. Trying to outguess, chart, or follow a financial guru in order to determine the next trend is a fool's paradise. The notion that anyone has special insights into the marketplace is sheer nonsense. Countless neutral and lengthy studies attest to this fact. If this is the case, what should we do?

Step 1: Categories That Have Historically Done Well
First we should look at those generic categories of investments that have historically done well over long periods of time. A time frame of at least fifteen or twenty years is recommended. True, your investment horizon may be a fraction of this, but keep in mind two points. First, fifteen or twenty years includes good as well as bad times. Second, bad results cannot be hidden when you are studying the long term. Even the investor looking at a one- or two-year holding period should ask, "Do I want something that does phenomenally well one out of every five years, or do I want something that has a very good return in eight or nine out of every ten years?" Unless you are a gambler, the answer is obvious.

All investments can be categorized as either debt or equity instruments. Debt instruments in this book include corporate bonds, government bonds, high-yield bonds, international bonds, money market accounts, and municipal bonds. Equity instruments include growth, growth and income, international stocks, metals, and utility funds. Four other categories are hybrid instruments: asset allocation, balanced, convertible, and multi-asset global funds. In this book, these four categories are combined under the heading "balanced."

Throughout history, *equity has outperformed debt*. The longer the time frame reviewed, the better equity vehicles look. Over the past half century, the worst 15-year holding period performance for stocks (+4.3 percent a year) was very similar to the average 15-year holding period performance for long-term government bonds (+4.9 percent a year). For 20-year holding periods, the worst period for common stocks has been more than 40 percent better than the average for long-term government bonds. Indeed, stocks have outperformed bonds in every decade. Look at it this way: would you rather have loaned Henry Ford or Bill Gates the money to start their companies, or would you rather have given them money in return for a piece of the action?

Step 2: Review Your Objectives

Decide what you are trying to do with your portfolio. Everyone wants one of the following: growth, current income, or a combination of growth and income. Don't assume that if you are looking for current income your money should go into a bond or money market fund. There is a way to set up an equity fund so that it will give you a high monthly income. This is known as a "systematic withdrawal program" and is discussed in Appendix D. The growth-oriented investor, on the other hand, should consider certain categories of debt instruments or hybrid securities to help add more stability to a portfolio.

Objectives are certainly important, but so is the element of time. The shorter the time frame and the greater the need for assurances, the greater the likelihood that debt instruments should be used. A growth investor who is looking at a single-year time frame and wants a degree of safety is probably better off in a series of bond and/or money market accounts. On the other hand, the longer the commitment, the better equities look. Thus, even a cautious investor who has a life expectancy (or whose spouse has a life expectancy) of ten years or more should seriously consider having at least a moderate portion of his or her portfolio in equities.

A retired couple in their sixties should realize that one or both of them will probably live at least fifteen more years. Since this is the case, and since we know that equities have almost always outperformed bonds when looking at a horizon of ten years or more, their emphasis should be in this area.

The conservative investor may say that stocks are too risky. True, the day-to-day or year-to-year volatility of equities can be quite disturbing. However, it is also true that the medium- and long-term effects of inflation and the resulting diminished purchasing power of a fixed-income investment are even more devastating. At least with an equity there is a better than 50–50 chance that it will go up in value. In the case of inflation, what do you think are the chances that the cost of goods and services will go *down* during the next 1, 3, 5, or 10 years? The answer is "not likely."

Step 3: Ascertain Your Risk Level

No investment is worthwhile if you stay awake at night worrying about it. If you do not already know or are uncertain about your risk level, contact your financial advisor. These professionals usually have some kind of questionnaire that you can answer. Your responses will give a good indication of which investments are proper for you and which should be avoided. If you do not deal with a financial advisor, try the test below. Your score, and what it means, are shown at the end of the questionnaire.

Test for Determining Your Risk Level

1. "I invest for the long term, five to ten years or more. The final result is more important than daily, monthly, or annual fluctuations in value."

(10) Totally disagree. (20) Willing to accept some volatility, but not loss of principal. (30) Could accept a moderate amount of yearly fluctuation in return for a good *total* return. (40) Would accept an *occasional* negative year if the final results were good. (50) Agree.

2. Rank the importance of current income.

(10) Crucial, the exact amount must be known. (20) Important, but I am willing to have the amount vary each period. (30) Fairly important, but other aspects of investing are also of concern. (40) Only a modest amount of income is needed. (50) Current income is unimportant.

3. Rank the amount of loss you could tolerate in a single *quarter*.

(10) None. (20) A little, but over a year's time the total value of the investment should not decline. (30) Consistency of total return is more important than trying to get big gains. (40) One or two quarters of negative returns are the price you must pay when looking at the total picture. (50) Unimportant.

4. Rank the importance of beating inflation.

(10) Factors such as preservation of principal and current income are much more important. (20) I am willing to have a slight variance in my returns, *on a quarterly basis only*, in order to have at least a partial hedge against inflation. (30) Could accept some annual volatility in order to offset inflation. (40) I consider inflation to be important, but have mixed feelings about how much volatility I could accept from one year to the next. (50) The long-term effects of inflation are devastating and should not be ignored by anyone.

5. Rank the importance of beating the stock market over any given two-to-three-year period.

(10) Irrelevant. (20) A small concern. (30) Fairly important. (40) Very important. (50) Absolutely crucial.

Add up your score from questions 1 through 5. Your risk, as defined by your total point score, is as follows: 0–50 points = extremely conservative; 50–100 points = somewhat conservative; 100–150 points = moderate; 150–200 points = somewhat aggressive; 200–250 points = very aggressive.

Step 4: Review Your Current Holdings

Everyone has heard the expression, "Don't put all your eggs in one basket." This advice also applies to investing. No matter how much we like investment X, if a third of our net worth is already in X, we probably should not add any more to this investment. After all, there is more than one good investment.

Since no single investment category is the top performer every year, it makes sense to diversify into several *fundamentally* good categories. By using *proper* diversification, we have an excellent chance of being number one with a portion of our portfolio every year. Babe Ruth may have hit more home runs than almost anyone, but he also struck out more. As investors, we should be content with consistently hitting doubles and triples.

Trying to hit a homer every time may result in financial ruin. Never lose track of the fact that losses always have a greater impact than gains. An investment that goes up 50 percent the first year and falls 50 percent the next year still has a net loss of 25 percent. This philosophy is emphasized throughout the book.

Step 5: Implementation

There is no such thing as the perfect time to invest. No matter how strongly you or some "expert" individual or publication believes that the market is going to go up or down, no one actually knows.

Once you have properly educated yourself, *now* is the right time to invest. If you are afraid to make the big plunge, consider some form of dollar-cost averaging (see Appendix C). This is a disciplined approach to investing; it also reduces your risk exposure significantly.

Reading investment books and attending classes are encouraged, but some people may be tempted to remain on the sidelines indefinitely. For such people, there is no perfect time to invest. If the stock market drops two hundred points, they are waiting for the next hundred-point drop. If stocks or bonds are up 15 percent, they say things are peaking and they will invest as soon as it drops by 10 percent. If the stock or bond market does drop by that magical figure, these same investors are now certain that it will drop another 10 percent.

The "strategy" described above is frustrating. More important, it is wrong. One can look back in history and find lots of reasons not to have invested. But the fact is that all of the investments in this book have gone up almost every year. The "wait and see" approach is a poor one; the same reasons for not investing will still exist in the present and throughout the future.

Remember, your money is doing something right now. It is invested somewhere. If it is under the mattress, it is being eaten away by inflation. If it is in a "risk-free" investment, such as an insured savings account, bank CD, or U.S. Treasury bill, it is being subjected to taxation and the cumulative effects of reduced purchasing power. Do not think you can hide by having your money in some safe haven. Once you understand that there can be things worse than market swings, you will become an educated investor who knows there is no such thing as a truly risk-free place or investment.

If you are still not convinced, consider the story of Louie the Loser. There is only one thing you can say about Louie's timing: It is *always* awful. So it is no surprise that when he decided to invest $10,000 a year in a fund featured in this book, he managed to pick the *worst* possible times. *Every year* for the past twenty years (1980–1999), he has invested on the very day that the stock market *peaked*. How has he done? He has over $1,123,000, which means his money has grown at an average rate of 16.2 percent a year (a cumulative investment of $200,000; 20 years times $10,000 invested each year).

Yet even by picking the *worst* possible days, Louie still came out way ahead of the $379,000 he would have had if he had put his money in U.S. Treasury bills twenty years ago. Even though his timing was terrible, he still fared much better than if he had done what many people are doing today: waiting for the "perfect" time to invest.

After asking you a series of questions, your investment advisor can give you a framework within which to operate. Investors who do not have a good advisor may wish to look at the different sample portfolios below. These general recommendations will provide you with a sense of direction.

The Conservative Investor
15 percent balanced
10 percent utilities
15 percent growth & income
10 percent world bond
10 percent international equities
10 percent money market or short-term bonds
30 percent intermediate-term municipal or government bonds
    (depending upon your tax bracket)

This portfolio would give you a weighting of 43 percent in equities (stocks) and 57 percent in debt instruments (bonds and cash equivalents). Investors who are not in a high federal income tax bracket may wish to avoid municipal bonds completely and use government bonds instead.

If your tax bracket is such that you are not sure whether you should own tax-free or taxable bonds (if, that is, the after-tax return on government bonds is similar to what a similarly maturing, high-quality municipal bond pays), lean toward a municipal bond fund—they are almost always less volatile than a government bond fund that has the same or a similar average maturity.

The Moderate Investor
10 percent small-company growth
 5 percent balanced/convertibles
15 percent growth
20 percent growth & income
10 percent high-yield bond
10 percent world bond
15 percent global equities
10 percent technology
 5 percent natural resources

This portfolio would give you a weighting of 80 percent in equities (common stocks) and 20 percent in debt instruments. The figures are a little misleading since high-yield bonds are more of a hybrid investment—part stock and part bond. The price, or value, of high-yield bonds is influenced by economic (macro and micro) news as well as interest rate changes. Whereas government, municipal, and high-quality corporate bonds often react favorably to bad economic news such as a recession, increases in the jobless rate, a slowdown in housing starts, and so on, high-yield bonds have a tendency to view such news positively. Thus, taking into account that high-yield bonds are about halfway between traditional bonds and stocks, the weighting distribution is more in the range of 85 percent equities and 15 percent bonds.

The Aggressive Investor
15 percent aggressive growth
20 percent small-company growth
20 percent growth
10 percent growth & income
15 percent international equities
20 percent technology

This portfolio would give you a weighting of 100 percent in equities. Bond fund categories, with the possible exception of high-yield and international, are not recommended for the aggressive investor because they usually do not have enough appreciation potential.

Readers of the previous editions of this book may notice that this edition weighs equities (the different stock categories) more heavily than it has in the past. This is because bonds cannot experience the appreciation or total return for the balance of the 1990s that they saw in the 1980s and very early 1990s. For the most part, bonds increase in value because of falling interest rates. In 1981, the prime interest rate briefly peaked at 21.5 percent; for more than a dozen years this benchmark figure dropped. During the balance of the 1990s, it would be literally impossible for the prime interest rate to drop 13 points (it cannot drop below zero).

Stocks, on the other hand, could end up doing worse than bonds, the same, or better. At least conceptually, however, equities have the possibility of exceeding their performance over the past 10 years. The 1980s and early 1990s (whatever 10-year period you wish to use during this time horizon) were not the best 10 years in a row for stocks. It is certainly possible that the next 10 years, or the 10 years beginning in 1998 or 1999, will be the best. When you look at the state of the world, the conditions certainly seem more favorable now for tremendous economic and stock market growth for the next several decades.

Step 6: Review

After implementation, it is important that you keep track of how you are doing. One of the beauties of mutual funds is that, if you choose a fund with good management, managers will do their job and you can spend your time on something else. Nevertheless, review your situation at least quarterly. Once you feel comfortable with your portfolio, only semiannual or annual reviews are recommended.

Daily or weekly tracking is pointless. If a particular investment goes up or down 5 percent, that does not mean you should rush out and buy more or sell off. That same investment may do just the opposite the following week or month. By watching your investments too closely, you will be defeating a major attribute of mutual funds: professional management. Presumably these fund managers know a lot more about their particular investments than you do. If they do not, you should either choose another fund or start your own mutual fund.

Step 7: Relax

If you do your homework by reading this book, you will be in fine shape. There are several thousand mutual funds. Some funds are just plain bad. Most mutual funds are mediocre. And, as with everything else in this world, a small portion are truly excellent. This book has taken those thousands of funds and eliminated all of the bad, mediocre, and fairly good. What are left are only excellent mutual funds.

If you would like help in designing a portfolio or picking a specific fund, telephone the Institute of Business & Finance (800/848-2029). The institute will be able to give you the names and telephone numbers of Certified Fund Specialists (CFS) in your area. To become a CFS, one must complete a rigorous one-year educational program, pass a comprehensive exam, adhere to a professional code of ethics, and meet annual continuing education requirements.

VII.
Fund Features

Advantages of Mutual Funds

Listed below are some of the features of mutual funds—advantages not found in other kinds of investments.

Ease of Purchase. Mutual fund shares are easy to buy. For those who prefer to make investment decisions themselves, mutual funds are as close as the telephone or the mailbox. Those who would like help in choosing a fund can draw upon a wide variety of sources.

Many funds sell their shares through stockbrokers, financial planners, or insurance agents. These representatives can help you analyze your financial needs and objectives and recommend appropriate funds. For these professional services, you may be charged a sales commission, usually referred to as a "load." This charge is expressed as a percentage of the total purchase price of the fund shares. In some cases, there is no initial sales charge, or load, but there may be an annual fee and/or another charge if shares are redeemed during the first few years of ownership.

Other funds distribute their shares directly to the public. They may advertise in magazines and newspapers; most can be reached through toll-free telephone numbers. Because there are no sales agents involved, most of these funds, often called "no loads," charge a much lower fee or no sales commission at all. With these funds it is generally up to you to do your investment homework.

In order to attract new shareholders, some funds have adopted 12b-1 plans (named after a federal government rule). These plans enable the fund to pay its own distribution costs. Distribution costs are those costs associated with marketing the fund, either through sales agents or through advertising. The 12b-1 fee is charged against fund assets and is paid indirectly by existing shareholders. Annual distribution fees of this type usually range between 0.1 percent and 1.25 percent of the value of the account.

Fees charged by a fund are described in the prospectus. In addition, a fee table listing all transactional fees and all annual fund expenses can be found at the front of the prospectus.

Access to Your Money (Marketability). Mutual funds, by law, must stand ready on any business day to redeem any or all of your shares at their current net asset value (NAV). Of course, the value may be greater or less than the price you originally paid, depending on the market.

To sell shares back to the fund, all you need to do is give the fund proper notification, as explained in the prospectus. Most funds will accept such notification by telephone; some funds require a written request. The fund will then send your check promptly. In most instances the fund will issue a check when it receives the notification; by law it must send you the check within seven business days. You receive the price your shares are worth *on the day* the fund gets proper notice of redemption from you. If you own a money market fund, you can also redeem shares by writing checks directly against your fund balance.

Disciplined Investment. The majority of funds allow you to set up what is known as a "check-o-matic plan." Under such a program a set amount of money is automatically deducted from your checking account each month and sent directly to the mutual fund of your choice. Your bank (or credit union) will not charge you for this service. Mutual funds also offer such programs free of charge. Automatic investment plans can be changed or terminated at any time, again at no charge.

Exchange Privileges. As the economy or your own personal circumstances change, the kinds of funds you hold may no longer be the ones you need. Many mutual funds are part of a "family of funds" and offer a feature called an exchange privilege. Within a family of funds there may be several choices, each with a different investment objective, varying from highly conservative funds to more aggressive funds that carry a higher degree of risk. An exchange privilege allows you to transfer all or part of your money from one of these funds to another. Exchange policies vary from fund to fund. The fee for an exchange is nominal, five dollars or less. For the specifics about a fund's exchange privilege, check the prospectus.

Automatic Reinvestment. You can elect to have any dividends and capital gains distributions from your mutual fund investment turned back into the fund, automatically buying new shares and expanding your current holdings. Most shareholders opt for the reinvestment privilege. There is usually no cost or fee involved.

Automatic Withdrawal. You can make arrangements with the fund to automatically send you, or anyone you designate, checks from the fund's earnings or principal. This system works well for retirees, families who want to arrange for payments to their children at college, or anyone needing monthly income checks. See Appendix D for a more detailed example as to how a systematic withdrawal plan (SWP) works.

Detailed Record Keeping. The fund will handle all the paperwork and record keeping necessary to keep track of your investment transactions. A typical statement will note such items as your most recent investment or withdrawal and any dividends or capital gains paid to you in cash or reinvested in the fund. The fund will also report to you on the tax status of your earnings. If you lose any paperwork, the fund will send you copies of current or past statements.

Retirement Plans. Financial experts have long viewed mutual funds as appropriate vehicles for retirement investing; indeed, they are quite commonly used for this purpose. For retirees over the age of seventy and a half, mutual fund companies will recompute the minimum amount that needs to be taken out each year, as dictated by the IRS. Mutual funds are ideal for Keoghs, IRAs, 401(k) plans, and other employer-sponsored retirement plans. Many funds offer prototype retirement plans and standard IRA agreements. Having your own retirement plan drafted by a law firm would cost you thousands of dollars, not to mention what you would be charged for the updates that would be needed every time the laws change. Mutual funds offer these plans and required updates for free.

Accountability. There are literally dozens of sources that track and monitor mutual funds. It is easy for you to determine a fund's track record and volatility over several different time periods. Federal regulatory bodies such as the NASD (National Association of Securities Dealers) and SEC (Securities and Exchange Commission) have strict rules concerning performance figures and what appears in advertisements, brochures, and prospectuses.

Flexibility. Investment choices are almost endless: domestic stocks, foreign debt, international equities, government obligations, money market instruments, convertible securities, short- and intermediate-term bonds, real estate, gold, and natural resources. Your only limitation is the choices offered by the fund family or families you are invested in. And because you can move part or all of your money from one mutual fund to another fund within the same family, usually for only a minimal transfer fee, your portfolio can become more aggressive, conservative, or moderate with a simple phone call.

Economies of Scale. As a shareholder (investor) in a fund, you automatically get the benefit of reduced transaction charges. Since a fund is often buying or selling thousands of shares of stock at a time, it is able to conduct its transactions at dramatically reduced costs. The fees a fund pays are far lower than what you would pay even if you were buying several hundred shares of a stock from a discount broker. The same thing is true when it comes to bonds. Funds are able to add them to their portfolio without any markup. When you buy a bond through a broker, even a discounter, there is always a markup; it is hidden in the price you pay and sell the bond for. The savings for bond investors ranges anywhere from less than 1 percent all the way up to 5 percent.

Risk Reduction: Importance of Diversification

If there is one ingredient to successful investing that is universally agreed upon, it is the benefit of diversification. This concept is also backed by a great deal of research and market experience. The benefit provided by diversification is risk reduction. Risk to investors is frequently defined as volatility of return—in other words, how much an investment's return might vary. Investors prefer returns that are relatively predictable, which is to say, less volatile. On the other hand, they want returns to be high. Diversification eliminates most of the risk without reducing potential returns.

A fund's portfolio manager(s) will normally invest the fund's pool of money in 50 to 150 different securities to spread the fund's holdings over a number of investments. This diversification is an important principle in lessening the fund's overall investment risk. Such diversification is typically beyond the financial capacity of most individual investors. The table below shows the relationship between diversification and investment risk, defined as the variability of annual returns of a stock portfolio.

number of stocks	risk ratio
1	6.6
2	3.8
4	2.4
10	1.6
50	1.1
100	1.0

Note that the variability of return, or risk, associated with holding just one stock is more than six times that of a 100-stock portfolio. Yet the *increased* potential return found in a portfolio made up of a small number of stocks is minimal.

VIII.
Reading a Mutual Fund Prospectus

The purpose of the fund's prospectus is to provide the reader with full and complete disclosure. The prospectus covers the following key points:

- The fund's investment objective: what the managers are trying to achieve.
- The investment methods it uses in trying to achieve this objective.
- The name and address of its investment advisor and a brief description of the advisor's experience.
- The level of investment risk the fund is willing to assume in pursuit of its investment objective.
- Any investments the fund will *not* make (for example, real estate, options, or commodities).
- Tax consequences of the investment for the shareholder.
- How to purchase shares of the fund, including the cost of investing.
- How to redeem shares.
- Services provided, such as IRAs, automatic investment of dividends and capital gains distributions, check writing, withdrawal plans, and any other features.
- A condensed financial statement (in tabular form, covering the last 10 years or the period the fund has been in existence if less than 10 years) called "Per Share Income and Capital Changes." The fund's performance may be calculated from the information given in this table.
- A tabular statement of any fees charged by the fund and their effect on earnings over time.

IX.
Commonly Asked Questions

Q. Are mutual funds a new kind of investment?

No. In fact, they have roots in eighteenth-century Scotland. The first U.S. mutual fund was organized in Boston in 1924. This fund, Massachusetts Investors Trust, is still in existence today. Several mutual fund companies have been in operation for over half a century.

Q. How much money do you need to invest in a mutual fund?

Literally anywhere from a few dollars to several million. Many funds have no minimum requirements for investing. A few funds are open to large institutional accounts only. The vast majority of funds require a minimum investment of between $250 and $1,000.

Q. Do mutual funds offer a fixed rate of return?

No. Mutual funds invest in securities such as stocks, bonds, and money market accounts whose yields and values fluctuate with market conditions.

Mutual funds can make money for their shareholders in three ways. First, they pay their shareholders dividends earned from the fund's investments. Second, if a security held by a fund is sold at a profit, funds pay their shareholders capital gains distributions. And third, if the value of the securities held by the fund increases, the value of each mutual fund share also increases.

In none of these cases, however, can a return be guaranteed. In fact, it is against the law for a mutual fund to make a claim as to its future performance. Ads quoting returns are based on past performance and should not be interpreted as a fixed-rate yield. Past performance should not be taken as a predictor of future earnings.

Q. What are the risks of mutual fund investing?

Mutual funds are investments in financial securities with fluctuating values. The value of the securities in a fund's portfolio, for example, will rise and fall according to general economic conditions and the fortunes of the particular companies that issue those securities. Even the most conservative assets, such as U.S. government obligations, will fluctuate in value as interest rates change. These are risks that investors should be aware of when purchasing mutual fund shares.

Q. How can I evaluate a fund's long-term performance?

You can calculate a fund's performance by referring to the section in the prospectus headed "Per Share Income and Capital Changes." This section will give you the figures needed to compute the annual rates of return earned by the fund each year for the past 10 years (or for the life of the fund if less than 10 years). There are also several periodicals that track the performance of funds on a regular basis. You can also telephone the fund and they will give you performance figures.

Q. What's the difference between *yield* and *total return*?

Yield is the income per share paid to a shareholder from the dividends and interest over a specified period of time. Yield is expressed as a percent of the current offering price per share.

Total return is a measure of the per-share change in total value from the beginning to the end of a specified period, usually a year, including distributions paid to shareholders. This measure includes income received from dividends and interest, capital gains distributions, and any unrealized capital gains or losses. Total return looks at the whole picture: appreciation (or loss) of principal plus any dividends or income. Total return provides the best measure of overall fund performance; *do not be misled by an enticing yield*.

Q. How much does it cost to invest in a mutual fund?

A mutual fund normally contracts with its management company to provide for most of the needs of a normal business. The management company is paid a fee for these services, which usually include managing the fund's investments.

In addition, the fund may pay directly for some of its costs, such as printing, mailing, accounting, and legal services. Typically, these two annual charges average 1.5 percent. In such a fund you would be paying $10 to $15 a year on every $1,000 invested.

Some fund directors have adopted plans (with the approval of the fund's shareholders) that allow them to pay certain distribution costs (the costs of advertising, for example) directly from fund assets. These costs may range from 0.1 percent to 1.25 percent annually.

There may also be other charges involved—for example, in exchanging shares. Some funds may charge a redemption fee when a shareholder redeems his or her shares, usually within five years of purchasing them. All costs and charges assessed by the fund organization are disclosed in its prospectus.

Q. Is the management fee part of the sales charge?

No, the management fee paid by the fund to its investment advisor is for services rendered in managing the fund's portfolio. An average fee ranges from 0.5 percent to 1 percent of the fund's total assets each year. As described above, the management fee and other business expenses generally total somewhere between 1 percent and 1.5 percent. These expenses are paid from the fund's assets and are reflected in the price of the fund shares. In contrast, most sales charges are deducted from your initial investment.

Q. Is my money locked up for a certain period of time in a mutual fund?

Unlike some other types of financial accounts, mutual funds are liquid investments. That means that any shares an investor owns may be redeemed freely on any day the fund is open for business. Since a mutual fund stands ready to buy back its shares at their current net asset value, you always have a buyer for your shares at current market value.

Q. How often do I get statements from a mutual fund?

Mutual funds ordinarily send immediate confirmation statements when an investor purchases or redeems (sells) shares. Statements alerting shareholders to reinvested dividends are sent out periodically. At least semiannually, investors also receive statements on the status of the fund's investments. Tax statements, referred to as "substitute 1099s," are mailed annually. Some funds automatically send out quarterly reports.

Q. I've already purchased shares of a mutual fund. How can I tell how well my investment is doing?

Figuring out how well your fund is faring is a two-step procedure. First you need to know how many shares you *now* own. The "now" is emphasized because if you have asked the fund to plow any dividends and capital gains distributions back into the fund for you, it will do so by issuing you more shares, thereby increasing the value of your investment. Once you know how many shares you own, look up the fund's net assets value (sometimes called the sell or bid price) in the financial section of a major metropolitan daily newspaper. Next, multiply the net asset value by the number of shares you own to figure out the value of your investment as of that date. Compare today's value against your beginning value.

You will need to keep the confirmation statements you receive when you first purchase shares and as you make subsequent purchases in order to compare present value to the original purchase value. You will also need these statements for tax purposes.

Q. Do investment experts recommend mutual funds for IRAs and other qualified plans?

Financial experts view many mutual funds as compatible with the long-term objectives of saving for retirement. Indeed, fund shareholders cite this reason for investing more than any other. Many kinds of funds work best when allowed to ride out the ups and downs of market cycles over long periods of time.

Funds can also offer the owner of an IRA, Keogh, pension plan, 401(k), or 403(b) flexibility. By using the exchange privilege within a family of funds, the investor can shift investments from one kind of security to another in response to changes in personal finances or the economic outlook, or as retirement approaches.

Q. Are money market funds a good investment?

No. If I were to recommend an investment to you that lost money in 17 of the last 25 calendar years (adjusted for income taxes and inflation), you would probably balk. Yet this is the track record of CDs, money market accounts, and T-bills. Money market funds are an excellent place to park your money for the short term— some period less than two years.

Q. Why don't more people invest in foreign (international) securities?

Ignorance. The reality is that foreign securities (stocks and bonds), when added to domestic investments, actually reduce the portfolio's level of risk. Stock and bond markets around the world rarely move up and down at the same time. This random correlation is what helps lower risk and volatility: When U.S. stocks (or bonds) are going down, securities in other parts of the world may well be moving sideways or going up.

Q. Is standard deviation the correct way to measure risk?

No. Standard deviation measures volatility (or predictability) of returns. The standard deviation for each of the mutual funds in this book is ranked under the star system next to the heading "predictability of returns." The system used in this book for measuring risk is different, punishing funds for performance that is less than that offered by T-bills, a figure commonly referred to as the "risk-free rate of return." To me this makes more sense than a system that punishes a fund for volatility by translating its high standard deviation figure as "high risk." This is what most financial writers do, whether the volatility the fund experienced was upward or downward volatility. I have yet to meet an investor who is upset that he or she did better than expected. No one minds *upward* volatility.

Q. Why not simply invest in those funds that were the best performers over the past 1, 3, 5, or 10 years?

This would be a big mistake. There is little relationship (or correlation) between the performance of one fund or fund category from one year to the next. This, by the way, is the way most investors and advisors select investments—making this one of the biggest and costliest mistakes one could make. Unfortunately, no one knows what the next best performing fund or category will be.

Q. Speaking of common stocks, what are the odds of making money in the market?

If you think investing in the market is too risky, what are the odds that:

You will win a state lottery?	1 in 4 million
You will be dealt a royal flush poker hand?	1 in 649,739
The Earth will be struck by a huge meteor during your lifetime?	1 in 9,000
You will be robbed this year?	1 in 500
The airlines will lose your luggage?	1 in 186
You will be audited by the IRS?	1 in 100
You will roll dice and get snake eyes?	1 in 36
You will go to Disney World this year?	1 in 9
The next bottled water you buy will be nothing more than tap water?	1 in 4
You will eat out today?	1 in 2
An investment in stocks will make money in any given year?	7 in 10

Source: *What the Odds Are*, Les Krantz (Harper Perennial, 1992)

X.
How the 100 Best Funds Were Determined

With an entry field that numbers over 13,000, it is no easy task to determine the 100 best mutual funds. Magazines and newspapers report on the "best" by relying on performance figures over a specific period, usually 1, 3, 5, or 10 years. Investors often rely on these sources and invest accordingly, only to be disappointed later.

Studies from around the world bear out what investors typically experience: that there is no correlation between the performance of a stock or bond from one year to the next. The same can be said for individual money managers—and sadly, for most mutual funds.

The criteria used to determine the 100 best mutual funds are unique and far-reaching. In order for a fund to be considered for this book, it must pass several tests. First, all stock and bond funds that have had managers for less than five years were excluded; in the case of money market funds, the only remaining category, the criterion was liberalized since overhead costs have a much greater bearing on net returns than management's expertise.

This first step alone eliminated well over half the contenders. The reasoning for the cutoff is simple: A fund is often only as good as its manager. An outstanding 10-year track record may be cited in a periodical, but how relevant is this performance if the manager who oversaw the fund left a year or two ago? This criterion was liberalized in selecting money market funds because this category of funds normally requires less expertise.

Second, any fund that places in the bottom (worst) half of its *category's* risk ranking is excluded. No matter how profitable the finish line looks, the number of investors will be sparse if the fund demonstrates too much negative activity. In most cases, a little performance was gladly given up if a great deal of risk was eliminated. This reflects the book's philosophy that returns must be viewed in relation to the amount of risk that was taken. In most cases the funds described in the book possess outstanding risk management. Those few selected funds where risk control has been less than stellar have shown tremendous performance, and their risky nature has been highlighted to warn the reader.

Virtually all sources measure risk by something known as *standard deviation*. Determining an investment's standard deviation is not as difficult as you might imagine. First you calculate the asset's average annual return. Usually, the most recent three years are used, updated each quarter. Once an average annual rate of return is determined, a line is drawn on a graph, representing this return.

Next, the monthly returns are plotted on the graph. Since three years is a commonly accepted time period for such calculations, a total of 36 individual points are plotted—one for each month over the past three years. After all of these points are plotted, the standard deviation can be determined. Quite simply, standard deviation measures the variance of returns from the norm (the line drawn on a graph).

There is a problem in using standard deviation to determine the risk level of any investment, including a mutual fund. The shortcoming of this method is that standard deviation punishes *good* as well as bad results. An example will help expose the problem.

Suppose there were two different investments, X and Y. Investment X went up almost every month by exactly 1.5 percent but had a few months each year when it went down 1 percent. Investment Y went up only 1 percent most months, but it always went up 6 percent for each of the final months of the year. The standard deviation of Y would be substantially higher than X. It might be so high that we would avoid it because it was classified as "high risk." The fact is that we would love to own such an investment. No one ever minds *upward* volatility or surprises; it is only negative or downward volatility that is cause for alarm.

The system used for determining risk in this book is not widely used, but it is certainly a fairer and more meaningful measurement. The book's method for determining risk is to see how many months over the past three years a fund underperformed what is popularly referred to as a "risk-free vehicle," something like a bank CD or U.S. Treasury bill. The more months a fund falls below this safe return, the greater the fund will be punished in its risk ranking.

Third, the fund must have performed well for the last three and five years. A one- or two-year time horizon could be attributed to luck or nonrecurring events. A 10- or 15-year period would certainly be better, if not for the reality that the overwhelming majority of funds are managed by a different person today than they were even six years ago.

Finally, the fund must either possess an excellent risk-adjusted return or have had superior returns with no more than average levels of risk. It is assumed that most readers are equally concerned with risk and reward. Thus, the foundation of the text is based on which mutual funds have the best *risk-adjusted returns*.

Sadly, some funds were excluded, despite their superior performance and risk control, because they were either less than five years old, had new management, or were closed to new investors.

XI.
The 100 Best Funds

This section describes the 100 very best funds. As discussed, the methodology used to narrow down the universe of funds is based on performance, risk, and management.

Every one of these 100 funds is a superlative choice. However, there must still be a means to compare and rank each of the funds within its peer group. Each one of the 100 funds is first categorized by its investment objective. The category breakdown is as follows:

category of mutual fund	number
aggressive growth	11
balanced	10
corporate bond	5
global equity	11
government bond	5
growth	13
growth & income	10
high-yield bond	5
metals/natural resources	2
money market	7
municipal bond	7
technology	5
utilities	5
world bond	4
total	**100 funds**

There are five areas to be ranked: (1) total return, (2) risk/volatility, (3) management, (4) tax minimization (current income in the case of bond, hybrid, and money market funds), and (5) expense control. Of these five classifications, management, risk/volatility, and total return are the most important.

The track record of a fund is only as good as its management, which is why extensive space is given to this section for each fund. The areas of concern are the length of time the manager, or team, has overseen the fund and the management's background and investment philosophy.

The risk/volatility of the fund is the second biggest concern. Investors like to be in things that have somewhat predictable results—that aren't up 60 percent one year and down 25 percent the next. A few such highly volatile funds are included, but the risk associated with such a fund is clearly highlighted, informing the prospective investor.

Total return was the third concern. When all is said and done, people like to make lots of money with an acceptable level of risk, or at least get decent returns by taking little, if any, risk. This is also known as the *risk-adjusted return*. So, although the very safest funds within each category were preferred, this safety had to be combined with impressive returns.

The fourth category, current income, was of lesser importance. Income is important to a lot of people but often gets in the way of selecting the proper investment; preservation of capital should also be considered. There is a better way to get current income than to rely on monthly dividend or interest checks. This is known as a systematic withdrawal plan (SWP). A 66-year example of a SWP is shown in Appendix D. Current-income-oriented investors will truly be amazed when they see how such a system works.

In the case of equity funds, "tax minimization" was substituted for the category "current income." This was done for two reasons. First, there is no reason why a fund whose objective is capital appreciation should be punished simply because it does not throw off a high dividend. Once you are familiar with the benefits of using a systematic withdrawal plan, you will no longer care whether a certain aggressive growth or even a growth and income fund pays much in the form of dividends. Second, unless your money is sheltered in a qualified retirement plan (IRA, pension plan, etc.), income taxes are a real concern. Funds should be rewarded for minimizing shareholder tax liability. This is why every mutual fund in the book is rated, one way or another, when it comes to personal income taxes.

Tax-conscious investors want to downplay current income as much as possible. For them, a high current income simply means paying more in taxes. For other categories, such as growth and income, utilities, and balanced, a healthy current income stream often translates into lower risk. And for still other categories, such as corporate bonds, government bonds, international bonds, money market, and municipal bonds, current income is, and rightfully should be, a major determinant for selection.

The final category, expenses, rates how effective management is in operating the fund. High expense ratios for a given category mean that the advisors are either too greedy or simply do not know or care about running an efficient operation. The actual expenses incurred by a fund are not directly seen by the client, but such costs are deducted from the portfolio's gross returns, which is important.

In addition to looking at the expense ratio of a fund, the turnover rate is studied. The turnover rate shows how often the fund buys and sells its securities. There is a real cost when such a transaction occurs. These transaction costs, also known as commissions, are borne by the fund and eat into the gross return figures. Expense ratios do not include transaction costs incurred when management decides to replace or add a security. Thus, expense ratios do not tell the whole story. By scrutinizing the turnover rate, the rankings take into account excessive trading. A fund's turnover rate may represent a larger true cost to the investor than the fund's expense ratio.

Each fund is ranked in each one of these five categories. The rating ranges from zero to five points (stars) in each category. The points can be transcribed as follows: zero points = poor, one point = fair, two points = good, three points = very good, four points = superior, and five points = excellent.

All of the rankings for each fund are based on how such a fund fared against its peer group category in the book. Thus, even though a given rating may only be fair or even poor, it is within the context of the category and its peers that have made the book—a category that only includes the very best. There is a strong likelihood that a fund in the book that is given a low score in one category would still rate as great when compared to the entire universe of funds or even compared to other funds within the same category but not included in this book.

Do not be fooled by a low rating for any fund in any of the five areas. All 100 of these funds are true winners. Keep in mind that only about one in one hundred funds can appear in the book. The purpose of the ratings is to show the best of the best.

Aggressive Growth Funds

These funds focus strictly on appreciation, with no concern about generating income. Aggressive growth funds strive for maximum capital growth, frequently using such trading strategies as leveraging, purchasing restricted securities, or buying stocks of emerging growth companies. Portfolio composition is almost exclusively U.S. stocks.

Aggressive growth funds can go up in value quite rapidly during favorable market conditions. These funds will often outperform other categories of U.S. stocks during bull markets but suffer greater percentage losses during bear markets.

Over the past 15 years, small stocks, which are included in the aggressive growth category, have *underperformed* common stocks by 6.1 percent per year, as measured by the Standard & Poor's 500 Stock Index. From 1985 through 1999, small stocks averaged 12.7 percent, while common stocks averaged 18.9 percent compounded per year. A $10,000 investment in small stocks grew to $66,670 over the past 15 years; a similar initial investment in the S & P 500 grew to $134,740.

During the past 20 years, there have been 16 five-year periods (1980–1984, 1981–1985, etc.). The Small Stock Index, made up from the smallest 20 percent of companies listed on the NYSE, as measured by market capitalization, outperformed the S & P 500 in just four of those 16 five-year periods. During these same 20 years, there have been 11 10-year periods (1978–1987, 1979–1988, etc.). The Small Stock Index never outperformed the S & P 500 during any one of those 11 10-year periods.

During the past 30 years, there have been 11 20-year periods (1970–1989, 1971–1990, etc.). The Small Stock Index outperformed the S & P 500 in nine of those 11 20-year periods.

Over the past 50 years, there have been 46 five-year periods (1950–1954, 1951–1954, etc.). The Small Stock Index outperformed the S & P 500 in 26 of those 46 five-year periods. Over the past 50 years, there have been 41 10-year periods (1950–1959, 1951–1960, etc.). The Small Stock Index outperformed the S & P 500 in 27 of those 41 10-year periods, the last such period being 1988–1997.

A dollar invested in small stocks for the past 50 years grew to $1,062 by the end of 1999 (versus $589 for $1 invested in the S & P 500). For small stocks, this translates into an average compound return of 15.0 percent per year. Over the past 50 years, the worst year for small stocks was 1973, when a loss of 31 percent was suffered. Two years later these same stocks posted a gain of almost 53 percent in one year. The best year so far has been 1967, when small stocks posted a gain of 84 percent. The best five years in a row for this category were 1975 to 1979, when the rate of return averaged 40 percent per year. The worst five-year period over the past half century has been 1969 to 1973, when this group lost an average of 11 percent per year. For 10-year periods, the best has been 1975 to 1984 (30 percent per year); the worst has been 1965 to 1974 (3 percent per year).

In order to obtain the kinds of returns described above, investors would have needed quite a bit of patience and understanding. During the 1990s, small-company stocks had a standard deviation (variation of return) of 20.2 percent, compared to 15.8 percent for common stocks and 8.9 percent for long-term government bonds.

During the past three years, aggressive growth funds have outperformed the S & P 500 by 10.7 percent per year. Over the past five years, this fund category has outperformed the S & P 500 by an average of a little under 1 percent per year. Average turnover during the last three years has been 120 percent.

The p/e ratio is 46 for the typical aggressive growth fund, 25 percent higher than the S & P 500. The typical stock in these portfolios is less than 20 percent the size of the average stock in the S & P 500. The average beta is 1.0, which means the group has a market-related risk that is almost identical to that of the S & P 500. There is over $220 billion in all aggressive growth funds combined. The average aggressive growth fund throws virtually no annual income stream. The typical annual expense ratio for this group is 1.6 percent.

The p/e ratio for the typical small-company fund is 32, a figure about 15 percent lower than the S & P 500. Yet the typical stock in these portfolios is only about 2 percent the size of the average stock in the S & P 500. The average beta is 0.9, which means the group's market-related risk is 10 percent less than the S & P 500. There is about $220 billion in all small-company funds combined. The average small-company growth fund throws off an income stream of close to zero annually. The typical annual expense ratio for this group is 1.5 percent.

There are 125 funds that make up the aggressive growth category. The small-company stock category, which has 725 funds, has been combined with aggressive growth. Thus, for this section, there were a total of 850 possible candidates. Total market capitalization of these two categories combined is $440 billion.

Over the past three years, aggressive growth funds (which include small-company stock funds) have had an average compound return of 27 percent per year (24 percent for small-company stock funds alone). The annual return has been 22 percent for the past five years (20 percent for small-company stock funds), 17 percent for the past decade (17 percent per year for small-company stock funds), and 16 percent per year for the past 15 years (15 percent for small-company stock funds).

The standard deviation for this combined category (aggressive growth and small-company stock) has been 35 percent over the past three years. This means that these funds have been more volatile than any other category except technology (standard deviation of 63 percent) and metals (standard deviation of 36 percent). Aggressive growth funds are certainly not for the faint of heart.

Aggressive Growth Funds

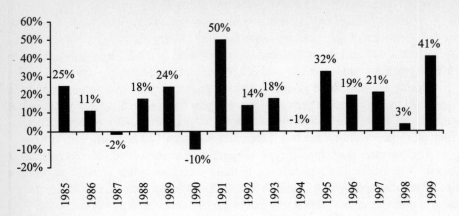

Alger Capital Appreciation B

1 World Trade Center Suite 9333
New York, NY 10048
800-992-3863
www.algerfunds.com

total return	★★★★★
risk reduction	★★★★
management	★★★★
tax minimization	★★★★★
expense control	★
symbol ACAPX	19 points
up-market performance	excellent
down-market performance	fair
predictability of returns	excellent

Total Return ★★★★★

Over the past five years, Alger Capital Appreciation B has taken $10,000 and turned it into $57,735 ($33,750 over the past three years). This translates into an annualized return of 42 percent over the past five years and 50 percent over the past three years. Over the past five years, this fund has outperformed 99 percent of all mutual funds; within its general category it has done better than 97 percent of its peers. Aggressive growth funds have averaged 22 percent annually over these same five years (all periods ending March 31, 2000).

Risk/Volatility ★★★★

Over the past five years, Capital Appreciation has only been safer than 10 percent of all aggressive growth funds. Since its inception, the fund has had one negative year, while the S & P 500 has also had one (off 3 percent in 1990); the Russell 2000 fell three times (off 20 percent in 1990, 2 percent in 1994, and 3 percent in 1998). The fund has underperformed the S & P 500 and the Russell 2000 three times since the fund's inception.

	last 5 years		since inception	
worst year	14%	1996	-2%	1994
best year	79%	1995	79%	1995

In the past, Alger Capital Appreciation B has done better than 95 percent of its peer group in up markets and outperformed 40 percent of its competition in down markets. Consistency, or predictability, of returns for Capital Appreciation can be described as excellent. This fund's risk-related return is excellent.

Management ★★★★

There are 50 stocks in this $1.2 billion portfolio. The average aggressive growth fund today is $480 million in size. Close to 100 percent of the fund's holdings are in stocks. The stocks in this portfolio have an average price-earnings (p/e) ratio of 49 and a median market capitalization of $76 billion. Technology represents over

60 percent of the fund's holdings, followed by non-durables (9 percent) and services (6 percent). The portfolio's equity holdings can be categorized as large-cap and growth-oriented issues. The fund has a correlation of just roughly 55 percent to the S & P 500 (versus 55 percent for aggressive growth funds).

David Alger has managed this fund for the past six years; Seilai Khoo came on board as comanager in early 1995. A team of over forty analysts, each of whom is assigned a specific industry, looks for high growth or a corporation that has made major changes. A security is sold if any of the following occurs: (1) deterioration of fundamentals, (2) stock has become overvalued, or (3) there is a better alternative. Management seeks long-term growth by using a bottom-up approach. There are 19 funds besides Capital Appreciation within the Alger family. Overall, the fund family's risk-adjusted performance can be described as excellent.

Tax Minimization   ★★★★★
During the past five years, a $10,000 initial investment grew to $54,440 after taxes, assuming a 39.6 percent income tax bracket (state and federal combined) and a capital gains rate of 28 percent. This means that investors in this fund were able to preserve 94 percent of their total returns. Compared to other equity funds, this fund's tax savings are considered to be excellent.

Expenses   ★
Alger Capital Appreciation B's expense ratio is 2.2 percent; it has averaged 2.3 percent annually over the past three calendar years. The average expense ratio for the 950 funds in this category is 1.5 percent. This fund's turnover rate over the past year has been 180 percent, while its peer group average has been 95 percent.

Summary
Alger Capital Appreciation B is an excellent choice for growth investors who like large company stocks. The folks at Alger are known for their independent, "non-herd" mentality, way of thinking. Alger has trained a number of managers who are considered tops in their field. Performance for this fund has been superb and so have after-tax returns; overall risk is surprisingly low considering the kind of returns.

Profile
minimum initial investment $1
subsequent minimum investment . . . $25
available in all 50 states. . . . . yes
telephone exchanges. . . . . yes
number of funds in family 20

IRA accounts available . . . . yes
IRA minimum investment $1
date of inception . . . . Oct. 1993
dividend/income paid . . . . annually
largest sector weighting . . . technology

Bridgeway Aggressive Growth
5650 Kirby Drive, Suite 141
Houston, TX 77005
800-661-3550
www.bridgewayfund.com

total return	★★★★★
risk reduction	★★
management	★★★★
tax minimization	★★★★★
expense control	★★★
symbol BRAGX	19 points
up-market performance	good
down-market performance	n/a
predictability of returns	excellent

Total Return   ★★★★★
Over the past five years, Bridgeway Aggressive Growth has taken $10,000 and turned it into $59,800 ($37,240 over the past three years). This translates into an annualized return of 43 percent over the past five years and 55 percent over the past three years. Over the past five years, this fund has outperformed 98 percent of all mutual funds; within its general category it has done better than 96 percent of its peers. Aggressive growth funds have averaged 22 percent annually over these same five years (all periods ending March 31, 2000).

Risk/Volatility   ★★
Over the past five years, Bridgeway has been safer than 80 percent of all aggressive growth funds. Since its inception, the fund has had no negative years, while the S & P 500 has had one (off 3 percent in 1990); the Russell 2000 fell three times (off 20 percent in 1990, 2 percent in 1994, and 3 percent in 1998). The fund has underperformed the S & P 500 and the Russell 2000 three times since the fund's inception.

	last 5 years		since inception	
worst year	18%	1997	18%	1997
best year	121%	1999	121%	1999

In the past, Bridgeway has done better than 65 percent of its peer group in up markets and outperformed 99 percent of its competition in down markets. Consistency, or predictability, of returns for Bridgeway can be described as excellent. This fund's risk-related return is also excellent.

Management   ★★★★
There are 35 stocks in this $30 million portfolio. The average aggressive growth fund today is $480 million in size. Close to 98 percent of the fund's holdings are in stocks. The stocks in this portfolio have an average price-earnings (p/e) ratio of 31 and a median market capitalization of $38 billion. Technology represents over half of the portfolio, followed by retail trade (12 percent of the holdings) and health

care (10 percent). The portfolio's equity holdings can be categorized as large-cap and growth-oriented issues. The fund has a correlation of just roughly 25 percent to the S & P 500 (versus 55 percent for aggressive growth funds in general).

John Montgomery has managed this fund for the past six years. Montgomery uses a bottom-up approach, examining growth rates, earnings prospects, comparative valuations, as well as downside risk potential. Management's fee drops if the fund's trailing five-year return lags the S & P 500. The fund strives to maintain a long-term risk level that is similar to the overall market. However, over the short term, the portfolio can be quite concentrated. There are four funds besides Aggressive Growth within the Bridgeway family. Overall, the fund family's risk-adjusted performance can be described as excellent.

Tax Minimization   ★★★★★
During the past five years, a $10,000 initial investment grew to $55,015 after taxes, assuming a 39.6 percent income tax bracket (state and federal combined) and a capital gains rate of 28 percent. This means that investors in this fund were able to preserve 92 percent of their total returns. Compared to other equity funds, this fund's tax savings are considered to be excellent.

Expenses   ★★★
Bridgeway's expense ratio is 1 percent; it has averaged 1.7 percent annually over the past three calendar years. The average expense ratio for the 950 funds in this category is 1.5 percent. This fund's turnover rate over the past year has been 210 percent, while its peer group average has been 95 percent.

Summary
Bridgeway Aggressive Growth has some of the highest returns in its sector. Equally important, returns remain quite high on an after-tax basis. One of the more appealing aspects of this portfolio is how management is punished if it trails the returns of the S & P 500 over an extended period. This, coupled with the fact that manager Montgomery sometimes bets heavily on just a couple of stocks, makes this a compelling choice for the moderate-to-aggressive investor.

Profile

minimum initial investment $2,000	*IRA accounts available* . . . . yes
subsequent minimum investment . . $500	*IRA minimum investment* $2,000
available in all 50 states. . . . . yes	*date of inception* . . . . Aug. 1994
telephone exchanges. . . . . yes	*dividend/income paid* . . . . annually
number of funds in family 5	*largest sector weighting* . . . technology

Citizens Emerging Growth
230 Commerce Way Suite 300
Portsmouth, NH 03801
800-223-7010
www.citizensfunds.com

total return	★★★★★
risk reduction	★★★★
management	★★★★
tax minimization	★★★
expense control	★
symbol WAEGX	19 points
up-market performance	excellent
down-market performance	very good
predictability of returns	excellent

Total Return   ★★★★★
Over the past five years, Citizens Emerging Growth has taken $10,000 and turned it into $51,890 ($38,700 over the past three years). This translates into an annualized return of 39 percent over the past five years and 57 percent over the past three years. Over the past five years, this fund has outperformed 98 percent of all mutual funds; within its general category it has done better than 94 percent of its peers. Aggressive growth funds have averaged 22 percent annually over these same five years (all periods ending March 31, 2000).

Risk/Volatility   ★★★★
Over the past five years, Emerging Growth has been safer than 85 percent of all aggressive growth funds. Since its inception, the fund has had no negative years, while the S & P 500 has had one (off 3 percent in 1990); the Russell 2000 fell three times (off 20 percent in 1990, 2 percent in 1994, and 3 percent in 1998). The fund has underperformed the S & P 500 and the Russell 2000 twice since the fund's inception.

	last 5 years		since inception	
worst year	14%	1996	14%	1996
best year	68%	1999	68%	1999

In the past, Emerging Growth has done better than 85 percent of its peer group in up markets and outperformed 80 percent of its competition in down markets. Consistency, or predictability, of returns for Citizens Emerging Growth can be described as excellent. This fund's risk-related return is also excellent.

Management   ★★★★
There are 30 stocks in this $175 million portfolio. The average aggressive growth fund today is $480 million in size. Close to 93 percent of the fund's holdings are in stocks. The stocks in this portfolio have an average price-earnings (p/e) ratio of 44 and a median market capitalization of $6 billion. Technology represents close to half of the portfolio, followed by services (17 percent of the holdings) and health

care (16 percent). The portfolio's equity holdings can be categorized as mid-cap and growth-oriented issues. The fund has a correlation of 70 percent to the S & P 500 (versus 50 percent for small company growth funds in general).

Richard Little has managed this fund for the past six years. Management first focuses on earnings momentum. The portfolio has been highly concentrated in just a couple of industry groups in the past and will repeat this strategy in the future. There are four funds besides Emerging Growth within the Citizens family. Overall, the fund family's risk-adjusted performance can be described as excellent.

Tax Minimization   ★★★★
During the past five years, a $10,000 initial investment grew to $45,145 after taxes, assuming a 39.6 percent income tax bracket (state and federal combined) and a capital gains rate of 28 percent. This means that investors in this fund were able to preserve 87 percent of their total returns. Compared to other equity funds, this fund's tax savings are considered to be very good.

Expenses   ★
Emerging Growth's expense ratio is 1.8 percent; it has averaged 1.9 percent annually over the past three calendar years. The average expense ratio for the 950 funds in this category is 1.5 percent. This fund's turnover rate over the past year has been 205 percent, while its peer group average has been 95 percent.

Summary
Citizens Emerging Growth is the only "socially responsible" aggressive growth fund in the book. It is also one of the best performers over the past three and five years. The fund does well in every area except expenses and turnover (the costs of which are not shown in any fund's expense ratio). Still, risk-adjusted returns have been amazingly good and the fund has been safer than 85 percent of its peers. Citizens is a small fund family that provides other portfolios that also have excellent risk-adjusted returns.

Profile

minimum initial investment $2,500	*IRA accounts available* . . . . yes
subsequent minimum investment $1	*IRA minimum investment* $1,000
available in all 50 states. . . . . yes	*date of inception* . . . . Feb. 1994
telephone exchanges. . . . . yes	*dividend/income paid* . . . . annually
number of funds in family 5	*largest sector weighting* . . . technology

Franklin Small Cap Growth A

777 Mariners Island Boulevard
San Mateo, CA 94403
800-342-5236
www.franklin-templeton.com

total return	★★★
risk reduction	★★
management	★★★
tax minimization	★★★★★
expense control	★★★★★
symbol FRSGX	18 points
up-market performance	excellent
down-market performance	good
predictability of returns	very good

Total Return   ★★★

Over the past five years, Franklin Small Cap Growth A has taken $10,000 and turned it into $41,620 ($28,635 over the past three years). This translates into an annualized return of 33 percent over the past five years and 42 percent over the past three years. Over the past five years, this fund has outperformed 96 percent of all mutual funds; within its general category it has done better than 90 percent of its peers. Aggressive growth funds have averaged 22 percent annually over these same five years (all periods ending March 31, 2000).

Risk/Volatility   ★★

Over the past five years, Small Cap Growth has been safer than 85 percent of all aggressive growth funds. Since its inception, the fund has had one negative year, while the S & P 500 has also had one (off 3 percent in 1990); the Russell 2000 fell three times (off 20 percent in 1990, 2 percent in 1994, and 3 percent in 1998). The fund has underperformed the S & P 500 twice and the Russell 2000 once since the fund's inception.

	last 5 years		since inception	
worst year	0%	1998	0%	1998
best year	97%	1999	97%	1999

In the past, Small Cap Growth has done better than 90 percent of its peer group in up markets and outperformed 50 percent of its competition in down markets. Consistency, or predictability, of returns for Franklin Small Cap Growth A can be described as very good. This fund's risk-related return is good.

Management   ★★★

There are 330 stocks in this $15 billion portfolio. The average aggressive growth fund today is $480 million in size. Close to 92 percent of the fund's holdings are in stocks. Roughly half the portfolio is in technology issues, followed by industrial cyclicals (9 percent of the holdings) and financials (8 percent). The stocks in this portfolio have an average price-earnings (p/e) ratio of 34 and a median market capitalization of $3.2 billion. The portfolio's equity holdings can be categorized as mid-cap and growth-oriented issues. The fund has a correlation of just under 40 percent to the S & P 500 (versus 50 percent for small company growth funds in general).

A team has managed this fund for the past six years. There are 78 funds besides Small Cap Growth within the Franklin Templeton family. Management targets emerging companies that have the potential for significant appreciation. Security selection is partially based on the use of computer models as well as fundamental analysis. Overall, the fund family's risk-adjusted performance can be described as very good.

Tax Minimization   ★★★★★
During the past five years, a $10,000 initial investment grew to $39,120 after taxes, assuming a 39.6 percent income tax bracket (state and federal combined) and a capital gains rate of 28 percent. This means that investors in this fund were able to preserve 94 percent of their total returns. Compared to other equity funds, this fund's tax savings are considered to be excellent.

Expenses   ★★★★★
Small Cap Growth's expense ratio is .9 percent; it has averaged .9 percent annually over the past three calendar years. The average expense ratio for the 950 funds in this category is 1.5 percent. This fund's turnover rate over the past year has been 45 percent, while its peer group average has been 95 percent.

Summary
Franklin Small Cap Growth A has managed to outperform over 95 percent of all mutual funds as well as 90 percent of its peer group. Despite these impressive figures, capital preservation (tax minimization) and low overhead are the two areas where this fund receives its highest marks. This fund is part of the Franklin Templeton group, one of the largest and oldest fund families in the country.

Profile
minimum initial investment $1,000	*IRA accounts available* . . . . yes
subsequent minimum investment . . . $50	*IRA minimum investment* $250
available in all 50 states. . . . . yes	*date of inception* . . . . Feb. 1992
telephone exchanges. . . . . yes	*dividend/income paid* . . . semi-annually
number of funds in family 79	*largest sector weighting* . . . technology

Fremont U.S. Micro-Cap
50 Beale Street, Suite 100
San Francisco, CA 94105
800-548-4539
www.fremontfunds.com

total return	★★★★★
risk reduction	★★
management	★★★
tax minimization	★★★★
expense control	★★
symbol FUSMX	16 points
up-market performance	excellent
down-market performance	poor
predictability of returns	very good

Total Return   ★★★★★
Over the past five years, Fremont U.S. Micro-Cap has taken $10,000 and turned it into $64,100 ($33,750 over the past three years). This translates into an annualized return of 45 percent over the past five years and 50 percent over the past three years. Over the past five years, this fund has outperformed 99 percent of all mutual funds; within its general category it has also done better than 99 percent of its peers. Aggressive growth funds have averaged 22 percent annually over these same five years (all periods ending March 31, 2000).

Risk/Volatility   ★★★★★
Over the past five years, U.S. Micro-Cap has been safer than 75 percent of all aggressive growth funds. Since its inception, the fund has had no negative years, while the S & P 500 has had one (off 3 percent in 1990); the Russell 2000 fell three times (off 20 percent in 1990, 2 percent in 1994, and 3 percent in 1998). The fund has underperformed the S & P 500 twice and the Russell 2000 once since the fund's inception.

	last 5 years		since inception	
worst year	3%	1998	3%	1998
best year	130%	1999	130%	1999

In the past, Fremont U.S. Micro-Cap has done better than 99 percent of its peer group in up markets but outperformed only 5 percent of its competition in down markets. Consistency, or predictability, of returns for Fremont U.S. Micro-Cap can be described as very good. This fund's risk-related return is excellent.

Management   ★★★★★
There are 72 stocks in this $1.3 billion portfolio. The average aggressive growth fund today is $480 million in size. Close to 72 percent of the fund's holdings are in stocks. The stocks in this portfolio have an average price-earnings (p/e) ratio of 25 and a median market capitalization of $400 million. Approximately 37 percent of the portfolio is in technology issues, followed by industrial cyclicals (11 percent of the holdings) and health care (8 percent). The portfolio's equity holdings

can be categorized as small-cap and growth-oriented issues. The fund has a correlation of under 30 percent to the S & P 500 (versus 50 percent for small company funds in general).

Robert Kern has managed this fund for the past six years. Most of the fund's holdings are in micro-cap issues. Management focuses on the bottom 5 percent of the market-capitalization spectrum (caps that typically range from $10–$500 million). Stocks are sold if the company's fundamentals deteriorate or valuation becomes too rich. There are six funds besides U.S. Micro-Cap within the Fremont family. Overall, the fund family's risk-adjusted performance can be described as very good.

Tax Minimization   ★★★★★
During the past five years, a $10,000 initial investment grew to $57,690 after taxes, assuming a 39.6 percent income tax bracket (state and federal combined) and a capital gains rate of 28 percent. This means that investors in this fund were able to preserve 90 percent of their total returns. Compared to other equity funds, this fund's tax savings are considered to be very good.

Expenses   ★★
U.S. Micro-Cap's expense ratio is 1.8 percent; it has averaged 1.9 percent annually over the past three calendar years. The average expense ratio for the 950 funds in this category is 1.5 percent. This fund's turnover rate over the past year has been 160 percent, while its peer group average has been 95 percent.

Summary
Fremont U.S. Micro-Cap leads the pack as the five-year best-performing aggressive growth/small company stock fund in the book. After-tax earnings of 90 percent also make this an appealing fund from a tax minimization perspective. This is not the kind of fund you would want to own during a market downturn, but it certainly is the top choice for the investor with an eye toward the long term or anyone who can ride out the ups and downs of the market.

Profile
minimum initial investment $2,000	*IRA accounts available* . . . . yes
subsequent minimum investment . . $100	*IRA minimum investment* $1,000
available in all 50 states. . . . . yes	*date of inception*. . . . . June 1994
telephone exchanges. . . . . yes	*dividend/income paid* . . . . annually
number of funds in family 7	*largest sector weighting* . . . technology

Invesco Dynamics
P.O. Box 173706
Denver, CO 80217
800-525-8085
www.invesco.com

total return	★★★★
risk reduction	★★★★★
management	★★★★★
tax minimization	★★★★
expense control	★★★
symbol FIDYX	21 points
up-market performance	very good
down-market performance	fair
predictability of returns	very good

Total Return   ★★★★
Over the past five years, Invesco Dynamics has taken $10,000 and turned it into $44,840 ($33,090 over three years and $100,860 over the past 10 years). This translates into an annualized return of 35 percent over the past five years, 49 percent over the past three years, and 26 percent for the decade. Over the past five years, this fund has outperformed 97 percent of all mutual funds; within its general category it has done better than 88 percent of its peers. Aggressive growth funds have averaged 22 percent annually over these same five years (all periods ending March 31, 2000).

Risk/Volatility   ★★★★★
Over the past five years, Dynamics has been safer than 95 percent of all aggressive growth funds. Over the past decade, the fund has had two negative years, while the S & P 500 has had one (off 3 percent in 1990); the Russell 2000 fell three times (off 20 percent in 1990, 2 percent in 1994, and 3 percent in 1998). The fund has underperformed the S & P 500 five times and the Russell 2000 three times in the last 10 years.

	last 5 years		last 10 years	
worst year	15%	1996	-2%	1994
best year	72%	1999	72%	1999

In the past, Dynamics has done better than 80 percent of its peer group in up markets and outperformed 40 percent of its competition in down markets. Consistency, or predictability, of returns for Dynamics can be described as very good. This fund's risk-related return is excellent.

Management   ★★★★★
There are 150 stocks in this $6.8 billion portfolio. The average aggressive growth fund today is $480 million in size. Close to 95 percent of the fund's holdings are in stocks. Approximately 45 percent of the portfolio is in technology issues, followed

by nondurables (10 percent of the holdings) and health care (9 percent). The stocks in this portfolio have an average price-earnings (p/e) ratio of 43 and a median market capitalization of $8.9 billion. The portfolio's equity holdings can be categorized as mid-cap and growth-oriented issues. The fund has a correlation of a little more than 40 percent to the S & P 500 (versus 55 percent for aggressive growth funds in general).

Timothy Miller and Thomas Wald have comanaged this fund for the past five years. Management favors companies with valuations of $2–$15 billion. Strategically, the fund tries to maintain long-term "core" holdings with the 40 percent balance in more speculative issues. There are 19 funds besides Dynamics within the Invesco family. Overall, the fund family's risk-adjusted performance can be described as very good.

Tax Minimization   ★★★★
During the past five years, a $10,000 initial investment grew to $38,115 after taxes, assuming a 39.6 percent income tax bracket (state and federal combined) and a capital gains rate of 28 percent. This means that investors in this fund were able to preserve 85 percent of their total returns. Compared to other equity funds, this fund's tax savings are considered to be very good.

Expenses   ★★★
Invesco Dynamics's expense ratio is 1 percent; it has averaged 1.1 percent annually over the past three calendar years. The average expense ratio for the 950 funds in this category is 1.5 percent. This fund's turnover rate over the past year has been 175 percent, while its peer group average has been 95 percent.

Summary
Invesco Dynamics is one the very lowest risk funds in its category (beating out 95 percent of its competition) plus has turned in impressive three- and five-year return figures. Capital preservation and low overhead are also areas in which the fund has done a very good job. You should check out some of the other offerings within the Invesco family; overall, the group is rated quite high on a risk-adjusted return basis.

Profile
minimum initial investment $1,000
subsequent minimum investment . . . $50
available in all 50 states. . . . . yes
telephone exchanges. . . . . yes
number of funds in family 20

IRA accounts available . . . . yes
IRA minimum investment $250
date of inception . . . . Sept. 1967
dividend/income paid . . . . annually
largest sector weighting . . . technology

Pin Oak Aggressive Stock
P.O. Box 419441
Kansas City, MO 64141
888-462-5386
www.oakassociates.com

total return	★★★★★
risk reduction	★
management	★★★★
tax minimization	★★★★★
expense control	★★★★★
symbol POGSX	20 points
up-market performance	excellent
down-market performance	very good
predictability of returns	very good

Total Return ★★★★★
Over the past five years, Pin Oak Aggressive Stock has taken $10,000 and turned it into $61,920 ($51,780 over the past three years). This translates into an annualized return of 44 percent over the past five years and 73 percent over the past three years. Over the past five years, this fund has outperformed 98 percent of all mutual funds; within its general category it has done better than 95 percent of its peers. Aggressive growth funds have averaged 22 percent annually over these same five years (all periods ending March 31, 2000).

Risk/Volatility ★
Over the past five years, Pin Oak Aggressive Stock has only been safer than 10 percent of all aggressive growth funds. Over the past decade, the fund has had no negative years, while the S & P 500 has had one (off 3 percent in 1990); the Russell 2000 fell three times (off 20 percent in 1990, 2 percent in 1994, and 3 percent in 1998). The fund has underperformed the S & P 500 five times and the Russell 2000 three times in the last 10 years.

	last 5 years		since inception	
worst year	1%	1997	0%	1994
best year	98%	1999	98%	1999

In the past, Aggressive Stock has done better than 99 percent of its peer group in up markets and outperformed 80 percent of its competition in down markets. Consistency, or predictability, of returns for Aggressive Stock can be described as very good. This fund's risk-related return is very good.

Management ★★★★
There are 25 stocks in this $460 million portfolio. The average aggressive growth fund today is $480 million in size. Over 90 percent of the fund's holdings are in stocks. Approximately 85 percent of the portfolio is in technology issues, followed by financials (8 percent of the holdings) and industrial cyclicals (4 percent). The

stocks in this portfolio have an average price-earnings (p/e) ratio of 48 and a median market capitalization of $37 billion. The portfolio's equity holdings can be categorized as large-cap and growth-oriented issues. The fund has a correlation of a little more than 30 percent to the S & P 500 (versus 50 percent for small company growth funds in general).

James Oelschlager has managed this fund for the past eight years. Management starts with a top-down approach, seeking high-growth industries; once sectors are selected, specific equities are chosen based on comparisons of several ratios against the S & P 500. Securities are sold if there are signs of poor fundamentals, downward revisions in earnings estimates, or if a predetermined price target has been hit. There are two funds besides Aggressive Stock within the Oak Associates family. Overall, the fund family's risk-adjusted performance can be described as excellent.

Tax Minimization   ★★★★★
During the past five years, a $10,000 initial investment grew to $61,920 after taxes, assuming a 39.6 percent income tax bracket (state and federal combined) and a capital gains rate of 28 percent. This means that investors in this fund were able to preserve 100 percent of their total returns. Compared to other equity funds, this fund's tax savings are considered to be excellent.

Expenses   ★★★★★
Aggressive Stock's expense ratio is 1 percent; it has averaged 1 percent annually over the past three calendar years. The average expense ratio for the 950 funds in this category is 1.5 percent. This fund's turnover rate over the past year has been 10 percent, while its peer group average has been 95 percent.

Summary
Pin Oak Aggressive Stock ranks number one in performance over the past three years and number two over the past five years. After-tax returns are 100 percent, making this the most tax-efficient fund in its broad category. Overall risk level is higher than any of its peers in the book, but the fund has certainly rewarded patient investors. It is a highly recommended choice whether one is dealing with sheltered or nonsheltered investment dollars.

Profile
minimum initial investment $2,000	*IRA accounts available* . . . . yes
subsequent minimum investment . . . $50	*IRA minimum investment* $2,000
available in all 50 states. . . . . yes	*date of inception* . . . . Aug. 1992
telephone exchanges. . . . . yes	*dividend/income paid* . . . . annually
number of funds in family 3	*largest sector weighting* . . . technology

Putnam New Opportunities A

One Post Office Square
Boston, MA 02109
800-225-1581
www.putnaminv.com

total return	★★★★
risk reduction	★★★★
management	★★★★★
tax minimization	★★★★★
expense control	★★★★★
symbol PNOPX	23 points
up-market performance	very good
down-market performance	fair
predictability of returns	very good

Total Return   ★★★★

Over the past five years, Putnam New Opportunities A has taken $10,000 and turned it into $44,840 ($32,420 over the past three years). This translates into an annualized return of 35 percent over the past five years and 48 percent over the past three years. Over the past five years, this fund has outperformed 97 percent of all mutual funds; within its general category it has done better than 89 percent of its peers. Aggressive growth funds have averaged 22 percent annually over these same five years (all periods ending March 31, 2000).

Risk/Volatility   ★★★★

Over the past five years, New Opportunities has only been safer than 10 percent of all aggressive growth funds. Over the past decade, the fund has had no negative years, while the S & P 500 has had one (off 3 percent in 1990); the Russell 2000 fell three times (off 20 percent in 1990, 2 percent in 1994, and 3 percent in 1998). The fund has underperformed the S & P 500 three times and the Russell 2000 once in the last 10 years.

	last 5 years		last 10 years	
worst year	11%	1996	3%	1994
best year	70%	1999	70%	1999

In the past, New Opportunities has done better than 80 percent of its peer group in up markets and outperformed 40 percent of its competition in down markets. Consistency, or predictability, of returns for New Opportunities can be described as very good. This fund's risk-related return is excellent.

Management   ★★★★★

There are 195 stocks in this $21 billion portfolio. The average aggressive growth fund today is $480 million in size. Close to 100 percent of the fund's holdings are in stocks. The stocks in this portfolio have an average price-earnings (p/e) ratio of 53 and a median market capitalization of $71 billion. Approximately 60 percent of the portfolio is in technology issues, followed by nondurables (13 percent of the holdings) and industrial retail (5 percent). The portfolio's equity holdings can be categorized as large-cap and growth-oriented issues. The fund has a correlation of a little more than 50 percent to the S & P 500 (versus 55 percent for aggressive growth funds in general).

Daniel Miller has been manager since 1990; Jeffrey Lindsey came on board as comanager in 1998. Management uses a thematic, top-down approach, looking first to industry groups that have the best growth prospects. A bottom-up approach is then used to select corporations that have a dominant position, market niche, freedom from excessive government regulation, management ownership of stock, as well as minimum growth rate of 17 percent. There are 178 funds besides New Opportunities within the Putnam family. Overall, the fund family's risk-adjusted performance can be described as very good.

Tax Minimization   ★★★★★
During the past five years, a $10,000 initial investment grew to $43,940 after taxes, assuming a 39.6 percent income tax bracket (state and federal combined) and a capital gains rate of 28 percent. This means that investors in this fund were able to preserve 98 percent of their total returns. Compared to other equity funds, this fund's tax savings are considered to be excellent.

Expenses   ★★★★★
New Opportunities' expense ratio is .9 percent; it has averaged .9 percent annually over the past three calendar years. The average expense ratio for the 950 funds in this category is 1.5 percent. This fund's turnover rate over the past year has been 77 percent, while its peer group average has been 95 percent.

Summary
Putnam New Opportunities A has a great management team. Miller concentrates on stocks with a $2–$20 billion cap while comanager Lindsey invests the remaining third of the portfolio in large caps. Returns have been very good for this fund and tax minimization as well as expense control have been exceptional. This fund is highly recommended, as evidenced by its near-perfect score.

Profile

minimum initial investment $500	*IRA accounts available* .... yes
subsequent minimum investment ... $50	*IRA minimum investment* $250
available in all 50 states.......... yes	*date of inception* .... Aug. 1990
telephone exchanges............. yes	*dividend/income paid* .... annually
number of funds in family 179	*largest sector weighting* ... technology

Sit Small Cap Growth
4600 Norwest Center
90 South 7th Street
Minneapolis, MN 55402
800-332-5580
www.sitfunds.com

total return	★★★★
risk reduction	★★
management	★★★
tax minimization	★★★★★
expense control	★★★★
symbol SSMGX	18 points
up-market performance	excellent
down-market performance	excellent
predictability of returns	excellent

Total Return   ★★★★
Over the past five years, Sit Small Cap Growth has taken $10,000 and turned it into $46,530 ($33,750 over the past three years). This translates into an annualized return of 36 percent over the past five years and 50 percent over the past three years. Over the past five years, this fund has outperformed 95 percent of all mutual funds; within its general category it has done better than 87 percent of its peers. Aggressive growth funds have averaged 22 percent annually over these same five years (all periods ending March 31, 2000).

Risk/Volatility   ★★
Over the past five years, Sit Small Cap Growth has been safer than 65 percent of all aggressive growth funds. Since its inception, the fund has had no negative years, while the S & P 500 has had one (off 3 percent in 1990); the Russell 2000 fell three times (off 20 percent in 1990, 2 percent in 1994, and 3 percent in 1998). The fund has underperformed the S & P 500 three times and the Russell 2000 twice since the fund's inception.

	last 5 years		since inception	
worst year	2%	1998	2%	1998
best year	109%	1999	109%	1999

In the past, Small Cap Growth has done better than 95 percent of its peer group in up markets and outperformed 85 percent of its competition in down markets. Consistency, or predictability, of returns for Small Cap Growth can be described as excellent. This fund's risk-related return is very good.

Management   ★★★
There are 60 stocks in this $80 million portfolio. The average aggressive growth fund today is $480 million in size. Close to 95 percent of the fund's holdings are in stocks. The stocks in this portfolio have an average price-earnings (p/e) ratio of

51 and a median market capitalization of $3.3 billion. Technology represents close to 60 percent of the fund's holdings, followed by services (21 percent) and health care (11 percent). The portfolio's equity holdings can be categorized as mid-cap and growth-oriented issues. The fund has a correlation of approximately 50 percent to the S & P 500 (versus 55 percent for aggressive growth funds in general).

Eugene Sit has managed this fund for the past six years. Management is interested in three kinds of stocks: fast growers, conservative growers, and cyclical growers. There are nine funds besides Small Cap Growth within the Sit family. Overall, the fund family's risk-adjusted performance can be described as excellent.

Tax Minimization   ★★★★★
During the past five years, a $10,000 initial investment grew to $43,735 after taxes, assuming a 39.6 percent income tax bracket (state and federal combined) and a capital gains rate of 28 percent. This means that investors in this fund were able to preserve 94 percent of their total returns. Compared to other equity funds, this fund's tax savings are considered to be excellent.

Expenses   ★★★★
Small Cap Growth's expense ratio is 1.5 percent; it has averaged 1.5 percent annually over the past three calendar years. The average expense ratio for the 950 funds in this category is also 1.5 percent. This fund's turnover rate over the past year has been 70 percent, while its peer group average has been 95 percent.

Summary
Sit Small Cap Growth has very good returns and excellent after-tax gains. This is one of the few funds that receives an "excellent" rating in up and down markets as well as for predictability of returns. Management has been able to outdo 95 percent of its competitors in bull markets and 85 percent during bear periods. This 10-fund family has a number of other fantastic offerings that investors should strongly consider.

Profile
minimum initial investment $2,000	*IRA accounts available* . . . . no
subsequent minimum investment . . $100	*IRA minimum investment* . . . . n/a
available in all 50 states . . . . yes	*date of inception* . . . . July 1994
telephone exchanges . . . . yes	*dividend/income paid* . . . . annually
number of funds in family 10	*largest sector weighting* . . . technology

Smith Barney Aggressive Growth A

388 Greenwich Street, 37th Floor
New York, NY 10013
800-451-2010
www.smithbarney.com

total return	★★★★
risk reduction	★★★★★
management	★★★★★
tax minimization	★★★★★
expense control	★★★★★
symbol SHRAX	24 points
up-market performance	excellent
down-market performance	very good
predictability of returns	good

Total Return   ★★★★
Over the past five years, Smith Barney Aggressive Growth A has taken $10,000 and turned it into $44,840 ($33,080 over three years and $79,260 over the past 10 years). This translates into an annualized return of 35 percent over the past five years, 49 percent over the past three years, and 23 percent for the decade. Over the past five years, this fund has outperformed 97 percent of all mutual funds; within its general category it has done better than 90 percent of its peers. Aggressive growth funds have averaged 22 percent annually over these same five years (all periods ending March 31, 2000).

Risk/Volatility   ★★★★★
Over the past five years, Aggressive Growth has only been safer than 15 percent of all aggressive growth funds. Over the past decade, the fund has had two negative years, while the S & P 500 has had one (off 3 percent in 1990); the Russell 2000 fell three times (off 20 percent in 1990, 2 percent in 1994, and 3 percent in 1998). The fund has underperformed the S & P 500 six times and the Russell 2000 three times in the last 10 years.

	last 5 years		last 10 years	
worst year	3%	1996	-6%	1990
best year	64%	1999	64%	1999

In the past, Aggressive Growth has done better than 85 percent of its peer group in up markets and outperformed 70 percent of its competition in down markets. Consistency, or predictability, of returns for Aggressive Growth can be described as good. This fund's risk-related return is excellent.

Management   ★★★★★
There are 82 stocks in this $1.3 billion portfolio. The average aggressive growth fund today is $480 million in size. Close to 98 percent of the fund's holdings are in stocks. The stocks in this portfolio have an average price-earnings (p/e) ratio of 44 and a

median market capitalization of $56 billion. Approximately 35 percent of the portfolio is in technology issues, followed by services (35 percent of holdings) and financials (9 percent). The portfolio's equity holdings can be categorized as large-cap and growth-oriented issues. The fund has a correlation of a little more than 50 percent to the S & P 500 (versus 55 percent for aggressive growth funds in general).

Richard Freeman has managed this fund since 1986. Management looks for companies whose growth rate is greater than those found in the S & P 500. Freeman is particularly interested in undervalued stocks in high-growth industries. Long-term holdings are emphasized. There are 172 funds besides Aggressive Growth within the Salomon Smith Barney family. Overall, the fund family's risk-adjusted performance can be described as good.

Tax Minimization   ★★★★★
During the past five years, a $10,000 initial investment grew to $43,050 after taxes, assuming a 39.6 percent income tax bracket (state and federal combined) and a capital gains rate of 28 percent. This means that investors in this fund were able to preserve 96 percent of their total returns. Compared to other equity funds, this fund's tax savings are considered to be excellent.

Expenses   ★★★★★
Aggressive Growth's expense ratio is 1.2 percent; it has also averaged 1.2 percent annually over the past three calendar years. The average expense ratio for the 950 funds in this category is 1.5 percent. This fund's turnover rate over the past year has been 8 percent, while its peer group average has been 95 percent.

Summary
Smith Barney Aggressive Growth A has ranked in the top quartile of performance in three of the past four years (through June of 2000). The fund ranks as the second best in its category when it comes to risk and predictability of returns. Capital preservation on an after-tax basis is also exceptional. This fund receives 24 out of 25 points, making its near-perfect score one of the very best funds in any category.

Profile

minimum initial investment $1,000	*IRA accounts available* . . . . yes
subsequent minimum investment . . . $50	*IRA minimum investment* $250
available in all 50 states. . . . . yes	*date of inception* . . . . Oct. 1983
telephone exchanges. . . . . yes	*dividend/income paid* . . . . annually
number of funds in family 173	*largest sector weighting* . . . . health

USAA Aggressive Growth
USAA Building
San Antonio, TX 78288
800-382-8722
www.usaa.com

total return	★★★★
risk reduction	★★
management	★★★★
tax minimization	★★★★★
expense control	★★★★★
symbol USAUX	20 points
up-market performance	excellent
down-market performance	fair
predictability of returns	very good

Total Return   ★★★★
Over the past five years, USAA Aggressive Growth has taken $10,000 and turned it into $48,260 ($33,750 over three years and $79,260 over the past 10 years). This translates into an annualized return of 37 percent over the past five years, 50 percent over the past three years, and 23 percent for the decade. Over the past five years, this fund has outperformed 98 percent of all mutual funds; within its general category it has done better than 93 percent of its peers. Aggressive growth funds have averaged 22 percent annually over these same five years (all periods ending March 31, 2000).

Risk/Volatility   ★★
Over the past five years, Aggressive Growth has been safer than 40 percent of all aggressive growth funds. Over the past decade, the fund has had three negative years, while the S & P 500 has had one (off 3 percent in 1990); the Russell 2000 fell three times (off 20 percent in 1990, 2 percent in 1994, and 3 percent in 1998). The fund has underperformed the S & P 500 seven times and the Russell 2000 four times in the last 10 years.

	last 5 years		last 10 years	
worst year	8%	1997	-12%	1990
best year	91%	1999	91%	1999

In the past, Aggressive Growth has done better than 90 percent of its peer group in up markets and outperformed 25 percent of its competition in down markets. Consistency, or predictability, of returns for Aggressive Growth can be described as very good. This fund's risk-related return is very good.

Management   ★★★★
There are 250 stocks in this $1.9 billion portfolio. The average aggressive growth fund today is $480 million in size. Close to 98 percent of the fund's holdings are in stocks. The stocks in this portfolio have an average price-earnings (p/e) ratio of

37 and a median market capitalization of $18 billion. Approximately 50 percent of the portfolio is in technology issues, followed by health care (16 percent of hold-ings) and services (8 percent). The portfolio's equity holdings can be categorized as large-cap and growth-oriented issues. The fund has a correlation of 30 percent to the S & P 500 (versus 55 percent for aggressive growth funds in general).

Eric Efron and John Cabell have managed this fund for the past six years. The managers look for corporations that are taking advantage of changes in society and in the economy, which are broken down into six themes: telecom, lifestyles, effi-ciency, computing, consolidation, and new products and services. There are 26 funds besides Aggressive Growth within the USAA family. Overall, the fund family's risk-adjusted performance can be described as very good.

Tax Minimization   ★★★★★
During the past five years, a $10,000 initial investment grew to $44,400 after taxes, assuming a 39.6 percent income tax bracket (state and federal combined) and a capital gains rate of 28 percent. This means that investors in this fund were able to preserve 92 percent of their total returns. Compared to other equity funds, this fund's tax savings are considered to be excellent.

Expenses   ★★★★★
USAA Aggressive Growth's expense ratio is .7 percent; it has averaged .7 percent annually over the past three calendar years. The average expense ratio for the 950 funds in this category is 1.5 percent. This fund's turnover rate over the past year has been 35 percent, while its peer group average has been 95 percent.

Summary
USAA Aggressive Growth has turned in very impressive return figures for the past three and five years, but its eye toward keeping expenses down (the lowest of its peers in the book) and tax minimization (92 percent) are where this fund really shines. Check out other members in the fund family; overall, the group's risk-adjusted returns are quite good.

Profile
minimum initial investment . . . . . $3,000   *IRA accounts available* . . . . yes
subsequent minimum investment . . . $50   *IRA minimum investment* $250
available in all 50 states. . . . . yes   *date of inception* . . . . July 1981
telephone exchanges. . . . . yes   *dividend/income paid* . . . . annually
number of funds in family 27   *largest sector weighting* . . . technology

Balanced Funds

The objective of balanced funds, also referred to as total return funds, is to provide both growth and income. Fund management purchases common stocks, bonds, and convertible securities. Portfolio composition is almost always exclusively U.S. securities. The weighting of stocks compared to bonds depends upon the portfolio manager's perception of the stock market, interest rates, and risk levels. It is rare for less than 30 percent of the fund's holdings to be in stocks or bonds.

Balanced funds offer neither the best nor worst of both worlds. These funds will often outperform the different categories of bond funds during bull markets but suffer greater percentage losses during stock market declines. On the other hand, when interest rates are on the rise, balanced funds will typically decline less on a total return basis (current yield plus or minus principal appreciation) than a bond fund. When rates are falling, balanced funds will also outperform bond funds if stocks are also doing well.

Over the past 10 years, the average balanced fund had 69 percent of the return of growth funds (12.1 percent versus 17.5 percent) with 54 percent less risk. Balanced funds are the perfect choice for the investor who cannot decide between stocks and bonds. This hybrid security is a middle-of-the-road approach, ideal for someone who wants a fund manager to determine the portfolio's weighting of stocks, bonds, and convertibles.

Balanced Funds

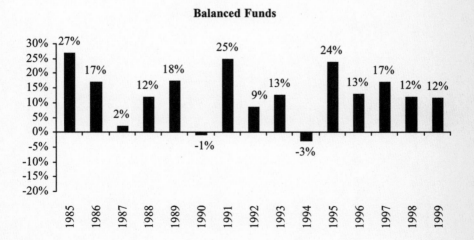

The price-earnings ratio for stocks in a typical balanced fund is 33, a little more than 10 percent lower than the S & P 500's p/e ratio. The average beta is 0.6, which means that this group has only 60 percent of the market-related risk of the S & P 500. During the past three years, balanced funds have lagged the performance of the S & P 500 by over 13 percent annually. Over the past five years, this benchmark has outperformed balanced funds by an average of 12 percent per year. The figure falls to 7 percent annually for the past decade. Average turnover during the last three years has been 80 percent per annum. Balanced funds throw off an income stream of less than 2.5 percent annually. The typical annual expense ratio for this group is 1.3 percent.

Over 450 funds make up the balanced category; market capitalization is $180 billion. Three other categories—asset allocation (300 funds, total market capitalization of $85 billion), multi-asset global (100 funds, total market capitalization of $40 billion), and convertible (60 funds, total market capitalization of $9 billion)—have been combined with balanced. Thus, for this section there were a total of 910 possible candidates. Total market capitalization of these four categories combined is $314 billion.

BlackRock Balanced

Four Falls Corporate Center, 6th Floor
West Conshohoken, PA 19428
800-441-7762
www.blackrock.com

total return	★★★★
risk reduction	★★★★
management	★★★★
current income	★★★
expense control	★★
symbol PCBAX	17 points
up-market performance	very good
down-market performance	very good
predictability of returns	excellent

Total Return   ★★★★

Over the past five years, BlackRock Balanced has taken $10,000 and turned it into $22,880 ($16,850 over three years). This translates into an annualized return of 18 percent over the past five years and 19 percent over the past three years. Over the past five years, this fund has outperformed 76 percent of all mutual funds; within its general category it has done better than 87 percent of its peers. Balanced funds have averaged 15 percent annually over these same five years (all periods ending March 31, 2000).

During the past five years, a $10,000 initial investment grew to $20,360 after taxes, assuming a 39.6 percent income tax bracket (state and federal combined) and a capital gains rate of 28 percent. This means that investors in this fund were able to preserve 89 percent of their total returns. Compared to other fixed-income funds, this fund's tax savings are considered to be very good.

Risk/Volatility   ★★★★

Over the past five years, BlackRock has been safer than 60 percent of all balanced funds. Over the past decade, the fund has had one negative year, while the S & P 500 has had one (off 3 percent in 1990); the Lehman Brothers Aggregate Bond Index fell twice (off 3 percent in 1994 and 1 percent in 1999). The fund has underperformed the S & P 500 seven times and the Lehman Brothers Aggregate Bond Index once in the last 10 years.

	last 5 years		last 10 years	
worst year	11%	1999	-4%	1994
best year	27%	1995	27%	1995

In the past, BlackRock has done better than 65 percent of its peer group in up markets and down markets. Consistency, or predictability, of returns for BlackRock Balanced can be described as excellent. This fund's risk-related return is also excellent.

Management   ★★★★

There are 75 stocks and 280 fixed-income securities in this $160 million portfolio. The average balanced fund today is $350 million in size. Close to 65 percent of this fund's holdings are in stocks and 35 percent in bonds. The stocks in this portfolio have an average price-earnings (p/e) ratio of 35 and a median market capitalization of $130 billion. Approximately 20 percent of the equity holdings are in technology issues, followed by finance (10 percent of holdings) and industrial cyclicals (7 percent). The fund's equities have a correlation of 97 percent to the S & P 500 (versus 95 percent for its category). The average maturity of the bonds in this account is 17 years; the weighted coupon rate averages 6.8 percent. The portfolio's equity holdings can be categorized as large-cap and a blend of growth and value stocks. The portfolio's fixed-income holdings can be categorized as long-term, very high-quality debt.

A team has managed this fund for the past five years. A policy committee looks at macroeconomic data and input from the fund's advisor. Target weightings are 60 percent in stocks similar to the S & P 500 and 40 percent in debt instruments similar to those found in the Salomon Bond Investment Grade Index. There are 94 funds besides Balanced within the BlackRock family. Overall, the fund family's risk-adjusted performance can be described as very good.

Current Income   ★★★

Over the past year, BlackRock Balanced had a 12-month yield of 1.8 percent. During this same 12-month period, the typical balanced fund had a yield that averaged 2.4 percent.

Expenses   ★★

BlackRock Balanced's expense ratio is 1.3 percent; it has averaged 1.3 percent annually over the past three calendar years. The average expense ratio for the 910 funds in this category is 1.4 percent. This fund's turnover rate over the past year has been 120 percent, while its peer group average has been 95 percent.

Summary

BlackRock Balanced is a solid choice. It scores very well in the three most important categories: return, risk, and management. Predictability of returns has been superb, which is exactly what you want in a balanced fund. Management has been able to preserve after-tax returns at such a level as to make it one of the best in its category. Look to other BlackRock offerings for similar quality.

Profile

minimum initial investment $500	*IRA accounts available* . . . . yes
subsequent minimum investment . . . $50	*IRA minimum investment* $500
available in all 50 states. . . . . yes	*date of inception*. . . . . May 1990
telephone exchanges. . . . . yes	*dividend/income paid* . . . . quarterly
number of funds in family 95	*largest sector weighting* . . . technology

Guardian Asset Allocation A

201 Park Avenue South
New York, NY 10003
800-343-0817
www.guardianfund.com

total return	★★★★
risk reduction	★★★★★
management	★★★★★
current income	★★★
expense control	★★★★★
symbol GUAAX	22 points
up-market performance	excellent
down-market performance	good
predictability of returns	excellent

Total Return   ★★★★

Over the past five years, Guardian Asset Allocation A has taken $10,000 and turned it into $24,880 ($17,720 over three years). This translates into an annualized return of 20 percent over the past five years and 21 percent over the past three years. Over the past five years, this fund has outperformed 80 percent of all mutual funds; within its general category it has done better than 95 percent of its peers. Balanced funds have averaged 15 percent annually over these same five years (all periods ending March 31, 2000).

During the past five years, a $10,000 initial investment grew to $20,400 after taxes, assuming a 39.6 percent income tax bracket (state and federal combined) and a capital gains rate of 28 percent. This means that investors in this fund were able to preserve 82 percent of their total returns. Compared to other fixed-income funds, this fund's tax savings are considered to be very good.

Risk/Volatility   ★★★★★

Over the past five years, Asset Allocation has been safer than 80 percent of all balanced funds. Since its inception, the fund has had one negative year, while the S & P 500 has also had one (off 3 percent in 1990); the Lehman Brothers Aggregate Bond Index fell twice (off 3 percent in 1994 and 1 percent in 1999). The fund has underperformed the S & P 500 six times and has outperformed the Lehman Brothers Aggregate Bond Index every year since the fund's inception.

	last 5 years		since inception	
worst year	13%	1999	-2%	1994
best year	25%	1995	25%	1995

In the past, Asset Allocation has done better than 90 percent of its peer group in up markets and outperformed 55 percent of its competition in down markets. Consistency, or predictability, of returns for Asset Allocation can be described as excellent. This fund's risk-related return is also excellent.

Management   ★★★★★

This $250 million portfolio is divided as follows: 50 percent in bonds, 30 percent in cash, and 20 percent in stocks. The average balanced fund today is $350 million in size. The two largest holdings of this portfolio are other Guardian funds; half of the money is in Guardian Park Avenue and about 17 percent is in a Guardian high-quality bond fund. The stocks in this portfolio have an average price-earnings (p/e) ratio of 35 and a median market capitalization of $130 billion. The fund's equities have a correlation of 60 percent to the S & P 500 (versus 85 percent for asset allocation funds in general).

Jonathan Junks has managed this fund for the past six years. Management's style is mostly passive, largely relying on the performance of two other Guardian offerings, neither of which invest in foreign securities. Overall, equities are selected based on relative value and earnings momentum. The bond portion attempts to maintain a constant maturity similar to that found in the Lehman Brothers Aggregate Bond Index; value is added by adjusting the weighting of corporate, government, and mortgage-backed securities. The dollars committed to each Guardian fund and cash is determined by a computer model. There are 13 funds besides Asset Allocation within the Guardian family. Overall, the fund family's risk-adjusted performance can be described as very good.

Current Income   ★★★

Over the past year, Asset Allocation had a 12-month yield of 2.2 percent. During this same 12-month period, the typical balanced fund had a yield that averaged 2.4 percent.

Expenses   ★★★★★

Asset Allocation's expense ratio is .6 percent; it has averaged .7 percent annually over the past three calendar years. The average expense ratio for the 910 funds in this category is 1.4 percent. This fund's turnover rate over the past year has been 23 percent, while its peer group average has been 95 percent.

Summary

Guardian Asset Allocation A has ranked in the top one or two performance quartiles in almost every year since its inception. Performance in positive markets, control over expenses, and predictability of returns have all been exceptional. The fund is somewhat of an odd bird since it relies heavily on a model that allocates its assets between two other Guardian funds and money market instruments. However, the overall fund family's ratings are strong enough so as not to make this a concern.

Profile

minimum initial investment $1,000	*IRA accounts available* . . . . yes
subsequent minimum investment . . $100	*IRA minimum investment* $1,000
available in all 50 states. . . . . yes	*date of inception* . . . . Feb. 1993
telephone exchanges. . . . . yes	*dividend/income paid* . . . semi-annually
number of funds in family 14	*largest sector weighting* . . . technology

Nations Capital Income Investor A

One Bank of America Plaza, 33rd Floor
Charlotte, NC 28255
800-321-7854
www.nationsbank.com/nationsfunds

total return	★★★★
risk reduction	★★★★
management	★★★★
current income	★★★
expense control	★★★★★
symbol PACIX	20 points
up-market performance	good
down-market performance	excellent
predictability of returns	excellent

Total Return   ★★★★

Over the past five years, Nations Capital Income Investor A has taken $10,000 and turned it into $25,940 ($18,160 over three years). This translates into an annualized return of 21 percent over the past five years and 22 percent over the past three years. Over the past five years, this fund has outperformed 76 percent of all mutual funds; within its general category it has done better than 70 percent of its peers. Balanced funds have averaged 15 percent annually over these same five years (all periods ending March 31, 2000).

During the past five years, a $10,000 initial investment grew to $20,750 after taxes, assuming a 39.6 percent income tax bracket (state and federal combined) and a capital gains rate of 28 percent. This means that investors in this fund were able to preserve 80 percent of their total returns. Compared to other fixed-income funds, this fund's tax savings are considered to be very good.

Risk/Volatility   ★★★★

Over the past five years, Income Investor has been safer than 70 percent of all balanced funds. Over the past decade, the fund has had two negative years, while the S & P 500 has had one (off 3 percent in 1990); the Lehman Brothers Aggregate Bond Index fell twice (off 3 percent in 1994 and 1 percent in 1999). The fund has underperformed the S & P 500 six times and the Lehman Brothers Aggregate Bond Index three times in the last 10 years.

	last 5 years		last 10 years	
worst year	7%	1998	-6%	1994
best year	27%	1999	38%	1991

In the past, Income Investor has done better than 60 percent of its peer group in up markets and outperformed 85 percent of its competition in down markets. Consistency, or predictability, of returns for Income Investor can be described as excellent. This fund's risk-related return is very good.

Management   ★★★★

There are 45 fixed-income securities in this $350 million portfolio. The average balanced fund today is $350 million in size. Close to 55 percent of the fund's holdings are in convertibles, 12 percent in stocks, and 30 percent in bonds. The stocks in this portfolio have an average price-earnings (p/e) ratio of 45 and a median market capitalization of $45 billion. The fund's equities have a correlation of 60 percent to the S & P 500 (versus 50 percent for convertible funds in general). The average maturity of the bonds in this account is five years; the weighted coupon rate averages 3.7 percent. The portfolio's equity holdings can be categorized as large-cap and growth-oriented issues. The portfolio's fixed-income holdings can be categorized as short-term, medium-quality debt.

Ed Cassens has managed this fund for the past six years. There are 210 funds in addition to Income Investor within the Nations family. Overall, the fund family's risk-adjusted performance can be described as good.

Current Income   ★★★

Over the past year, Nations Capital Income Investor A had a 12-month yield of 1.9 percent. During this same 12-month period, the typical balanced fund had a yield that averaged 2.4 percent.

Expenses   ★★★★★

Income Investor's expense ratio is 1.2 percent; it has averaged 1.1 percent annually over the past three calendar years. The average expense ratio for the 910 funds in this category is 1.4 percent. This fund's turnover rate over the past year has been 65 percent, while its peer group average has been 95 percent.

Summary

Nations Capital Income Investor A is one of the few funds that invests heavily in convertibles. The fund scores highly in every category but does a particularly great job when it comes to keeping expenses low and turning in appealing results during bear market cycles. Predictability of returns has been excellent. This is the kind of balanced, or convertible, fund that attracts conservative-to-somewhat moderate investors.

Profile

minimum initial investment $1,000	*IRA accounts available* . . . . yes
subsequent minimum investment . . $100	*IRA minimum investment* $500
available in all 50 states. . . . . yes	*date of inception* . . . . Sept. 1987
telephone exchanges. . . . . yes	*dividend/income paid* . . . . quarterly
number of funds in family 211	*largest sector weighting* . . . technology

Oppenheimer Global Growth & Income A

P.O. Box 5270
Denver, CO 80217
800-525-7048
www.oppenheimerfunds.com

total return	★★★★★
risk reduction	★
	★★★
	★★
	★★★
	14 points
	excellent
	good
	good

★★★★★

...wth & Income A has taken
...e years). This translates into
...years and 43 percent over the
...s outperformed 97 percent of
...one better than 99 percent of
...nnually over these same five

...estment grew to $35,790 after
...ate and federal combined) and
...vestors in this fund were able
...d to other fixed-income funds,
...od.

★

...has been safer than 40 percent
...nd has had two negative years,
...n 1990); the Lehman Brothers
...994 and 1 percent in 1999). The
...imes and the Lehman Brothers
...ars.

	last 5 years		last 10 years	
worst year	13%	1998	-6%	1992
best year	87%	1999	87%	1999

In the past, Global Growth & Income has done better than 96 percent of its peer group in up markets and outperformed 50 percent of its competition in down markets. Consistency, or predictability, of returns for Global Growth & Income can be described as good. This fund's risk-related return is excellent.

Management   ★★★

There are 80 stocks and 15 fixed-income securities in this $1.3 billion portfolio. The average balanced fund today is $350 million in size. Close to 80 percent of this fund's holdings are in stocks and 16 percent in bonds. The stocks in this portfolio have an average price-earnings (p/e) ratio of 43 and a median market capitalization of $5.6 billion. The fund's equities have a correlation of 15 percent to the S & P 500 (versus 65 percent for global equity funds in general). The average maturity of the bonds in this account is 25 years; the weighted coupon rate averages zero percent (the bond portion of the portfolio is largely in zero-coupon issues). The portfolio's equity holdings can be categorized as mid-cap and growth-oriented issues. The portfolio's fixed-income holdings can be categorized as long-term, very high-quality debt.

Frank Jennings has managed this fund for the past six years. The fund invests in both foreign as well as domestic stocks and bonds. Manager Jennings looks for equities that are likely to benefit from trends, based on a bottom-up approach. A strong growth rate coupled with a bargain price for the stock is what management strives for—small- and mid-cap neglected companies are highly favored. There are 140 funds besides Global Growth & Income within the Oppenheimer family. Overall, the fund family's risk-adjusted performance can be described as good.

Current Income   ★★

Over the past year, Global Growth & Income had a 12-month yield of .9 percent. During this same 12-month period, the typical balanced fund had a yield that averaged 2.4 percent.

Expenses   ★★★

Global Growth & Income's expense ratio is 1.3 percent; it has also averaged 1.3 percent annually over the past three calendar years. The average expense ratio for the 910 funds in this category is 1.4 percent. This fund's turnover rate over the past year has been 98 percent, while its peer group average has been 95 percent.

Summary

Oppenheimer Global Growth & Income A has ranked in the top quintile of performance for three of the past four years. This is also the number one performer within its broad category over the past three- and five-year periods. Volatility is high for this type of portfolio, but investors sure have been rewarded—the fund has outperformed 99 percent of its peer group.

Profile

minimum initial investment $1,000	*IRA accounts available* . . . . yes
subsequent minimum investment . . . $25	*IRA minimum investment* $250
available in all 50 states . . . . yes	*date of inception* . . . . Oct. 1990
telephone exchanges . . . . yes	*dividend/income paid* . . . . quarterly
number of funds in family 141	*largest sector weighting* . . . technology

Phoenix-Engemann Balanced Return A

State Street Bank
P.O. Box 8301
Boston, MA 02266
800-243-4361
www.phoenixfunds.com

total return	★★★★
risk reduction	★★★
management	★★★
current income	★
expense control	★★
symbol PABRX	13 points
up-market performance	excellent
down-market performance	good
predictability of returns	excellent

Total Return   ★★★★

Over the past five years, Phoenix-Engemann Balanced Return A has taken $10,000 and turned it into $27,030 ($19,530 over three years). This translates into an annualized return of 22 percent over the past five years and 25 percent over the past three years. Over the past five years, this fund has outperformed 80 percent of all mutual funds. Balanced funds have averaged 15 percent annually over these same five years (all periods ending March 31, 2000).

During the past five years, a $10,000 initial investment grew to $24,325 after taxes, assuming a 39.6 percent income tax bracket (state and federal combined) and a capital gains rate of 28 percent. This means that investors in this fund were able to preserve 90 percent of their total returns. Compared to other fixed-income funds, this fund's tax savings are considered to be very good.

Risk/Volatility   ★★★

Over the past five years, Balanced Return has been safer than 97 percent of all balanced funds. Over the past decade, the fund has had two negative years, while the S & P 500 has had one (off 3 percent in 1990); the Lehman Brothers Aggregate Bond Index fell twice (off 3 percent in 1994 and 1 percent in 1999). The fund has underperformed the S & P 500 seven times and the Lehman Brothers Aggregate Bond Index four times in the last 10 years.

	last 5 years		last 10 years	
worst year	18%	1996	-4%	1994
best year	29%	1998	39%	1991

In the past, Balanced Return has done better than 95 percent of its peer group in up markets and outperformed 50 percent of its competition in down markets. Consistency, or predictability, of returns for Balanced Return can be described as excellent. This fund's risk-related return is also excellent.

Management   ★★★

There are 60 stocks and 40 fixed-income securities in this $140 million portfolio. The average balanced fund today is $350 million in size. Close to 60 percent of this fund's holdings are in stocks and 40 percent in bonds. The stocks in this portfolio have an average price-earnings (p/e) ratio of 48 and a median market capitalization of $170 billion. Technology represents close to 40 percent of the fund's equity holdings, followed by retail trade (10 percent) and health care (9 percent). The fund's stock holdings have a correlation of roughly 85 percent to the S & P 500 (versus 95 percent for balanced funds in general). The average maturity of the bonds in this account is 20 years; the weighted coupon rate averages 6.0 percent. The portfolio's equity holdings can be categorized as large-cap and growth-oriented issues. The portfolio's fixed-income holdings can be categorized as long-term, very high-quality debt.

James Mair and John Tilson have managed this fund for the past 14 years. Management concentrates its holdings in government securities and quality growth stocks. Securities are sold when there has been a change in the original factors used in its selection. There are 20 funds besides Balanced Return within the Phoenix family. Overall, the fund family's risk-adjusted performance can be described as good.

Current Income   ★

Over the past year, Balanced Return had a 12-month yield of .4 percent. During this same 12-month period, the typical balanced fund had a yield that averaged 2.4 percent.

Expenses   ★★

Balanced Return's expense ratio is 1.6 percent; it has also averaged 1.6 percent annually over the past three calendar years. The average expense ratio for the 910 funds in this category is 1.4 percent. This fund's turnover rate over the past year has been 120 percent, while its peer group average has been 95 percent.

Summary

Phoenix-Engemann Balanced Return A has ranked in the top quintile of performance for its category for four of the past five years. Compared to its peer group, returns for this fund are extremely predictable and bull market performance is exceedingly strong. The fund has also been safer than 97 percent of its category.

Profile

minimum initial investment $500	*IRA accounts available* .... yes
subsequent minimum investment ... $25	*IRA minimum investment* $25
available in all 50 states. .... yes	*date of inception.* .... June 1987
telephone exchanges. .... yes	*dividend/income paid* .... annually
number of funds in family 21	*largest sector weighting* ... technology

Preferred Asset Allocation

P.O. Box 8320
Boston, MA 02266
800-662-4769
www.preferredgroup.com

total return	★★★★
risk reduction	★★★★★
management	★★★★
current income	★★★
expense control	★★★★★
symbol PFAAX	21 points
up-market performance	good
down-market performance	excellent
predictability of returns	excellent

Total Return   ★★★★

Over the past five years, Preferred Asset Allocation has taken $10,000 and turned it into $23,860 ($16,430 over three years). This translates into an annualized return of 19 percent over the past five years and 18 percent over the past three years. Over the past five years, this fund has outperformed 75 percent of all mutual funds; within its general category it has done better than 88 percent of its peers. Balanced funds have averaged 15 percent annually over these same five years (all periods ending March 31, 2000).

During the past five years, a $10,000 initial investment grew to $19,810 after taxes, assuming a 39.6 percent income tax bracket (state and federal combined) and a capital gains rate of 28 percent. This means that investors in this fund were able to preserve 83 percent of their total returns. Compared to other fixed-income funds, this fund's tax savings are considered to be very good.

Risk/Volatility   ★★★★★

Over the past five years, Asset Allocation has been safer than 90 percent of all balanced funds. Since its inception, the fund has had one negative year, while the S & P 500 has also had one (off 3 percent in 1990); the Lehman Brothers Aggregate Bond Index fell twice (off 3 percent in 1994 and 1 percent in 1999). The fund has underperformed the S & P 500 six times and has outperformed the Lehman Brothers Aggregate Bond Index every year since the fund's inception.

	last 5 years		since inception	
worst year	1%	1999	-3%	1994
best year	33%	1995	33%	1995

In the past, Asset Allocation has done better than 45 percent of its peer group in up markets and outperformed 95 percent of its competition in down markets. Consistency, or predictability, of returns for Asset Allocation can be described as excellent. This fund's risk-related return is also excellent.

Management   ★★★★

There are 450 stocks and 35 fixed-income securities in this $220 million portfolio. The average balanced fund today is $350 million in size. Close to 35 percent of this fund's holdings are in stocks and 65 percent in bonds. The stocks in this portfolio have an average price-earnings (p/e) ratio of 38 and a median market capitalization of $150 billion. Technology represents close to 15 percent of the fund's equity holdings, followed by finance (4 percent of the stock holdings) and industrial cyclicals (3 percent). The fund's stock holdings have a correlation of roughly 75 percent to the S & P 500 (versus 85 percent for asset allocation funds in general). The average maturity of the bonds in this account is 22 years; the weighted coupon rate averages 8.3 percent. The portfolio's equity holdings can be categorized as large-cap and value-oriented issues. The portfolio's fixed-income holdings can be categorized as long-term, high-quality debt.

Thomas Hazuka and Edgar Peters have managed this fund for the past nine years. Each manager's asset allocation is 60 percent equities and 40 percent debt instruments. Hazuka uses a dividend-discount model to determine his weighting of stocks, bonds, and money market instruments. Comanager Peters relies on the Federal Reserve Signal (the 10-year bond yield versus the earnings-yield ratio of equities). There are six funds besides Asset Allocation within the Preferred family. Overall, the fund family's risk-adjusted performance can be described as very good.

Current Income   ★★★

Over the past year, Asset Allocation had a 12-month yield of 2.3 percent. During this same 12-month period, the typical balanced fund had a yield that averaged 2.4 percent.

Expenses   ★★★★★

Asset Allocation's expense ratio is .9 percent; it has also averaged .9 percent annually over the past three calendar years. The average expense ratio for the 910 funds in this category is 1.4 percent. This fund's turnover rate over the past year has been 6 percent, while its peer group average has been 95 percent.

Summary

Preferred Asset Allocation ranks number one when it comes to risk reduction, an amazing accomplishment when you consider the breadth of the category (which includes balanced, asset allocation, flexible, and convertible funds). Other ratings are very good. This fund is also a member of a fund family whose risk-adjusted returns are quite attractive.

Profile

minimum initial investment $1,000	*IRA accounts available* . . . . yes
subsequent minimum investment . . . $50	*IRA minimum investment* $250
available in all 50 states. . . . . yes	*date of inception.* . . . . June 1992
telephone exchanges. . . . . yes	*dividend/income paid* . . . . quarterly
number of funds in family 7	*largest sector weighting* . . . technology

Van Kampen Harbor A

One Parkview Plaza
Oakbrook Terrace, IL 60181
800-421-5666
www.vankampen.com

total return	★★★★
risk reduction	★★
management	★★★
current income	★★★
expense control	★★★
symbol ACHBX	15 points
up-market performance	excellent
down-market performance	poor
predictability of returns	good

Total Return ★★★★

Over the past five years, Van Kampen Harbor A has taken $10,000 and turned it into $28,150 ($21,470 over three years). This translates into an annualized return of 23 percent over the past five years and 29 percent over the past three years. Over the past five years, this fund has outperformed 79 percent of all mutual funds; within its general category it has done better than 76 percent of its peers. Balanced funds have averaged 15 percent annually over these same five years (all periods ending March 31, 2000).

During the past five years, a $10,000 initial investment grew to $23,090 after taxes, assuming a 39.6 percent income tax bracket (state and federal combined) and a capital gains rate of 28 percent. This means that investors in this fund were able to preserve 82 percent of their total returns. Compared to other fixed-income funds, this fund's tax savings are considered to be very good.

Risk/Volatility ★★

Over the past five years, Harbor has been safer than 40 percent of all balanced funds. Over the past decade, the fund has had two negative years, while the S & P 500 has had one (off 3 percent in 1990); the Lehman Brothers Aggregate Bond Index fell twice (off 3 percent in 1994 and 1 percent in 1999). The fund has under-performed the S & P 500 six times and the Lehman Brothers Aggregate Bond Index three times in the last 10 years.

	last 5 years		last 10 years	
worst year	8%	1998	-6%	1994
best year	50%	1999	50%	1999

In the past, Harbor has done better than 90 percent of its peer group in up markets and outperformed 15 percent of its competition in down markets. Consistency, or predictability, of returns for Harbor can be described as good. This fund's risk-related return is also good.

Management   ★★★

There are 25 stocks and 45 convertible securities in this $570 million portfolio. The average balanced fund today is $350 million in size. Close to 15 percent of this fund's holdings are in stocks and 75 percent in convertibles. The stocks in this portfolio have an average price-earnings (p/e) ratio of 52 and a median market capitalization of $67 billion. The fund's stock holdings have a correlation of roughly 35 percent to the S & P 500 (versus 50 percent for convertible funds in general). The portfolio's equity holdings can be categorized as large-cap and growth-oriented issues.

Christine Drusch has been the lead manager of this fund for the past nine years. Management favors convertibles and preferred stocks because of their comparatively high yields and subdued volatility compared to common stocks. Comanagers Stephen Boyd, Matthew Hart, and David McLaughlin seek out corporations that have solid sales and earnings growth; economically sensitive securities are emphasized when conditions warrant. Final selection or disposition is based on fundamentals. There are 121 funds besides Harbor within the Van Kampen family. Overall, the fund family's risk-adjusted performance can be described as good.

Current Income   ★★★

Over the past year, Harbor had a 12-month yield of 2 percent. During this same 12-month period, the typical balanced fund had a yield that averaged 2.4 percent.

Expenses   ★★★

Harbor's expense ratio is 1 percent; it has averaged 1 percent annually over the past three calendar years. The average expense ratio for the 910 funds in this category is 1.4 percent. This fund's turnover rate over the past year has been 155 percent, while its peer group average has been 95 percent.

Summary

Van Kampen Harbor A ranks as the second best performer in its broad category. It is the only fund selected for this book that emphasizes convertible securities—a nice risk reduction category for most investors. The fund really shines during bull markets but has not fared particularly well during bear periods. Thus, this is a highly recommended offering for the patient investor.

Profile

minimum initial investment $1,000	*IRA accounts available* . . . . yes
subsequent minimum investment . . . $25	*IRA minimum investment* $500
available in all 50 states. . . . . yes	*date of inception* . . . . Nov. 1956
telephone exchanges. . . . . yes	*dividend/income paid* . . . . quarterly
number of funds in family 122	*largest sector weighting*. . . . . n/a

Vanguard Asset Allocation
Vanguard Financial Center
P.O. Box 2600
Valley Forge, PA 19482
800-662-7447
www.vanguard.com

total return	★★★★
risk reduction	★★★★★
management	★★★★★
current income	★★★★★
expense control	★★★★★
symbol VAAPX	24 points
up-market performance	good
down-market performance	very good
predictability of returns	excellent

Total Return   ★★★★
Over the past five years, Vanguard Asset Allocation has taken $10,000 and turned it into $25,940 ($17,716 over three years). This translates into an annualized return of 21 percent over the past five years and 21 percent over the past three years. Over the past five years, this fund has outperformed 80 percent of all mutual funds; within its general category it has done better than 96 percent of its peers. Balanced funds have averaged 15 percent annually over these same five years (all periods ending March 31, 2000).

During the past five years, a $10,000 initial investment grew to $21,790 after taxes, assuming a 39.6 percent income tax bracket (state and federal combined) and a capital gains rate of 28 percent. This means that investors in this fund were able to preserve 84 percent of their total returns. Compared to other fixed-income funds, this fund's tax savings are considered to be very good.

Risk/Volatility   ★★★★★
Over the past five years, Vanguard Asset Allocation has been safer than 70 percent of all balanced funds. Over the past decade, the fund has had one negative year, while the S & P 500 has also had one (off 3 percent in 1990); the Lehman Brothers Aggregate Bond Index fell twice (off 3 percent in 1994 and 1 percent in 1999). The fund has underperformed the S & P 500 eight times and the Lehman Brothers Aggregate Bond Index twice in the last 10 years.

	last 5 years		last 10 years	
worst year	5%	1999	-2%	1994
best year	35%	1995	35%	1995

In the past, Asset Allocation has done better than 45 percent of its peer group in up markets and outperformed 75 percent of its competition in down markets. Consistency, or predictability, of returns for Asset Allocation can be described as excellent. This fund's risk-related return is excellent.

Management   ★★★★★

There are 500 stocks and 30 fixed-income securities in this $8.7 billion portfolio. The average balanced fund today is $350 million in size. Close to 40 percent of this fund's holdings are in stocks and 60 percent in bonds. The stocks in this portfolio have an average price-earnings (p/e) ratio of 35 and a median market capitalization of $110 billion. Technology represents 12 percent of the fund's equity holdings, followed by finance (5 percent of the stock holdings) and industrial cyclicals (4 percent). The fund's stock holdings have a correlation of roughly 90 percent to the S & P 500 (versus 85 percent for asset allocation funds in general). The average maturity of the bonds in this account is 21 years; the weighted coupon rate averages 8.2 percent. The portfolio's equity holdings can be categorized as large-cap, value-oriented issues. The portfolio's fixed-income holdings can be categorized as long-term, high-quality debt.

William Fouse and Thomas Loeb have managed this fund for the past 12 years. Unlike a large number of their peers, management is not restricted by percentage limits for any of the fund's asset categories. The managers utilize a proprietary, quantitative model for security selection. There are 77 funds besides Asset Allocation within the Vanguard family. Overall, the fund family's risk-adjusted performance can be described as very good.

Current Income   ★★★★★

Over the past year, Asset Allocation had a 12-month yield of 3.4 percent. During this same 12-month period, the typical balanced fund had a yield that averaged 2.4 percent.

Expenses   ★★★★★

Asset Allocation's expense ratio is .5 percent; it has averaged .5 percent annually over the past three calendar years. The average expense ratio for the 910 funds in this category is 1.4 percent. This fund's turnover rate over the past year has been 11 percent, while its peer group average has been 95 percent.

Summary

Vanguard Asset Allocation receives a near-perfect score of 24 out of 25 possible points, making this one of the very best funds you can buy, regardless of category. A small part of the fund's success is well-known by Vanguard followers: super-low overhead. Vanguard was, and remains, the pioneer in low expenses and fund industry reform. This vocal champion of investor rights has never received the full credit it deserves in its ongoing battle to make the world a better place for mutual fund investors. Look for a large number of other Vanguard offerings to fulfill your needs in other investment categories as well.

Profile

minimum initial investment $3,000	*IRA accounts available* . . . . yes
subsequent minimum investment . . $100	*IRA minimum investment* $1,000
available in all 50 states . . . . yes	*date of inception* . . . . Nov. 1988
telephone exchanges . . . . yes	*dividend/income paid* . . . semi-annually
number of funds in family 78	*largest sector weighting* . . . technology

Vanguard Tax-Managed Balanced
Vanguard Financial Center
P.O. Box 2600
Valley Forge, PA 19482
800-662-7447
www.vanguard.com

total return	★★★
risk reduction	★★★★★
management	★★★★★
current income	★★★
expense control	★★★★★
symbol VTMFX	21 points
up-market performance	very good
down-market performance	very good
predictability of returns	excellent

Total Return ★★★
Over the past five years, Vanguard Tax-Managed Balanced has taken $10,000 and turned it into $21,000 ($16,430 over three years). This translates into an annualized return of 16 percent over the past five years and 18 percent over the past three years. Over the past five years, this fund has outperformed 68 percent of all mutual funds; within its general category it has done better than 68 percent of its peers. Balanced funds have averaged 15 percent annually over these same five years (all periods ending March 31, 2000).

During the past five years, a $10,000 initial investment grew to $20,370 after taxes, assuming a 39.6 percent income tax bracket (state and federal combined) and a capital gains rate of 28 percent. This means that investors in this fund were able to preserve 97 percent of their total returns. Compared to other fixed-income funds, this fund's tax savings are considered to be excellent.

Risk/Volatility ★★★★★
Over the past five years, Vanguard Tax-Managed Balanced has been safer than 78 percent of all balanced funds. Since its inception, the fund has had no negative years, while the S & P 500 has had one (off 3 percent in 1990); the Lehman Brothers Aggregate Bond Index fell twice (off 3 percent in 1994 and 1 percent in 1999). The fund has underperformed the S & P 500 five times and has outperformed the Lehman Brothers Aggregate Bond Index every year since the fund's inception.

	last 5 years		since inception	
worst year	12%	1996	12%	1996
best year	25%	1995	25%	1995

In the past, Tax-Managed Balanced has done better than 80 percent of its peer group in up markets and outperformed 70 percent of its competition in down markets. Consistency, or predictability, of returns for Tax-Managed Balanced can be described as excellent. This fund's risk-related return is excellent.

Management   ★★★★★

There are 475 stocks and 140 fixed-income securities in this $360 million portfolio. The average balanced fund today is $350 million in size. Close to 47 percent of this fund's holdings are in stocks and 52 percent in bonds. The stocks in this portfolio have an average price-earnings (p/e) ratio of 38 and a median market capitalization of $40 billion. The average maturity of the bonds in this account is 6 years; the weighted coupon rate averages 5.4 percent. The portfolio's equity holdings can be categorized as large-cap and a blend of growth and value stocks. The portfolio's fixed-income holdings can be categorized as intermediate-term, high-quality debt.

Gus Sauter oversees the equity portion of the portfolio; Ian MacKinnon and Chris Ryon manage the bond portion. The bonds in the portfolio are municipal, which means three things: tax-free income, very good quality, and less interest rate risk than their corporate peers. On the stock side, manager Sauter tries to replicate the characteristics of the Russell 1000 Index while concentrating on low dividend-paying issues. There are 77 funds besides Tax-Managed Balanced within the Vanguard family. Overall, the fund family's risk-adjusted performance can be described as very good.

Current Income   ★★★

Over the past year, Tax-Managed Balanced had a 12-month yield of 2.3 percent. During this same 12-month period, the typical balanced fund had a yield that averaged 2.4 percent.

Expenses   ★★★★★

Tax-Managed Balanced's expense ratio is .2 percent; it has averaged .2 percent annually over the past three calendar years. The average expense ratio for the 910 funds in this category is 1.4 percent. This fund's turnover rate over the past year has been 7 percent, while its peer group average has been 95 percent.

Summary

Vanguard Tax-Managed Balanced may well be the best there is when it comes to a tax-managed domestic stock and bond fund. For the kind of investor this fund appeals to, this is a great choice. As is true with other Vanguard offerings, expenses are extremely low with this fund. Management is to be commended for having such a unique portfolio.

Profile

minimum initial investment $10,000	*IRA accounts available*. . . . . no
subsequent minimum investment . . $100	*IRA minimum investment* . . . . n/a
available in all 50 states. . . . . yes	*date of inception* . . . . Sept. 1994
telephone exchanges. . . . . yes	*dividend/income paid* . . . . quarterly
number of funds in family 78	*largest sector weighting* . . . technology

Wells Fargo Asset Allocation A

525 Market Street, 12th Floor
San Francisco, CA 94105
800-222-8222
www.wellsfargo.com

total return	★★★★
risk reduction	★★★★
management	★★★★
current income	★★★
expense control	★★★★
symbol SFAAX	19 points
up-market performance	very good
down-market performance	very good
predictability of returns	excellent

Total Return   ★★★★

Over the past five years, Wells Fargo Asset Allocation A has taken $10,000 and turned it into $23,860 ($18,160 over three years). This translates into an annualized return of 19 percent over the past five years and 22 percent over the past three years. Over the past five years, this fund has outperformed 75 percent of all mutual funds; within its general category it has done better than 88 percent of its peers. Balanced funds have averaged 15 percent annually over these same five years (all periods ending March 31, 2000).

During the past five years, a $10,000 initial investment grew to $19,570 after taxes, assuming a 39.6 percent income tax bracket (state and federal combined) and a capital gains rate of 28 percent. This means that investors in this fund were able to preserve 82 percent of their total returns. Compared to other fixed-income funds, this fund's tax savings are considered to be very good.

Risk/Volatility   ★★★★

Over the past five years, Asset Allocation has been safer than 50 percent of all balanced funds. Over the past decade, the fund has had one negative year, while the S & P 500 has also had one (off 3 percent in 1990); the Lehman Brothers Aggregate Bond Index fell twice (off 3 percent in 1994 and 1 percent in 1999). The fund has underperformed the S & P 500 eight times and the Lehman Brothers Aggregate Bond Index twice in the last 10 years.

	last 5 years		last 10 years	
worst year	9%	1999	-3%	1994
best year	29%	1995	29%	1995

In the past, Asset Allocation has done better than 70 percent of its peer group in up markets and outperformed 65 percent of its competition in down markets. Consistency, or predictability, of returns for Asset Allocation can be described as excellent. This fund's risk-related return is excellent.

Management   ★★★★

There are 500 stocks and 25 fixed-income securities in this $1.4 billion portfolio. The average balanced fund today is $350 million in size. Close to 62 percent of this fund's holdings are in stocks and 38 percent in bonds. The stocks in this portfolio have an average price-earnings (p/e) ratio of 34 and a median market capitalization of $112 billion. Technology represents 20 percent of the fund's equity holdings, followed by finance (8 percent of the stock holdings) and industrial cyclicals (7 percent). The fund's stock holdings have a correlation of roughly 95 percent to the S & P 500 (versus 85 percent for asset allocation funds in general). The average maturity of the bonds in this account is 24 years; the weighted coupon rate averages 7.2 percent. The portfolio's equity holdings can be categorized as large-cap and value-oriented issues.

A team has managed this fund for the past 12 years. There are 89 funds besides Asset Allocation within the Wells Fargo family. Security selection is based on forecasts of market values using an asset allocation model. Equities are chosen based on a dividend-discount model (discounted value of future dividends). When management feels that stocks and bonds are both fairly valued, investments will usually be 60 percent in equities and 40 percent in debt instruments. Overall, the fund family's risk-adjusted performance can be described as good.

Current Income   ★★★

Over the past year, Asset Allocation had a 12-month yield of 2 percent. During this same 12-month period, the typical balanced fund had a yield that averaged 2.4 percent.

Expenses   ★★★★

Asset Allocation's expense ratio is .9 percent; it has averaged .9 percent annually over the past three calendar years. The average expense ratio for the 910 funds in this category is 1.4 percent. This fund's turnover rate over the past year has been 31 percent, while its peer group average has been 95 percent.

Summary

Wells Fargo Asset Allocation A ranks in the top quintile of performance for three of the past four years. Ratings are very good in all major categories. The fund has been able to outperform nearly 90 percent of its peers while enjoying a below-average level of risk with predictability of returns that are superb.

Profile

minimum initial investment $1,000
subsequent minimum investment . . $100
available in all 50 states. . . . . yes
telephone exchanges. . . . . yes
number of funds in family 90

IRA accounts available . . . . yes
IRA minimum investment $250
date of inception . . . . Nov. 1986
dividend/income paid . . . . quarterly
largest sector weighting . . . technology

Corporate Bond Funds

Traditionally, bond funds are held by investors who require high current income and low risk. Interest income is normally paid on a monthly basis. Corporate bond funds are made up primarily of bonds issued by domestic corporations; government securities often represent a moderate part of these funds. Portfolio composition is almost always exclusively U.S. issues.

Bonds are normally purchased because of their income stream; one's principal in a bond fund fluctuates. The major influence on bond prices, and therefore the value of the fund's shares, is interest rates. There is an inverse relationship between interest rates and bond values; whatever one does, the other does the opposite. If interest rates rise, the price per share of a bond fund will fall, and vice versa.

The amount of appreciation or loss of a corporate bond fund primarily depends upon the average maturity of the bonds in the portfolio; the cumulative amount of interest rate movement and the typical yield of the bonds in the fund's portfolio are distant secondary concerns. *Short-term* bond funds, made up of debt instruments with an average maturity of five years or less, are subject to very little interest rate risk or reward. *Medium-term* bond funds, with maturities averaging between six and 10 years, are subject to one-third to one-half the risk level of long-term funds. A long-term corporate bond fund will average an 8 percent increase or decrease in share price for every cumulative 1 percent change in interest rates.

Often investors can tell what kind of corporate bond fund they are purchasing by its name. Unless the fund includes the term "short" in its title, chances are that it is a medium- or long-term bond fund. Investors would be wise to contact the fund or counsel with an investment advisor to learn more about the portfolio's average maturity; most bond funds will dramatically reduce their portfolio's average maturity during periods of interest-rate uncertainty.

The average weighted maturity for the bonds in these funds is just under eight years, the average coupon rate is 6.9 percent, and the average weighted price is $980 (meaning that the bonds are worth $20 less than face value, on average). A price, or value, of par ($1,000 per bond) means that the bonds in a portfolio are worth face value and are not currently being traded at a discount (a price less than $1,000 per bond) or at a premium (some figure above $1,000). The portfolio of the "average" corporate bond fund is made up of securities purchased at a $20-per-bond discount ($980 versus $1,000 for bonds bought at face value). A portfolio manager purchases bonds at a discount for one of two reasons: to decrease the portfolio's current income, or to increase the fund's volatility slightly (the lower the coupon rate, the more susceptible a bond is to the effects of interest-rate changes).

During the past five and 10 years, corporate bond funds have underperformed the Lehman Brothers Aggregate Bond Index by a little less than 1 percent per year.

Over the last three years the gap widens to a little over 1 percent. Average turnover during the last three years has been 140 percent, a surprisingly high figure given the general belief that stocks are traded (turned over) much more frequently than bonds. (The typical growth fund has a turnover rate of 100 percent annually.) The average corporate bond fund throws off an annual income stream of 6 percent. The typical annual expense ratio for this group is just under 1 percent.

Over the past 15 years, individual corporate bonds have underperformed common stocks by close to 10 percent per year. From 1985 through 1999, long-term corporate bonds averaged 8.6 percent compounded per year, compared to 18.4 percent for common stocks and 15.0 percent for small stocks. A $10,000 investment in corporate bonds grew to $44,640 over the past 15 years; a similar initial investment in common stocks grew to $134,740 and $66,700 for small stocks.

Over the past half century, corporate bonds have only outpaced inflation on a pre-tax basis. A dollar invested in corporate bonds at the beginning of 1950 grew to $18.13 by the end of 1999. This translates into an average compound return of 6.0 percent per year. During this same period, $1 inflated to $6.73; this translates into an average annual inflation rate of 4.0 percent. Over the past 50 years, the worst year for long-term corporate bonds, on a total return basis (yield plus or minus principal appreciation or loss), was 1969, when a loss of 8 percent was suffered. The best year so far has been 1982, when corporate bonds posted a gain of 43 percent.

Over 870 funds make up the corporate bonds category. Total market capitalization of this category is $235 billion. Over the past three and five years, corporate bond funds have had an average compound return of 6 percent per year. For the decade, corporate bond funds have averaged 7 percent per year and 9 percent per annum for the past 15 years. All of these figures represent total returns. This means that bond appreciation (or depreciation) was added (or subtracted) from current yield.

Corporate Bond Funds

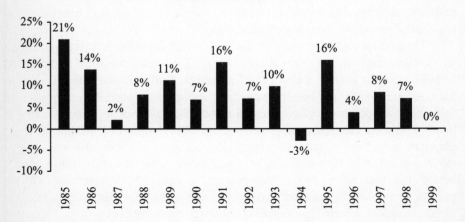

The standard deviation for corporate bond funds has been 3 percent over the past three years. As you may recall, a low standard deviation means a greater predictability of returns (fewer surprises—for better or worse). If a fund, or fund category, such as corporate bonds, has an average annual return of 10 percent and a standard deviation of 3 percent, this means that returns for every two out of three years should be roughly 10 percent, + or – 3 percent (one standard deviation). If you want to increase certainty of returns, then you must look at two standard deviations. This means that returns, for about 95 percent of the time, would be 10 percent + or – 6 percent (or +4 percent to +16 percent). These funds have been less volatile than any equity fund and have shown similar return variances (volatility) as government bond funds.

Alleghany/Chicago Trust

171 North Clark Street
Chicago, IL 60601
800-992-8151
www.alleghanyfunds.com

total return	★★★
risk reduction	★★★
management	★★★
current income	★★★★
expense control	★★★★★
symbol CHTBX	18 points
up-market performance	good
down-market performance	good
predictability of returns	very good

Total Return   ★★★

Over the past five years, Alleghany/Chicago Trust has taken $10,000 and turned it into $14,030 ($11,910 over three years). This translates into an annualized return of 7 percent over the past five years and 6 percent over the past three years. Over the past five years, this fund has outperformed 44 percent of all mutual funds; within its general category it has done better than 80 percent of its peers. Corporate bond funds have averaged 6 percent annually over these same five years (all periods ending March 31, 2000).

During the past five years, a $10,000 initial investment became $8,700 after taxes, assuming a 39.6 percent income tax bracket (state and federal combined) and a capital gains rate of 28 percent. This means that investors in this fund were able to preserve 62 percent of their total returns. Compared to other fixed-income funds, this fund's tax savings are considered to be very good.

Risk/Volatility   ★★★

Over the past five years, Chicago Trust has been safer than 90 percent of all corporate bond funds. Since its inception, the fund has had two negative years, while the Lehman Brothers Aggregate Bond Index has also had two (off 3 percent in 1994 and 1 percent in 1999); the Lehman Brothers Corporate Bond Index also fell once (off 4 percent in 1994). The fund has underperformed the Lehman Brothers Aggregate Bond Index twice and the Lehman Brothers Corporate Bond Index three times since the fund's inception.

	last 5 years		since inception	
worst year	0%	1999	-3%	1994
best year	18%	1995	18%	1995

In the past, Chicago Trust has done better than 50 percent of its peer group in up markets and outperformed 60 percent of its competition in down markets. Consistency, or predictability, of returns for Chicago Trust can be described as very good. This fund's risk-related return is good.

Management ★★★

There are 70 fixed-income securities in this $140 million portfolio. The average corporate bond fund today is $270 million in size. Close to 92 percent of the fund's holdings are in bonds, the balance is in cash equivalents. The average maturity of the bonds in this account is 11 years; the weighted coupon rate averages 6.7 percent. Over half of the bonds in the portfolio are U.S. Government or U.S. agency backed. The portfolio's fixed-income holdings can be categorized as long-term, very high-quality debt.

Thomas Marthaler has managed this fund for the past seven years. Management relies heavily on a bottom-up approach to security selection. However, before any bond is bought, a number of different economic hypotheticals are looked at. Although the vast majority of the fund's holdings are in mortgage-backed securities and debt instruments issued by the federal government, the fund is allowed to invest up to one-fifth of its assets in bonds rated as low as B. There are 12 funds besides Chicago Trust within the Alleghany family. Overall, the fund family's risk-adjusted performance can be described as good.

Current Income ★★★★

Over the past year, Chicago Trust had a 12-month yield of 6.4 percent. During this same 12-month period, the typical corporate bond fund had a yield that averaged 5.7 percent.

Expenses ★★★★★

Chicago Trust's expense ratio is .8 percent; it has averaged .8 percent annually over the past three calendar years. The average expense ratio for the more than 870 funds in this category is 1.0 percent. This fund's turnover rate over the past year has been 50 percent, while its peer group average has been 140 percent.

Summary

Alleghany/Chicago Trust has ranked in the top half of performance every year since its 1993 inception. During the last couple of years it has placed in the top quartile. The fund does a good job in all areas, but its eye toward overhead and low turnover are to be applauded. The portfolio has been safer than three-fourths of its peer group. This is a small fund that has unfortunately been overlooked by most investors. Do not make the same mistake.

Profile

minimum initial investment $2,500	*IRA accounts available* . . . . yes
subsequent minimum investment . . . $50	*IRA minimum investment* $500
available in all 50 states. . . . . yes	*date of inception*. . . . . Dec. 1993
telephone exchanges. . . . . yes	*dividend/income paid*. . . . . monthly
number of funds in family 13	*average credit quality* . . . . AAA

FPA New Income

11400 West Olympic Boulevard, Suite 1200
Los Angeles, CA 90064
800-982-4372

total return	★★★
risk reduction	★★★★
management	★★★★
current income	★★★★
expense control	★★★★★
symbol FPNIX	20 points
up-market performance	excellent
down-market performance	poor
predictability of returns	excellent

Total Return   ★★★

Over the past five years, FPA New Income has taken $10,000 and turned it into $14,030 ($11,910 over three years and $23,670 over the past 10 years). This translates into an annualized return of 7 percent over the past five years, 6 percent over the past three years, and 9 percent for the decade. Over the past five years, this fund has outperformed 45 percent of all mutual funds; within its general category it has done better than 82 percent of its peers. Corporate bond funds have averaged 6 percent annually over these same five years (all periods ending March 31, 2000).

During the past five years, a $10,000 initial investment became $8,275 after taxes, assuming a 39.6 percent income tax bracket (state and federal combined) and a capital gains rate of 28 percent. This means that investors in this fund were able to preserve 59 percent of their total returns. Compared to other fixed-income funds, this fund's tax savings are considered to be very good.

Risk/Volatility   ★★★★

Over the past five years, New Income has been safer than 99 percent of all corporate bond funds. Over the past decade, the fund has had no negative years, while the Lehman Brothers Aggregate Bond Index has had two (off 3 percent in 1994 and 1 percent in 1999); the Lehman Brothers Corporate Bond Index also fell once (off 4 percent in 1994). The fund has underperformed the Lehman Brothers Aggregate Bond Index four times and the Lehman Brothers Corporate Bond Index four times in the last 10 years.

	last 5 years		last 10 years	
worst year	3%	1999	1%	1994
best year	14%	1995	19%	1991

In the past, New Income has done better than 97 percent of its peer group in up markets and outperformed 15 percent of its competition in down markets. Consistency, or predictability, of returns for FPA New Income can be described as excellent. This fund's risk-related return is very good.

Management   ★★★★

There are 60 fixed-income securities in this $510 million portfolio. The average corporate bond fund today is $270 million in size. Close to 87 percent of the fund's holdings are in bonds. The average maturity of the bonds in this account is 8 years; the weighted coupon rate averages 5.4 percent. The portfolio's fixed-income holdings can be categorized as intermediate-term, high-quality debt.

Robert Rodriguez has managed this fund for the past 17 years. Three-fourths of the fund's holdings are always in U.S. Government securities. A very high percentage of the portfolio is in debt instruments selling at about a 10 percent discount to face value. There are three funds besides New Income within the FPA family. Overall, the fund family's risk-adjusted performance can be described as good.

Current Income   ★★★★

Over the past year, New Income had a 12-month yield of 6.6 percent. During this same 12-month period, the typical corporate bond fund had a yield that averaged 5.7 percent.

Expenses   ★★★★★

New Income's expense ratio is .6 percent; it has averaged .6 percent annually over the past three calendar years. The average expense ratio for the more than 870 funds. in this category is 1.0 percent. This fund's turnover rate over the past year has been 45 percent, while its peer group average has been 140 percent.

Summary

FPA New Income has turned in extremely impressive results over the past 1, 10, and 15 years. The fund has the second lowest risk level of its peer group in the book but beats out the lowest risk corporate bond offering when it comes to return. Overhead is quite low and so is turnover. The portfolio's bull market returns have been spectacular, but down-market results have been sub par. This offering is definitely for the conservative investor who is looking for high bond fund returns with little risk.

Profile

minimum initial investment $1,500	*IRA accounts available* . . . . yes
subsequent minimum investment . . $100	*IRA minimum investment* $100
available in all 50 states. . . . . yes	*date of inception* . . . . April 1969
telephone exchanges. . . . . yes	*dividend/income paid* . . . . quarterly
number of funds in family 4	*average credit quality.* . . . . AA

Fremont

50 Beale Street, Suite 100
San Francisco, CA 94102
800-548-4539
www.fremontfunds.com

total return	★★★★
risk reduction	★★
management	★★★
current income	★★★★
expense control	★★★
symbol FBDFX	16 points
up-market performance	very good
down-market performance	excellent
predictability of returns	very good

Total Return   ★★★★

Over the past five years, Fremont has taken $10,000 and turned it into $14,690 ($12,250 over three years). This translates into an annualized return of 8 percent over the past five years and 7 percent over the past three years. Over the past five years, this fund has outperformed 48 percent of all mutual funds; within its general category it has done better than 98 percent of its peers. Corporate bond funds have averaged 6 percent annually over these same five years (all periods ending March 31, 2000).

During the past five years, a $10,000 initial investment became $8,960 after taxes, assuming a 39.6 percent income tax bracket (state and federal combined) and a capital gains rate of 28 percent. This means that investors in this fund were able to preserve 61 percent of their total returns. Compared to other fixed-income funds, this fund's tax savings are considered to be very good.

Risk/Volatility   ★★

Over the past five years, Fremont has been safer than 55 percent of all corporate bond funds. Since its inception, the fund has had two negative years, while the Lehman Brothers Aggregate Bond Index has also had two (off 3 percent in 1994 and 1 percent in 1999); the Lehman Brothers Corporate Bond Index also fell once (off 4 percent in 1994). The fund has underperformed the Lehman Brothers Aggregate Bond Index twice and the Lehman Brothers Corporate Bond Index three times since the fund's inception.

	last 5 years		since inception	
worst year	-1%	1999	-4%	1994
best year	22%	1995	22%	1995

In the past, Fremont has done better than 65 percent of its peer group in up markets and outperformed 90 percent of its competition in down markets. Consistency, or predictability, of returns for Fremont can be described as very good. This fund's risk-related return is very good.

Management   ★★★

There are 86 fixed-income securities in this $160 million portfolio. The average corporate bond fund today is $270 million in size. Close to 99 percent of the fund's holdings are in bonds. The average maturity of the bonds in this account is eight years; the weighted coupon rate averages 6.6 percent. The portfolio's fixed-income holdings can be categorized as intermediate-term, high-quality debt.

The legendary William Gross has managed this fund for the past seven years. Gross is well-known as an accurate forecaster of macroeconomic events. There are six funds besides this corporate bond fund within the Fremont family. Overall, the fund family's risk-adjusted performance can be described as very good.

Current Income   ★★★★

Over the past year, Fremont had a 12-month yield of 6.2 percent. During this same 12-month period, the typical corporate bond fund had a yield that averaged 5.7 percent.

Expenses   ★★★

Fremont's expense ratio is .6 percent; it has averaged .6 percent annually over the past three calendar years. The average expense ratio for the more than 870 funds in this category is 1.0 percent. This fund's turnover rate over the past year has been 290 percent, while its peer group average has been 140 percent.

Summary

Fremont is the second-best performer in its category and has slightly less risk than its one superior. Management has done a wonderful job overseeing things during bad market declines; a trait not commonly seen in this conservative category. Turnover has been extremely high, but it is hard to argue with the investment style of a manager so widely praised as William H. Gross.

Profile

minimum initial investment $2,000	*IRA accounts available* . . . . yes
subsequent minimum investment . . $100	*IRA minimum investment* $1,000
available in all 50 states. . . . . yes	*date of inception* . . . . April 1993
telephone exchanges. . . . . yes	*dividend/income paid.* . . . . monthly
number of funds in family 7	*average credit quality.* . . . . AA

Harbor

One SeaGate
Toledo, OH 43666
800-422-1050
www.harborfund.com

total return	★★★★
risk reduction	★★★
management	★★★★
current income	★★★
expense control	★★★
symbol HABDX	17 points
up-market performance	very good
down-market performance	excellent
predictability of returns	very good

Total Return   ★★★★

Over the past five years, Harbor has taken $10,000 and turned it into $14,690 ($12,250 over three years and $23,670 over the past 10 years). This translates into an annualized return of 8 percent over the past five years, 7 percent over the past three years, and 9 percent for the decade. Over the past five years, this fund has outperformed 53 percent of all mutual funds; within its general category it has done better than 95 percent of its peers. Corporate bond funds have averaged 6 percent annually over these same five years (all periods ending March 31, 2000).

During the past five years, a $10,000 initial investment became $9,700 after taxes, assuming a 39.6 percent income tax bracket (state and federal combined) and a capital gains rate of 28 percent. This means that investors in this fund were able to preserve 66 percent of their total returns. Compared to other fixed-income funds, this fund's tax savings are considered to be excellent.

Risk/Volatility   ★★★

Over the past five years, Harbor has been safer than 60 percent of all corporate bond funds. Over the past decade, the fund has had two negative years, while the Lehman Brothers Aggregate Bond Index has had two (off 3 percent in 1994 and 1 percent in 1999); the Lehman Brothers Corporate Bond Index also fell once (off 4 percent in 1994). The fund has underperformed the Lehman Brothers Aggregate Bond Index three times and the Lehman Brothers Corporate Bond Index twice in the last 10 years.

	last 5 years		last 10 years	
worst year	0%	1999	-4%	1994
best year	19%	1995	20%	1991

In the past, Harbor has done better than 75 percent of its peer group in up markets and outperformed 85 percent of its competition in down markets. Consistency, or predictability, of returns for Harbor can be described as very good. This fund's risk-related return is very good.

Management   ★★★★
There are 140 fixed-income securities in this $640 million portfolio. The average corporate bond fund today is $270 million in size. Close to 70 percent of the fund's holdings are in bonds. The average maturity of the bonds in this account is seven years; the weighted coupon rate averages 6.5 percent. The portfolio's fixed-income holdings can be categorized as intermediate-term, high-quality debt.

William Gross has managed this fund for the past 14 years. Gross is perhaps the best-known bond fund manager in the United States and is highly respected. The quality rating of the bonds in the portfolio are broken down as follows: 50 percent AAA, 25 percent A, 15 percent AA, 8 percent BBB, and 8 percent BB. There are seven funds besides this corporate bond fund within the Harbor family. Overall, the fund family's risk-adjusted performance can be described as good.

Current Income   ★★★
Over the past year, Harbor had a 12-month yield of 5.4 percent. During this same 12-month period, the typical corporate bond fund had a yield that averaged 5.7 percent.

Expenses   ★★★
Harbor's expense ratio is .7 percent; it has averaged .7 percent annually over the past three calendar years. The average expense ratio for the more than 870 funds in this category is 1.0 percent. This fund's turnover rate over the past year has been 270 percent, while its peer group average has been 140 percent.

Summary
Harbor is the right choice for the nervous bond investor. The portfolio is overseen by the industry's most famous debt fund manager, bear market performance has been superb, and the average maturity of the portfolio gives it the best risk-adjusted return potential. Finally, the portfolio's tax efficiency is extremely good considering this is a bond fund.

Profile

minimum initial investment $2,000	*IRA accounts available* . . . . yes
subsequent minimum investment . . $500	*IRA minimum investment* $500
available in all 50 states. . . . . yes	*date of inception* . . . . Dec. 1987
telephone exchanges. . . . . yes	*dividend/income paid.* . . . . quarterly
number of funds in family 8	*average credit quality* . . . . AA

Strong Corporate

P.O. Box 2936
Milwaukee, WI 53201
800-368-1030
www.strongfunds.com

total return	★★★★★
risk reduction	★
management	★★★
current income	★★★★★
expense control	★★
symbol STCBX	16 points
up-market performance	very good
down-market performance	poor
predictability of returns	very good

Total Return   ★★★★★

Over the past five years, Strong Corporate has taken $10,000 and turned it into $15,390 ($12,250 over three years and $23,670 over the past 10 years). This translates into an annualized return of 9 percent over the past five years, 7 percent over the past three years, and 9 percent for the decade. Over the past five years, this fund has outperformed 50 percent of all mutual funds; within its general category it has done better than 90 percent of its peers. Corporate bond funds have averaged 6 percent annually over these same five years (all periods ending March 31, 2000).

During the past five years, a $10,000 initial investment grew to $10,309 after taxes, assuming a 39.6 percent income tax bracket (state and federal combined) and a capital gains rate of 28 percent. This means that investors in this fund were able to preserve 67 percent of their total returns. Compared to other fixed-income funds, this fund's tax savings are considered to be very good.

Risk/Volatility   ★

Over the past five years, Strong has been safer than 90 percent of all corporate bond funds. Over the past decade, the fund has had three negative years, while the Lehman Brothers Aggregate Bond Index has had two (off 3 percent in 1994 and 1 percent in 1999); the Lehman Brothers Corporate Bond Index also fell once (off 4 percent in 1994). The fund has underperformed the Lehman Brothers Aggregate Bond Index three times and the Lehman Brothers Corporate Bond Index three times in the last 10 years.

	last 5 years		last 10 years	
worst year	0%	1999	-6%	1990
best year	25%	1995	25%	1995

In the past, Corporate has done better than 75 percent of its peer group in up markets and outperformed 20 percent of its competition in down markets. Consistency, or predictability, of returns for Strong Corporate can be described as very good. This fund's risk-related return is also very good.

Management   ★★★

There are 140 fixed-income securities in this $850 million portfolio. The average corporate bond fund today is $270 million in size. Close to 90 percent of the fund's holdings are in bonds. The average maturity of the bonds in this account is 12 years; the weighted coupon rate averages 7.7 percent. The portfolio's fixed-income holdings can be categorized as long-term, medium-quality debt.

A team has managed this fund for the past six years. The quality rating of the bonds in the portfolio are broken down as follows: 60 percent BBB, 20 percent BB, 10 percent A, and the remaining 10 percent with ratings ranging from AAA to NR (not rated). There are 40 funds besides Corporate within the Strong family. Overall, the fund family's risk-adjusted performance can be described as very good.

Current Income   ★★★★★

Over the past year, Strong had a 12-month yield of 7.2 percent. During this same 12-month period, the typical corporate bond fund had a yield that averaged 5.7 percent.

Expenses   ★★

Strong's expense ratio is .9 percent; it has averaged .9 percent annually over the past three calendar years. The average expense ratio for the more than 870 funds in this category is 1.0 percent. This fund's turnover rate over the past year has been 360 percent, while its peer group average has been 140 percent.

Summary

Strong Corporate is the number one performer in its category and is also the best when it comes to tax minimization. The portfolio's overall level of risk is on the high side, but this should not pose much of a problem considering the nature of the fund's holdings as well as the seasoned experience of management. This is just one of several Strong funds that are recommended in this book, as well as in past editions.

Profile

minimum initial investment $2,500	*IRA accounts available* .... yes
subsequent minimum investment $0	*IRA minimum investment* $250
available in all 50 states .... yes	*date of inception* .... Dec. 1985
telephone exchanges .... yes	*dividend/income paid* .... monthly
number of funds in family 41	*average credit quality* .... BBB

Global Equity Funds

International, also known as "foreign," funds invest only in stocks of foreign companies, while global funds invest in both foreign and U.S. stocks. For the purposes of this book, the universe of global equity funds shown encompasses both foreign (international) and world (global) portfolios.

The economic outlook of foreign countries is the major factor in mutual fund management's decision as to which nations and industries are to be favored. A secondary concern is the future anticipated value of the U.S. dollar relative to foreign currencies. A strong or weak dollar can detract or add to an international fund's overall performance. A strong dollar will lower a foreign portfolio's return; a weak dollar will enhance international performance. Trying to gauge the direction of any currency is as difficult as trying to figure out what the U.S. stock market will do tomorrow, next week, or the following year.

Investors who do not wish to be subjected to currency swings may wish to use a fund family that practices currency hedging for their foreign holdings. Currency hedging means that management is buying a kind of insurance policy that pays off in the event of a strong U.S. dollar. Basically, the foreign or international fund that is being hurt by the dollar is making a killing in currency futures contracts. When done properly, the gains in the futures contracts, the insurance policy, offset some, most, or all security losses attributable to a strong dollar. Some people may feel that buying currency contracts is risky business for the fund; it is not.

Like automobile insurance, currency hedging only pays off if there is an accident; that is, if the U.S. dollar increases in value against the currencies represented by the portfolio's securities. If the dollar remains level or decreases in value, so much the better; the foreign securities increase in value and the currency contracts become virtually worthless. The price of these contracts becomes a cost of doing business; as with car insurance, the protection is simply renewed. In the case of a currency contract, the contract expires and a new one is purchased, covering another period of time.

To give you a tangible idea of how important currency hedging is on a risk-adjusted basis, consider how foreign and U.S. stock portfolios have fared against each other over the past 10 years. U.S. stocks have had a risk level of 16, compared to just over 17 for foreign equities. When currency hedging is added to the foreign portfolio, the international risk level drops to a 13, while the U.S. level remains at 16.

It is wise to consider investing abroad, since different economies experience prosperity and recession at different times. During the 1980s, foreign stocks were the number one performing investment, averaging a compound return of over 22 percent per year, compared to 18 percent for U.S. stocks and 5 percent for residential real estate. But during the past decade, U.S. stocks have outperformed foreign stocks (18.2 percent versus 9.4 percent). Over the past 15 years (ending March 31, 2000), U.S. stocks have had an average compound annual return of 18.4 percent versus 15.2 percent for foreign stocks. To give you a broader perspective, take a look at how U.S. securities have fared against their foreign counterparts over each of the last 25 years.

Why Global Stocks and Bonds Deserve a Place in Every Investor's Portfolio

The following table shows the total return for each investment category in each of the past 28 years.

Year	U.S. Stocks	U.S. Bonds	Non–U.S. Stocks	Non–U.S. Bonds
1972	+19.0	+ 7.3	+37.4	+ 4.4
1973	−14.6	+ 2.3	−14.2	+ 6.3
1974	−26.5	+ 0.2	−22.1	+ 5.3
1975	+37.2	+12.3	+37.0	+ 8.8
1976	+24.0	+15.6	+ 3.8	+10.5
1977	− 7.2	+ 3.0	+19.4	+38.9
1978	+ 6.5	+ 1.2	+34.3	+18.5
1979	+18.6	+ 2.3	+ 6.2	− 5.0
1980	+32.3	+ 3.1	+24.4	+13.7
1981	− 5.0	+ 7.3	− 1.0	− 4.6
1982	+21.5	+31.1	− 0.9	+11.9
1983	+22.6	+ 8.0	+24.6	+ 4.3
1984	+ 6.3	+15.0	+ 7.9	− 2.0
1985	+31.7	+21.3	+56.7	+37.2
1986	+18.6	+15.6	+67.9	+33.9
1987	+ 5.3	+ 2.3	+24.9	+36.1
1988	+16.6	+ 7.6	+28.6	+ 3.0
1989	+31.6	+14.2	+10.8	− 4.5
1990	− 3.1	+ 8.3	−14.9	+14.1
1991	+30.4	+16.1	+12.5	+17.9
1992	+ 7.7	+ 8.1	−12.2	+ 7.1
1993	+10.1	+18.2	+32.6	+15.1
1994	+ 1.3	− 7.8	+ 7.8	+ 6.7
1995	+37.4	+31.7	+11.2	+19.6
1996	+23.1	− 0.9	+6.1	+4.1
1997	+ 33.3	+ 16.0	+ 1.8	- 4.3
1998	+28.6	+13.1	+20.0	+17.8
1999	+21.0	− 9.0	+27.0	- 3.8

Number of years this category achieved the best results   10   4   9   5

Increasing your investment returns and reducing portfolio risk are two compelling reasons for investing worldwide. Global investing allows you to maximize your returns by investing in some of the world's best managed and most profitable companies. Japan, for example, is the world's leading producer of sophisticated electronics goods; Germany of heavy machinery; the United States of biotechnology; and Southeast Asia of commodity-manufactured goods.

Diversification reduces investment risk: Recent studies have once again proven this most basic investment principle. A 1996 study showed that the least volatile investment portfolio over the past 25 years (1972–1996) would have been composed of 60 percent U.S. equities and 40 percent foreign equities. These results reflect the importance of balancing a portfolio between U.S. and foreign equities.

Japan, the most economically mature country in the Pacific Basin, has become the dominant force behind the development of the newly industrialized countries (NICs) of Hong Kong, Korea, Thailand, Singapore, Malaysia, and Taiwan. As demand for Japanese products has grown and costs in Japan have risen, the search for affordable production of goods has caused Japanese investment to flow into neighboring countries, fostering their development as economically independent and prosperous nations.

The NICs, with some of the cheapest labor forces and richest untapped natural resources in the world, have recently experienced an enormous influx of international investment capital and today represent the world's fastest growing source of low-cost manufacturing. The Pacific Region, which includes Japan, Hong Kong, Korea, Taiwan, Thailand, Singapore, Malaysia, and Australia, has experienced outstanding economic growth and today represents 34 percent of the world's stock market capital—nearly double what it was 10 years ago.

The newly industrialized countries are favored locations for the manufacture and assembly of consumer electronics products. Displaced from high-cost countries such as the United States and Japan, electronics factories in these developing countries significantly benefit from reduced labor costs. Today, in fact, Korea is the world's third-largest manufacturer of semiconductors.

The Pacific Region yields yet another country with strong economic growth: China. Opportunities to benefit from the industrialization of China come from firms listed on the Hong Kong Stock Exchange, in such basic areas as electricity, construction materials, public transportation, and fundamental telecommunications. Indeed, these low-tech and essential industries, once growth industries in the United States, are now the foundation of a natural growth progression occurring in the NICs of Southeast Asia.

Companies such as China Light and Power (Hong Kong), Siam Cement (Thailand), and Hyundai (Korea) offer much the same profit potential today as their northern European counterparts did 100 years ago, their U.S. counterparts 40 years ago, and their Japanese counterparts as recently as 20 years ago.

Investors have long been familiar with the names of many of Europe's major producers—Nestlé, Olivetti, Shell, Bayer, Volkswagen, and Perrier, to name just a few. Europe's impressive manufacturing capacity, diverse industrial base, quality labor pools, and many leading, multinational, blue-chip corporations can make it an environment for growth, accessible to you through foreign funds.

With economic deregulation and the elimination of internal trade barriers, many European companies are, for the first time in history, investing in and competing for exposure to the whole European market. Companies currently restricted to manufacturing and distributing within their national boundaries will soon be able to locate facilities anywhere in Europe, maximizing the efficient employment of labor, capital, and raw materials.

The global stock category is made up of 1,400 funds: 310 "World" ($210 billion), 730 "Foreign" ($275 billion), 150 "European" ($27 billion), and 210 "Pacific" ($23 billion). Total market capitalization of this entire category is $535 billion. These funds typically throw off a dividend of less than 1 percent and have an expense ratio of 1.9 percent. The price-earnings (p/e) ratio is 36, versus a p/e ratio of 37 for the typical stock in the S & P 500.

Over the past three years, global equity funds have had an average compound return of 22 percent per year. The annual return for the past 5 years has been 20 percent, 13 percent for the past 10 years, and 15 percent for the last 15 years. The standard deviation for global equity funds has been 24 percent over the past three years. This means that global equity funds have experienced about 12 percent less volatility than growth funds.

International, or foreign, funds should be part of everyone's portfolio. They provide superior returns and reduce overall portfolio risk. As with any other fund category, this one should not be looked at in a vacuum. The real beauty of foreign funds shines through when they are combined with other categories of U.S. equities. According to a Stanford University study, one's overall risk level is cut in half when a global portfolio of stocks is used instead of one based on U.S. issues alone. Moreover, as already demonstrated, returns are greater when we look for opportunities worldwide instead of just domestically.

Global Equity Funds

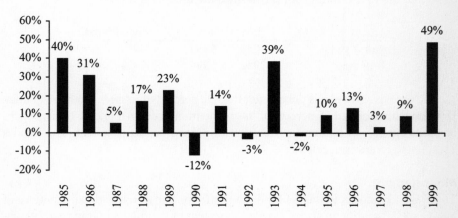

Acorn International
227 West Monroe Street, Suite 3000
Chicago, IL 60606
800-922-6769
www.wanger.com/fund.html

total return	★★★★
risk reduction	★★★★★
management	★★★★★
tax minimization	★★★★★
expense control	★★★★★
symbol ACINX	24 points
up-market performance	excellent
down-market performance	good
predictability of returns	excellent

Total Return   ★★★★
Over the past five years, Acorn International has taken $10,000 and turned it into $31,760 ($23,000 over three years). This translates into an annualized return of 26 percent over the past five years and 32 percent over the past three years. Over the past five years, this fund has outperformed 66 percent of all mutual funds; within its general category it has done better than 86 percent of its peers. Global equity funds have averaged 15 percent annually over these same five years (all periods ending March 31, 2000).

Risk/Volatility   ★★★★★
Over the past five years, Acorn has been safer than 90 percent of all global equity funds. Since its inception, the fund has had one negative year, while the S & P 500 has also had one (off 3 percent in 1990); the EAFE fell twice (off 23 percent in 1990 and 12 percent in 1992). The fund has underperformed the S & P 500 five times and the EAFE Index four times since the fund's inception.

	last 5 years		since inception	
worst year	0%	1997	-4%	1994
best year	79%	1999	79%	1999

In the past, Acorn has done better than 90 percent of its peer group in up markets and outperformed 55 percent of its competition in down markets. Consistency, or predictability, of returns for Acorn can be described as excellent. This fund's risk-related return is excellent.

Management   ★★★★★
There are 130 stocks in this $3.6 billion portfolio. The average global equity fund today is $380 million in size. Close to 98 percent of the fund's holdings are in foreign stocks. The stocks in this portfolio have an average price-earnings (p/e) ratio of 48 and a median market capitalization of $3.3 billion. The fund's four largest country weightings are as follows (shown as a percentage of the portfolio): U.K.

(14 percent), Japan (12 percent), Singapore (10 percent), and Italy (8 percent). The portfolio's equity holdings can be categorized as mid-cap and growth-oriented issues. The fund has a correlation of just roughly 15 percent to the S & P 500 (versus 50 percent for foreign equity funds in general).

Leah Zell and Margaret Forster have managed this fund for the past six years. Management highly favors foreign small- and mid-cap issues. Strong fundamentals are emphasized and a bottom-up approach is utilized. The managers look for companies that have a dominant industry position and positive cash flow. Manager Zell strongly favors a buy-and-hold philosophy in order to reduce operating expenses and increase tax efficiency. There are four funds besides International within the Acorn family. Overall, the fund family's risk-adjusted performance can be described as very good.

Tax Minimization ★★★★★
During the past five years, a $10,000 initial investment grew to $30,170 after taxes, assuming a 39.6 percent income tax bracket (state and federal combined) and a capital gains rate of 28 percent. This means that investors in this fund were able to preserve 95 percent of their total returns. Compared to other equity funds, this fund's tax savings are considered to be excellent.

Expenses ★★★★★
Acorn's expense ratio is 1.1 percent; it has averaged 1.1 percent annually over the past three calendar years. The average expense ratio for the 1,400 funds in this category is 1.9 percent. This fund's turnover rate over the past year has been 45 percent, while its peer group average has been 85 percent.

Summary
Acorn International scores an almost perfect score of 24 out of 25 possible points, making this one of the very best funds, regardless of category or objective. It is hard to imagine anything better than very good returns with extremely low risk. The fund is safer than 90 percent of its peer group. There is nothing not to like about Acorn International. Hopefully, this small fund family will add more funds to the fold.

Profile

minimum initial investment $1,000	*IRA accounts available* .... yes
subsequent minimum investment .. $100	*IRA minimum investment* $1,000
available in all 50 states .... yes	*date of inception* .... Sept. 1992
telephone exchanges .... yes	*dividend/income paid* ... semi-annually
number of funds in family 5	*largest sector weighting* ..... services

American Century International Growth Investor Shares

4500 Main Street
P.O. Box 419200
Kansas City, MO 64141
800-345-2021
www.americancentury.com

total return	★★★★
risk reduction	★★★★
management	★★★★
tax minimization	★★★★
expense control	★★★★
symbol TWIEX	20 points
up-market performance	very good
down-market performance	poor
predictability of returns	very good

Total Return   ★★★★

Over the past five years, American Century International Growth Investor Shares has taken $10,000 and turned it into $33,040 ($23,000 over three years). This translates into an annualized return of 27 percent over the past five years and 32 percent over the past three years. Over the past five years, this fund has outperformed 71 percent of all mutual funds; within its general category it has done better than 94 percent of its peers. Global equity funds have averaged 15 percent annually over these same five years (all periods ending March 31, 2000).

Risk/Volatility   ★★★★

Over the past five years, Investor Shares has been safer than 60 percent of all global equity funds. Since its inception, the fund has had one negative year, while the S & P 500 has also had one (off 3 percent in 1990); the EAFE fell twice (off 23 percent in 1990 and 12 percent in 1992). The fund has underperformed the S & P 500 six times and the EAFE Index twice since the fund's inception.

	last 5 years		since inception	
worst year	12%	1995	-5%	1994
best year	64%	1999	64%	1999

In the past, Investor Shares has done better than 75 percent of its peer group in up markets and outperformed 20 percent of its competition in down markets. Consistency, or predictability, of returns for Investor Shares can be described as very good. This fund's risk-related return is excellent.

Management   ★★★★

There are 130 stocks in this $6 billion portfolio. The average global equity fund today is $380 million in size. Close to 97 percent of the fund's holdings are in stocks. The stocks in this portfolio have an average price-earnings (p/e) ratio of 49 and a median market capitalization of $38 billion. The fund's four largest country weightings are as follows (shown as a percentage of the portfolio): Luxembourg (21 percent), Japan (17 percent), Netherlands (17 percent), and Switzerland (10 percent). The portfolio's equity holdings can be categorized as large-cap and growth-oriented issues. The fund has a correlation of just roughly 25 percent to the S & P 500 (versus 50 percent for foreign equity funds in general).

Mark Kopinski and Henrik Strabo have managed this fund for the past seven years. By mostly utilizing a bottom-up approach, management favors large-cap issues that have earnings and revenue acceleration. The analysis process begins with a computer program that screens through stocks worldwide comprising roughly 98 percent of the entire globe's equity capitalization. There are 86 funds besides Investor Shares within the American Century Investments family. Overall, the fund family's risk-adjusted performance can be described as very good.

Tax Minimization ★★★★
During the past five years, a $10,000 initial investment grew to $27,750 after taxes, assuming a 39.6 percent income tax bracket (state and federal combined) and a capital gains rate of 28 percent. This means that investors in this fund were able to preserve 84 percent of their total returns. Compared to other equity funds, this fund's tax savings are considered to be very good.

Expenses ★★★★
Investor Shares' expense ratio is 1.3 percent; it has averaged 1.3 percent annually over the past three calendar years. The average expense ratio for the 1,400 funds in this category is 1.9 percent. This fund's turnover rate over the past year has been 110 percent, while its peer group average has been 85 percent.

Summary
American Century International Growth Investor Shares has ranked in the top one or two performance quintiles for each of the past six years. This type of winning consistency is almost unheard of in the mutual fund industry, particularly when it comes to equity funds. Management does a very good job in every department—performance, risk reduction, expense control, and tax minimization. In fact, risk-adjusted returns are superb. And, speaking of top marks, look to other funds within this family for other highly rated portfolios.

Profile
minimum initial investment .... $,2,500	*IRA accounts available* .... yes
subsequent minimum investment $0	*IRA minimum investment* $1,000
available in all 50 states .... yes	*date of inception* .... May 1991
telephone exchanges .... yes	*dividend/income paid* .... annually
number of funds in family 87	*largest sector weighting* ..... services

IDEX JCC Global A

201 Highland Avenue
Largo, FL 34640
888-233-4339
www.idexfunds.com

total return	★★★★★
risk reduction	★★★★★
management	★★★★★
tax minimization	★★★★★
expense control	★★★
symbol IGLBX	23 points
up-market performance	excellent
down-market performance	fair
predictability of returns	excellent

Total Return   ★★★★★

Over the past five years, IDEX JCC Global A has taken $10,000 and turned it into
$41,620 ($26,281 over three years). This translates into an annualized return of 33
percent over the past five years and 38 percent over the past three years. Over the
past five years, this fund has outperformed 95 percent of all mutual funds; within
its general category it has also done better than 95 percent of its peers. Global
equity funds have averaged 15 percent annually over these same five years (all
periods ending March 31, 2000).

Risk/Volatility   ★★★★★

Over the past five years, JCC Global has been safer than 90 percent of all global
equity funds. Since its inception, the fund has had no negative years, while the S
& P 500 has had one (off 3 percent in 1990); the EAFE fell twice (off 23 percent
in 1990 and 12 percent in 1992). The fund has underperformed the S & P 500 four
times and the EAFE Index twice since the fund's inception.

	last 5 years		since inception	
worst year	20%	1995	1%	1994
best year	63%	1999	63%	1999

In the past, JCC Global has done better than 90 percent of its peer group in up
markets and outperformed 30 percent of its competition in down markets.
Consistency, or predictability, of returns for JCC Global can be described as excellent. This fund's risk-related return is also excellent.

Management   ★★★★★

There are 135 stocks in this $810 million portfolio. The average global equity fund
today is $380 million in size. Close to 99 percent of the fund's holdings are in stocks.
The stocks in this portfolio have an average price-earnings (p/e) ratio of 54 and a
median market capitalization of $82 billion. The portfolio's weighting by country is
as follows: United States (38 percent), Japan (11 percent), U.K. (9 percent), Finland

(6 percent), and Sweden (5 percent). The portfolio's equity holdings can be categorized as large-cap and growth-oriented issues.

Helen Young Hayes has managed this fund for the past eight years. Management uses a bottom-up approach for individual security selection. The fund is not concerned about an individual country's weighting. Stocks in the portfolio are sold if its growth potential changes. There are 54 funds besides JCC Global within the Idex family. Overall, the fund family's risk-adjusted performance can be described as very good.

Tax Minimization   ★★★★★
During the past five years, a $10,000 initial investment grew to $39,120 after taxes, assuming a 39.6 percent income tax bracket (state and federal combined) and a capital gains rate of 28 percent. This means that investors in this fund were able to preserve 94 percent of their total returns. Compared to other equity funds, this fund's tax savings are considered to be excellent.

Expenses   ★★★
JCC Global's expense ratio is 1.8 percent; it has averaged 1.9 percent annually over the past three calendar years. The average expense ratio for the 1,400 funds in this category is 1.9 percent. This fund's turnover rate over the past year has been 85 percent, while its peer group average has been 85 percent.

Summary
IDEX JCC Global A ranks in the top quintile overall as well as when it comes to performance over the past five years. Returns and risk minimization are both top-rated and some of the very best figures seen in the entire category. The same can be said about the fund's tax efficiency. This and other IDEX offerings are highly recommended.

Profile

minimum initial investment $500	*IRA accounts available* . . . . yes
subsequent minimum investment . . . $50	*IRA minimum investment* $1,000
available in all 50 states . . . . yes	*date of inception* . . . . Oct. 1992
telephone exchanges . . . . yes	*dividend/income paid* . . . . annually
number of funds in family 55	*largest sector weighting* . . . . . services

Janus Worldwide
100 Fillmore Street, Suite 300
Denver, CO 80206
800-525-8983
www.janus.com

total return	★★★★★
risk reduction	★★★★★
management	★★★★★
tax minimization	★★★★★
expense control	★★★★★
symbol JAWWX	25 points
up-market performance	excellent
down-market performance	fair
predictability of returns	excellent

Total Return   ★★★★★
Over the past five years, Janus Worldwide has taken $10,000 and turned it into $43,200 ($26,280 over three years). This translates into an annualized return of 34 percent over the past five years and 38 percent over the past three years. Over the past five years, this fund has outperformed 96 percent of all mutual funds; within its general category it has done better than 96 percent of its peers. Global equity funds have averaged 15 percent annually over these same five years (all periods ending March 31, 2000).

Risk/Volatility   ★★★★★
Over the past five years, Janus Worldwide has been safer than 90 percent of all global equity funds. Since its inception, the fund has had no negative years, while the S & P 500 has had one (off 3 percent in 1990); the EAFE fell twice (off 23 percent in 1990 and 12 percent in 1992). The fund has underperformed the S & P 500 three times and the EAFE Index twice since the fund's inception.

	last 5 years		since inception	
worst year	20%	1997	4%	1994
best year	64%	1999	64%	1999

In the past, Worldwide has done better than 90 percent of its peer group in up markets and outperformed 30 percent of its competition in down markets. Consistency, or predictability, of returns for Worldwide can be described as excellent. This fund's risk-related return is excellent.

Management   ★★★★★
There are 110 stocks in this $46 billion portfolio. The average global equity fund today is $380 million in size. Close to 90 percent of the fund's holdings are in stocks. The stocks in this portfolio have an average price-earnings (p/e) ratio of 54 and a median market capitalization of $94 billion. The fund's four largest country weightings are as follows (shown as a percentage of the portfolio): United States

(30 percent), Japan (12 percent), U.K. (10 percent), and Finland (5 percent). The fund has a correlation of just roughly 35 percent to the S & P 500 (versus 50 percent for global equity funds in general).

Helen Young Hayes has managed this fund since 1992, Laurence Chang came on board as comanager in 1999. These comanagers rely on fundamental bottom-up analysis, looking for stocks that are trading at a discount to their expected growth rate. Favored picks are companies whose management is making an effort to reduce debt, increase capital, and other methods of restructuring. There are 21 funds besides Worldwide within the Janus family. Overall, the fund family's risk-adjusted performance can be described as excellent.

Tax Minimization ★★★★★
During the past five years, a $10,000 initial investment grew to $41,040 after taxes, assuming a 39.6 percent income tax bracket (state and federal combined) and a capital gains rate of 28 percent. This means that investors in this fund were able to preserve 95 percent of their total returns. Compared to other equity funds, this fund's tax savings are considered to be excellent.

Expenses ★★★★★
Worldwide's expense ratio is .9 percent; it has averaged .9 percent annually over the past three calendar years. The average expense ratio for the 1,400 funds in this category is 1.9 percent. This fund's turnover rate over the past year has been 65 percent, while its peer group average has been 85 percent.

Summary
Janus Worldwide receives a perfect score, 25 out of 25 possible points. This fund is simply fantastic. Only a couple of funds in the entire book receive a perfect score and this is one of those very few. Performance wise, it ranks as number two within its large and broad category, but it has a third less volatility than the number one performer; its expense ratio is also less than half of the one fund that has a higher performance ranking. The fund also has tremendous consistency, ranking in the top quartile of performance for each of the past five years—a very rare accomplishment. One cannot say enough good things about this fund.

Profile
minimum initial investment $2,500	*IRA accounts available* .... yes
subsequent minimum investment .. $100	*IRA minimum investment* $500
available in all 50 states .... yes	*date of inception* .... May 1991
telephone exchanges .... yes	*dividend/income paid* .... annually
number of funds in family 22	*largest sector weighting* ... technology

Julius Baer International Equity A

Exchange Place
P.O. Box 1376
Boston, MA 02104
800-435-4659
www.juliusbaer.com

total return	★★★★
risk reduction	★★★★
management	★★★★
tax minimization	★★★★★
expense control	★★
symbol BJBIX	16 points
up-market performance	n/a
down-market performance	n/a
predictability of returns	excellent

Total Return   ★★★★

Over the past five years, Julius Baer International Equity A has taken $10,000 and turned it into $37,130 ($26,856 over three years). This translates into an annualized return of 30 percent over the past five years and 39 percent over the past three years. Over the past five years, this fund has outperformed 80 percent of all mutual funds; within its general category it has done better than 94 percent of its peers. Global equity funds have averaged 15 percent annually over these same five years (all periods ending March 31, 2000).

Risk/Volatility   ★★★★

Over the past five years, International Equity has been safer than 40 percent of all global equity funds. Since its inception, the fund has had two negative years, while the S & P 500 has had one (off 3 percent in 1990); the EAFE fell twice (off 23 percent in 1990 and 12 percent in 1992). The fund has underperformed the S & P 500 five times and the EAFE Index twice since the fund's inception.

	last 5 years		since inception	
worst year	0%	1995	-34%	1994
best year	77%	1999	77%	1999

Consistency, or predictability, of returns for International Equity can be described as excellent. This fund's risk-related return is very good.

Management   ★★★★

There are 60 stocks in this $140 million portfolio. The average global equity fund today is $380 million in size. Close to 90 percent of the fund's holdings are in stocks. The stocks in this portfolio have an average price-earnings (p/e) ratio of 44 and a median market capitalization of $19 billion. The portfolio's equity holdings can be categorized as large-cap and growth-oriented issues. The fund's four largest country weightings are as follows (shown as a percentage of the portfolio): Japan

(20 percent), U.K. (19 percent), France (14 percent), and Germany (14 percent). The fund has a correlation of just roughly 20 percent to the S & P 500 (versus 50 percent for foreign equity funds in general).

Rudolph-Riad Younes and Richard Pell have managed this fund for the past six years. These comanagers primarily invest in foreign industry market leaders, starting with a top-down approach for sector selection. Specific companies under consideration are compared against leading global counterparts. More often than not, the fund owns securities in roughly 40 different countries. There is one fund besides International Equity within the Julius Baer Investment family. Overall, the fund family's risk-adjusted performance can be described as very good.

Tax Minimization   ★★★★★
During the past five years, investors who initially invested $10,000 in this fund were able to preserve 96 percent of their total returns. Compared to other equity funds, this fund's tax savings are considered to be excellent.

Expenses   ★★
International Equity's expense ratio is 1.9 percent; it has averaged 1.8 percent annually over the past three calendar years. The average expense ratio for the 1,400 funds in this category is 1.9 percent. This fund's turnover rate over the past year has been 130 percent, while its peer group average has been 85 percent.

Summary
Julius Baer International Equity A's performance has been in the top quintile for each of the past four years. This is one of the more predictable and consistent foreign equity funds. Management scores well in every important category but does a particularly exceptional job when it comes to tax efficiency—investors have been able to preserve 96 percent of the high returns the fund has enjoyed over the past several years. This international offering is only one of two funds offered by this small family. Hopefully the people in charge at Julius Baer will add some more portfolios.

Profile

minimum initial investment $2,500	*IRA accounts available* . . . . yes
subsequent minimum investment $1,000	*IRA minimum investment* $100
available in all 50 states . . . . yes	*date of inception* . . . . Oct. 1993
telephone exchanges . . . . yes	*dividend/income paid* . . . . monthly
number of funds in family 2	*largest sector weighting* . . . . . services

Legg Mason EuropeFund-Class A
111 South Calvert Street
P.O. Box 1476
Baltimore, MD 21203
800-800-3609
www.leggmason.com

total return	★★★★
risk reduction	★★★★★
management	★★★★
tax minimization	★★★★
expense control	★★★
symbol LMEFX	20 points
up-market performance	good
down-market performance	good
predictability of returns	excellent

Total Return   ★★★★★

Over the past five years, Legg Mason EuropeFund-Class A has taken $10,000 and turned it into $31,760 ($20,000 over three years and $22,950 over the past 10 years). This translates into an annualized return of 26 percent over the past five years, 26 percent over the past three years, and 13 percent for the decade. Over the past five years, this fund has outperformed 91 percent of all mutual funds; within its general category it has done better than 93 percent of its peers. Global equity funds have averaged 15 percent annually over these same five years (all periods ending March 31, 2000).

Risk/Volatility   ★★★★★

Over the past five years, EuropeFund has been safer than 55 percent of all global equity funds. Over the past decade, the fund has had three negative years, while the S & P 500 has had one (off 3 percent in 1990); the EAFE fell twice (off 23 percent in 1990 and 12 percent in 1992). The fund has underperformed the S & P 500 six times and the EAFE Index four times in the last 10 years.

	last 5 years		last 10 years	
worst year	17%	1997	-22%	1990
best year	42%	1998	42%	1998

In the past, EuropeFund has done better than 50 percent of its peer group in up markets and outperformed 55 percent of its competition in down markets. Consistency, or predictability, of returns for EuropeFund can be described as excellent. This fund's risk-related return is also excellent.

Management   ★★★★★

There are 45 stocks in this $130 million portfolio. The average global equity fund today is $380 million in size. Close to 99 percent of the fund's holdings are in stocks. The stocks in this portfolio have an average price-earnings (p/e) ratio of 35 and a median market capitalization of $42 billion. Financials represent close to one-third of the fund's holdings, followed by services (20 percent) and technology (14 percent). The portfolio's equity holdings can be categorized as large-cap and a blend of growth and value stocks. The fund has a correlation of roughly 50 percent to the S & P 500 (versus 90 percent for European funds in general).

Neil Worsley and William Lovering have managed this fund for the past eight years. Management looks for companies with strong balance sheets; prospects that are expected to do better than their European counterparts. The fund also targets stocks that are likely to benefit from mergers and acquisitions. There are 20 funds besides EuropeFund within the Legg Mason family. Overall, the fund family's risk-adjusted performance can be described as very good.

Tax Minimization   ★★★★★
During the past five years, a $10,000 initial investment grew to $26,990 after taxes, assuming a 39.6 percent income tax bracket (state and federal combined) and a capital gains rate of 28 percent. This means that investors in this fund were able to preserve 85 percent of their total returns. Compared to other equity funds, this fund's tax savings are considered to be very good.

Expenses   ★★★
EuropeFund's expense ratio is 1.8 percent; it has averaged 1.8 percent annually over the past three calendar years. The average expense ratio for the 1,400 funds in this category is 1.9 percent. This fund's turnover rate over the past year has been 100 percent, while its peer group average has been 85 percent.

Summary
Legg Mason EuropeFund-Class A is one of only two European funds to make the book. This Europe offering is best suited for the low-risk foreign investor who wants to target a specific region. Tax minimization has also been outstanding. The fund scores well in every single category and has outperformed 93 percent of its peer group. Check out other Legg Mason offerings. This is a fund company that does a particularly good job on a risk-adjusted return basis.

Profile

minimum initial investment $1,000	*IRA accounts available* .... yes
subsequent minimum investment 10	*IRA minimum investment* $1,000
available in all 50 states .... yes	*date of inception* .... Aug. 1986
telephone exchanges .... yes	*dividend/income paid* .... annually
number of funds in family 21	*largest sector weighting* .... financials

Montgomery Global Opportunities R
101 California Street
San Francisco, CA 94111
800-572-3863
www.montgomeryfunds.com

total return	★★★★
risk reduction	★★★★
management	★★★★
tax minimization	★★★★
expense control	★★
symbol MNGOX	18 points
up-market performance	excellent
down-market performance	poor
predictability of returns	excellent

Total Return   ★★★★

Over the past five years, Montgomery Global Opportunities R has taken $10,000 and turned it into $37,130 ($24,600 over three years). This translates into an annualized return of 30 percent over the past five years and 35 percent over the past three years. Over the past five years, this fund has outperformed 90 percent of all mutual funds; within its general category it has done better than 90 percent of its peers. Global equity funds have averaged 15 percent annually over these same five years (all periods ending March 31, 2000).

Risk/Volatility   ★★★★

Over the past five years, Global Opportunities has been safer than 30 percent of all global equity funds. Since its inception, the fund has had one negative year, while the S & P 500 has also had one (off 3 percent in 1990); the EAFE fell twice (off 23 percent in 1990 and 12 percent in 1992). The fund has underperformed the S & P 500 four times and the EAFE Index once since the fund's inception.

	last 5 years		since inception	
worst year	11%	1997	-9%	1994
best year	58%	1999	58%	1999

In the past, Global Opportunities has done better than 90 percent of its peer group in up markets and outperformed just 10 percent of its competition in down markets. Consistency, or predictability, of returns for Global Opportunities can be described as excellent. This fund's risk-related return is also excellent.

Management   ★★★★

There are 75 stocks in this $100 million portfolio. The average global equity fund today is $380 million in size. Close to 90 percent of the fund's holdings are in stocks. The stocks in this portfolio have an average price-earnings (p/e) ratio of 37 and a median market capitalization of $18 billion. The portfolio's equity holdings can be categorized as large-cap and growth-oriented issues. The fund's four largest country weightings are as follows (shown as a percentage of the portfolio): United States (25 percent), U.K. (13 percent), Japan (12 percent), and France (10 percent). The portfolio's equity holdings can be categorized as large-cap and growth-oriented issues. The fund has a correlation of just roughly 45 percent to the S & P 500 (versus 50 percent for global equity funds in general).

Oscar Castro and John Boich have managed this fund for the past eight years. With the exception of the United States, management cannot have any one country represent more than 40 percent of the portfolio. The comanagers get a lot of their ideas from the research they do for the Montgomery International Growth Fund, a portfolio they also manage. Security selection is based on a bottom-up approach that targets undervalued issues that management believes has a minimum appreciation potential of at least 25 percent annually. There are 25 funds besides Global Opportunities within the Montgomery family. Overall, the fund family's risk-adjusted performance can be described as good.

Tax Minimization ★★★★
During the past five years, a $10,000 initial investment grew to $31,930 after taxes, assuming a 39.6 percent income tax bracket (state and federal combined) and a capital gains rate of 28 percent. This means that investors in this fund were able to preserve 86 percent of their total returns. Compared to other equity funds, this fund's tax savings are considered to be very good.

Expenses ★★
Global Opportunities' expense ratio is 1.9 percent; it has averaged 1.9 percent annually over the past three calendar years. The average expense ratio for the 1,400 funds in this category is 1.9 percent. This fund's turnover rate over the past year has been 170 percent, while its peer group average has been 85 percent.

Summary
Montgomery Global Opportunities R has ranked in the top one or two quintiles of performance for each of the past three years. The fund scores very highly in all categories except expenses, where the fund is punished slightly due to its comparatively high turnover rate. Still, one cannot argue with success or the fund's management expertise. This fund is strongly recommended for the global equity investor. Predictability of returns and bull market performance are both superb.

Profile

minimum initial investment $1,000	*IRA accounts available* .... yes
subsequent minimum investment .. $100	*IRA minimum investment* $1,000
available in all 50 states .... yes	*date of inception* .... Sept. 1993
telephone exchanges .... yes	*dividend/income paid* .... annually
number of funds in family 26	*largest sector weighting* ..... services

Oppenheimer Global A

P.O. Box 5270
Denver, CO 80217
800-525-7048
www.oppenheimerfunds.com

total return	★★★★
risk reduction	★★★★★
management	★★★★
tax minimization	★★★★
expense control	★★★★
symbol OPPAX	21 points
up-market performance	excellent
down-market performance	fair
predictability of returns	excellent

Total Return   ★★★★

Over the past five years, Oppenheimer Global A has taken $10,000 and turned it into $33,040 ($23,530 over three years and $48,070 over the past 10 years). This translates into an annualized return of 27 percent over the past five years, 33 percent over the past three years, and 17 percent for the decade. Over the past five years, this fund has outperformed 87 percent of all mutual funds; within its general category it has done better than 85 percent of its peers. Global equity funds have averaged 15 percent annually over these same five years (all periods ending March 31, 2000).

Risk/Volatility   ★★★★★

Over the past five years, Oppenheimer has been safer than 75 percent of all global equity funds. Over the past decade, the fund has had three negative years, while the S & P 500 has had one (off 3 percent in 1990); the EAFE fell twice (off 23 percent in 1990 and 12 percent in 1992). The fund has underperformed the S & P 500 seven times and the EAFE Index three times in the last 10 years.

	last 5 years		last 10 years	
worst year	13%	1998	-14%	1992
best year	58%	1999	58%	1999

In the past, Oppenheimer has done better than 90 percent of its peer group in up markets and outperformed 45 percent of its competition in down markets. Consistency, or predictability, of returns for Oppenheimer can be described as excellent. This fund's risk-related return is also excellent.

Management   ★★★★

There are 85 stocks in this $6.5 billion portfolio. The average global equity fund today is $380 million in size. Close to 90 percent of the fund's holdings are in stocks. The stocks in this portfolio have an average price-earnings (p/e) ratio of 42 and a median market capitalization of $13 billion. The fund's four largest country weightings are as follows (shown as a percentage of the portfolio): United States (40 percent), U.K. (13 percent), France (9 percent), and Japan (8 percent). The portfolio's equity holdings can be categorized as large-cap and growth-oriented issues. The fund has a correlation of just roughly 40 percent to the S & P 500 (versus 50 percent for global equity funds in general).

William Wilby has managed this fund for the past nine years. The manager invests in stocks, not markets. Management believes that by choosing specific companies, a high level of diversification can be obtained, regardless of geography. Wilby looks for industry groups that have solid long-term growth projections and then individual corporations that are the best in their category. He prefers those companies that are either underowned or underfollowed by the institutions. There are 140 funds besides Global within the Oppenheimer family. Overall, the fund family's risk-adjusted performance can be described as good.

Tax Minimization ★★★★
During the past five years, a $10,000 initial investment grew to $29,400 after taxes, assuming a 39.6 percent income tax bracket (state and federal combined) and a capital gains rate of 28 percent. This means that investors in this fund were able to preserve 89 percent of their total returns. Compared to other equity funds, this fund's tax savings are considered to be very good.

Expenses ★★★★
Oppenheimer's expense ratio is 1.2 percent; it has averaged 1.1 percent annually over the past three calendar years. The average expense ratio for the 1,400 funds in this category is 1.9 percent. This fund's turnover rate over the past year has been 65 percent, while its peer group average has been 85 percent.

Summary
Oppenheimer Global A has ranked in the top quintile of performance for three of the past four years. The fund is one of the very lowest risk in its category yet has been able to outperform 85 percent of its peer group. The fund scores very well in every category and really excels in three: risk reduction, predictability of returns, and bull market performance. Investors have been able to preserve close to 90 percent of the fund's returns.

Profile

minimum initial investment $1,000	*IRA accounts available* .... yes
subsequent minimum investment ... $25	*IRA minimum investment* $250
available in all 50 states .... yes	*date of inception* .... Dec. 1969
telephone exchanges .... yes	*dividend/income paid* .... annually
number of funds in family 141	*largest sector weighting* ... technology

Pilgrim International Small Cap Growth A
40 North Central Avenue, Suite 1200
Phoenix, AZ 85004
800-334-3444
www.pilgrimfunds.com

total return	★★★★★
risk reduction	★★★
management	★★★★
tax minimization	★★★★★
expense control	★★★
symbol NIGRX	20 points
up-market performance	excellent
down-market performance	good
predictability of returns	excellent

Total Return ★★★★★
Over the past five years, Pilgrim International Small Cap Growth A has taken $10,000 and turned it into $48,260 ($37,240 over three years). This translates into an annualized return of 37 percent over the past five years and 55 percent over the past three years. Over the past five years, this fund has outperformed 97 percent of all mutual funds; within its general category it has done better than 99 percent of its peers. Global equity funds have averaged 15 percent annually over these same five years (all periods ending March 31, 2000).

Risk/Volatility ★★★
Over the past five years, Pilgrim Small Cap has been safer than 80 percent of all global equity funds. Since its inception, the fund has had no negative years, while the S & P 500 has had one (off 3 percent in 1990); the EAFE fell twice (off 23 percent in 1990 and 12 percent in 1992). The fund has underperformed the S & P 500 three times and the EAFE Index once since the fund's inception.

	last 5 years		since inception	
worst year	5%	1995	5%	1995
best year	122%	1999	122%	1999

In the past, Pilgrim Small Cap has done better than 98 percent of its peer group in up markets and outperformed 50 percent of its competition in down markets. Consistency, or predictability, of returns for Pilgrim Small Cap can be described as excellent. This fund's risk-related return is excellent.

Management ★★★★
There are 110 stocks in this $290 million portfolio. The average global equity fund today is $380 million in size. Close to 92 percent of the fund's holdings are in stocks. The stocks in this portfolio have an average price-earnings (p/e) ratio of 50 and a median market capitalization of $3.3 billion. The fund's four largest country weightings are as follows (shown as a percentage of the portfolio): Japan.

(22 percent), U.K. (14 percent), France (14 percent), and Germany (13 percent). The portfolio's equity holdings can be categorized as mid-cap and growth-oriented issues. The fund has a correlation of just roughly 10 percent to the S & P 500 (versus 50 percent for foreign equity funds in general).

A team has managed this fund for the past six years. The fund is subadvised by Nicholas-Applegate. Management heavily invests in foreign stocks that are defined as being in the bottom 25 percent of the weighted market capitalization for each country in which it invests. The managers do not mind holding cash if they cannot find attractive issues. Individual securities are selected by using a bottom-up approach, looking for stocks that are growing faster than average due to some kind of sustainable corporate change. There are 95 funds besides International Small Cap Growth within the Pilgrim family. Overall, the fund family's risk-adjusted performance can be described as good.

Tax Minimization   ★★★★★
During the past five years, a $10,000 initial investment grew to $45,850 after taxes, assuming a 39.6 percent income tax bracket (state and federal combined) and a capital gains rate of 28 percent. This means that investors in this fund were able to preserve 95 percent of their total returns. Compared to other equity funds, this fund's tax savings are considered to be excellent.

Expenses   ★★★
Pilgrim Small Cap's expense ratio is 1.9 percent; it has averaged 1.9 percent annually over the past three calendar years. The average expense ratio for the 1,400 funds in this category is 1.9 percent. This fund's turnover rate over the past year has been 90 percent, while its peer group average has been 85 percent.

Summary
Pilgrim International Small Cap Growth A's performance has been in the top quintile for each of the past four years. This kind of consistency is almost unheard of, particularly when it comes to any kind of stock fund. The fund is also the number one performer in the book for its category over the past three and five years. Capital preservation, or tax efficiency, is also superb as is keeping overhead low.

Profile
minimum initial investment $1,000	*IRA accounts available* .... yes
subsequent minimum investment .. $100	*IRA minimum investment* $250
available in all 50 states .... yes	*date of inception* .... Aug. 1994
telephone exchanges .... yes	*dividend/income paid* .... annually
number of funds in family 96	*largest sector weighting* ... technology

Scudder Greater Europe Growth

Two International Place
Boston, MA 02110
800-225-2470
www.scudder.com

total return	★★★★
risk reduction	★★★★★
management	★★★★★
tax minimization	★★★★★
expense control	★★★★
symbol SCGEX	23 points
up-market performance	good
down-market performance	fair
predictability of returns	excellent

Total Return   ★★★★

Over the past five years, Scudder Greater Europe Growth has taken $10,000 and turned it into $35,720 ($21,470 over three years). This translates into an annualized return of 29 percent over the past five years and 29 percent over the past three years. Over the past five years, this fund has outperformed 93 percent of all mutual funds; within its general category it has done better than 95 percent of its peers. Global equity funds have averaged 15 percent annually over these same five years (all periods ending March 31, 2000).

Risk/Volatility   ★★★★★

Over the past five years, Greater Europe has been safer than 95 percent of all global equity funds. Since its inception, the fund has had no negative years, while the S & P 500 has had one (off 3 percent in 1990); the EAFE fell twice (off 23 percent in 1990 and 12 percent in 1992). The fund has underperformed the S & P 500 twice and has outperformed the EAFE Index every year since the fund's inception.

	last 5 years		since inception	
worst year	24%	1995	24%	1995
best year	35%	1999	35%	1999

In the past, Greater Europe has done better than 50 percent of its peer group in up markets and outperformed 30 percent of its competition in down markets. Consistency, or predictability, of returns for Greater Europe can be described as excellent. This fund's risk-related return is also excellent.

Management   ★★★★★

There are 100 stocks in this $1.4 billion portfolio. The average global equity fund today is $380 million in size. Close to 98 percent of the fund's holdings are in stocks. The stocks in this portfolio have an average price-earnings (p/e) ratio of 37 and a median market capitalization of $16 billion. Services stocks represent over 35 percent of the fund's holdings, followed by financials (17 percent) and industrials

(13 percent). The portfolio's equity holdings can be categorized as large-cap and growth-oriented issues. The fund has a correlation of roughly 40 percent to the S & P 500.

A team has managed this fund for the past six years. According to the prospectus, the fund must invest at least 80 percent of its assets in entities domiciled in European countries. Management first looks at macroeconomic conditions, such as projected rates of economic growth, interest rates, trade patterns, and currency trends. Specific stocks are selected based on whether the company has leading products, franchises, strong management, and financials. There are 38 funds besides Greater Europe within the Scudder family. Overall, the fund family's risk-adjusted performance can be described as good.

Tax Minimization   ★★★★★
During the past five years, a $10,000 initial investment grew to $34,650 after taxes, assuming a 39.6 percent income tax bracket (state and federal combined) and a capital gains rate of 28 percent. This means that investors in this fund were able to preserve 97 percent of their total returns. Compared to other equity funds, this fund's tax savings are considered to be excellent.

Expenses   ★★★★
Greater Europe's expense ratio is 1.5 percent; it has averaged 1.5 percent annually over the past three calendar years. The average expense ratio for the 1,400 funds in this category is 1.9 percent. This fund's turnover rate over the past year has been 90 percent, while its peer group average has been 85 percent.

Summary
Scudder Greater Europe Growth is one of only two European equity funds to make the book and it is the number one performer by quite a bit. The fund has very low risk, and risk-adjusted returns over the past three and five years have been outstanding. The fund receives a total of 23 out of 25 possible points, which is quite an accomplishment. The portfolio has shifted back and forth between value and growth plays over the years and the strategy has certainly paid off.

Profile
minimum initial investment $2,500	*IRA accounts available* . . . . yes
subsequent minimum investment . . $100	*IRA minimum investment* $1,000
available in all 50 states . . . . yes	*date of inception* . . . . Oct. 1994
telephone exchanges . . . . yes	*dividend/income paid* . . . . annually
number of funds in family 39	*largest sector weighting* . . . . . services

Smallcap World
333 South Hope Street
Los Angeles, CA 90071
800-421-4120
www.americanfunds.com

total return	★★★★
risk reduction	★★★★
management	★★★★
tax minimization	★★★★
expense control	★★★★★
symbol SMCWX	21 points
up-market performance	excellent
down-market performance	fair
predictability of returns	very good

Total Return   ★★★★

Over the past five years, Smallcap World has taken $10,000 and turned it into $30,520 ($21,970 over three years). This translates into an annualized return of 25 percent over the past five years and 30 percent over the past three years. Over the past five years, this fund has outperformed 75 percent of all mutual funds; within its general category it has done better than 56 percent of its peers. Global equity funds have averaged 15 percent annually over these same five years (all periods ending March 31, 2000).

Risk/Volatility   ★★★★

Over the past five years, Smallcap World has been safer than 99 percent of all global equity funds. Over the past decade, the fund has had one negative year, while the S & P 500 has also had one (off 3 percent in 1990); the EAFE fell twice (off 23 percent in 1990 and 12 percent in 1992). The fund has underperformed the S & P 500 six times and the EAFE Index three times in the last 10 years.

	last 5 years		last 10 years	
worst year	0%	1998	-3%	1994
best year	62%	1999	62%	1999

In the past, Smallcap has done better than 90 percent of its peer group in up markets and outperformed 45 percent of its competition in down markets. Consistency, or predictability, of returns for Smallcap World can be described as very good. This fund's risk-related return is excellent.

Management   ★★★★

There are 260 stocks in this $16 billion portfolio. The average global equity fund today is $380 million in size. Close to 90 percent of the fund's holdings are in stocks. The stocks in this portfolio have an average price-earnings (p/e) ratio of 35 and a median market capitalization of $1.3 billion. The fund's four largest country weightings are as follows (shown as a percentage of the portfolio): United States

(40 percent), Japan (7 percent), U.K. (6 percent), and Sweden (4 percent). The portfolio's equity holdings can be categorized as small-cap and growth-oriented issues. The fund has a correlation of just roughly 25 percent to the S & P 500 (versus 65 percent for global equity funds in general).

A team has managed this fund for the past five years. Management typically invests in stocks around the world that have a market cap of between $50 million and $1 billion. It is uncommon for the fund to have more than 50–60 percent of its holdings in foreign companies. Each member of the management company acts independently, selecting stocks for a small number of industry groups based on fundamental analysis; a large part of a manager's compensation is based on long-term performance. Such independence helps reduce overall risk. There are 28 funds besides Smallcap World within the American Funds family. Overall, the fund family's risk-adjusted performance can be described as very good.

Tax Minimization ★★★★
During the past five years, a $10,000 initial investment grew to $25,940 after taxes, assuming a 39.6 percent income tax bracket (state and federal combined) and a capital gains rate of 28 percent. This means that investors in this fund were able to preserve 85 percent of their total returns. Compared to other equity funds, this fund's tax savings are considered to be very good.

Expenses ★★★★★
Smallcap's expense ratio is 1.1 percent; it has averaged 1.1 percent annually over the past three calendar years. The average expense ratio for the 1,400 funds in this category is 1.9 percent. This fund's turnover rate over the past year has been 50 percent, while its peer group average has been 85 percent.

Summary
Smallcap World receives top marks when it comes to controlling expenses and up-market performance. All category ratings are either very good or superb. This is just one of several members of the American Funds family that is in this edition, as well as previous editions, of the book. As is true with most members of this family, the longer you own it, the better you will like the results and comparatively very low risk. This fund is highly recommended, particularly for the conservative or moderate investor.

Profile
minimum initial investment $1,000	*IRA accounts available* .... yes
subsequent minimum investment ... $50	*IRA minimum investment* $250
available in all 50 states .... yes	*date of inception* .... April 1990
telephone exchanges .... yes	*dividend/income paid* .... annually
number of funds in family 29	*largest sector weighting* ... technology

Government Bond Funds

These funds invest in direct and indirect U.S. government obligations. Government bond funds are made up of one or more of the following: T-bills, T-notes, T-bonds, GNMAs, and FNMAs. Treasury bills, notes, and bonds make up the entire marketable debt of the U.S. government. Such instruments are exempt from state income taxes.

Although GNMAs are considered an indirect obligation of the government, they are still backed by the full faith and credit of the United States. FNMAs are not issued by the government but are considered virtually identical in safety to GNMAs. FNMAs and GNMAs are both subject to state and local income taxes. All of the securities in a government bond fund are subject to federal income taxes.

The average maturity of securities found in government bond funds varies broadly depending upon the type of fund as well as on management's perception of risk and the future direction of interest rates. A more thorough discussion of interest rates and the volatility of bond fund prices can be found in the introductory pages of the corporate bond section.

Over the past 15 years (1985–1999), government bonds have returned an average compound return of 11 percent—versus 10.5 percent for corporate bonds. A $10,000 investment in U.S. government bonds grew to $47,730 over the past 15 years; a similar initial investment in corporate bonds grew to $44,640. During this same period, government bond funds have underperformed corporate bond funds, returning 8.2 percent, compared to 8.6 percent.

Looking at a longer time frame (1950–1999), government bonds have only slightly outperformed inflation. A dollar invested in governments at the beginning of 1950 grew to $14.94 by the end of 1999. This translates into an average compound return of 5.6 percent per year. Adjusted for inflation, the figure falls to $2.74. Over the past 50 years, the worst year for government bonds was 1967, when a loss of 9 percent was suffered. The second worst year was 1999, when the bonds suffered a loss of just under 9 percent. The best year so far has been 1982, when government bonds posted a gain of 40 percent. All of these figures are based on total return (current yield plus or minus any appreciation or loss of principal). The second best year was 1995, when these debt instruments had a total return of just under 32 percent.

Over the past half century, there have been 46 five-year periods (1951–1955, 1952–1956, etc.). On a pre-tax basis, government bonds have outperformed inflation during 27 of the 46 five-year periods. The last five-year period in which inflation outperformed long-term government bonds was 1979–1983 (8.4 percent versus 6.4 percent for bonds). Over the past 50 years, there have been 41 10-year periods (1950–1959, 1951–1960, etc.). On a pre-tax basis, government bonds have outperformed inflation during only 21 of the 41 10-year periods. The last 10-year period in which inflation outperformed long-term government bonds was 1975–1984 (7.3 percent versus 7.0 percent for bonds). Over the past half century, there have been 31 20-year periods (1946–1965, 1947–1966, etc.). On a pre-tax basis, government bonds have outperformed inflation during only 15 of these 31 periods. The last 20-year period in which inflation outperformed long-term government bonds was 1966–1985 (6.4 percent versus 6.0 percent for bonds).

Six hundred funds make up the government bonds category. Total market capitalization of this category is $110 billion.

Over the past three and five years (all periods ending March 31, 2000), government funds have had an average compound annual return of 5.6 and 5.9 percent, respectively. For the decade, these funds have averaged 7 percent a year; over the last 15 years, 8.2 percent a year. The standard deviation for government bond funds has been 3 percent over the past three years. This means that these funds have been less volatile than any other category except money market funds.

Government bond funds are the perfect choice for the conservative investor who wants to avoid any possibility of defaults. These securities should be avoided by even conservative investors who are in a high tax bracket or unable to shelter such an investment in a retirement plan or annuity. Such investors should first look at the advantages of municipal bond funds.

The prospective investor should always remember that government and corporate bonds are generally not a good investment once inflation and taxes are factored in. The investor who appreciates the cumulative effects of even low levels of inflation should probably avoid government and corporate bonds except as part of a retirement plan.

Government Bond Funds

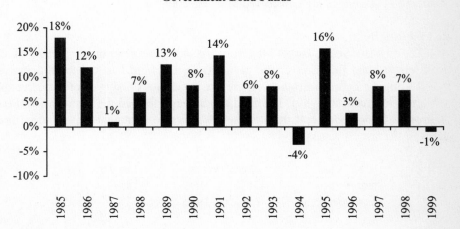

American Century Target Maturities Trust 2020
4500 Main Street
P.O. Box 419200
Kansas City, MO 64141
800-345-2021
www.americancentury.com

total return	★★★★★
risk reduction	
management	★★★
current income	★★★★
expense control	★★★★★
symbol BTTTX	17 points
up-market performance	excellent
down-market performance	poor
predictability of returns	fair

Total Return   ★★★★★
Over the past five years, has taken $10,000 and turned it into $19,250 ($15,609 over three years and $37,070 over the past 10 years). This translates into an annualized return of 14 percent over the past five years, 16 percent over the past three years, and 14 percent for the decade. Over the past five years, this fund has outperformed 57 percent of all mutual funds; within its general category it has done better than 99 percent of its peers. Government bond funds have averaged 6 percent annually over these same five years (all periods ending March 31, 2000).

During the past five years, a $10,000 initial investment grew to $13,480 after taxes, assuming a 39.6 percent income tax bracket (state and federal combined) and a capital gains rate of 28 percent. This means that investors in this fund were able to preserve 70 percent of their total returns. Compared to other fixed-income funds, this fund's tax savings are considered to be excellent.

Risk/Volatility
Over the past five years, Target Maturities has only been safer than 5 percent of all government bond funds. Over the past decade, the fund has had three negative years, while the Lehman Brothers Aggregate Bond Index had two (off 3 percent in 1994 and 1 percent in 1999). The fund has underperformed the Lehman Brothers Aggregate Bond Index and the Lehman Brothers Government Bond Index four times in the last 10 years.

	last 5 years		last 10 years	
worst year	-18%	1999	-18%	1999
best year	65%	1995	65%	1995

In the past, Target Maturities has done better than 97 percent of its peer group in up markets. Consistency, or predictability, of returns for Target Maturities Trust can be described as fair. This fund's risk-related return is excellent.

Management ★★★
There are 16 fixed-income securities in this $275 million portfolio. The average government bond fund today is $190 million in size. Close to 100 percent of the fund's holdings are in bonds. The average maturity of the bonds in this account is 21 years; the weighted coupon rate averages zero percent. The portfolio's fixed-income holdings can be categorized as long-term, high-quality debt.

A team has managed this fund for the past seven years. Management only invests in zero-coupon U.S. Treasury securities that will mature in the year 2020. These securities pay no current income to investors (shareholders) but interest is accreted daily. The price per share of the fund reflects the current value of the securities plus all accrued (accreted) interest. There are 86 funds besides Target Maturities Trust 2020 within the American Century family. Overall, the fund family's risk-adjusted performance can be described as very good.

Current Income ★★★★
Over the past year, Target Maturities had a 12-month yield of 5.9 percent. During this same 12-month period, the typical government bond fund had a yield that averaged 5.5 percent.

Expenses ★★★★★
Target Maturities' expense ratio is .6 percent; it has averaged .6 percent annually over the past three calendar years. The average expense ratio for the 600 funds in this category is 1.1 percent. This fund's turnover rate over the past year has been 30 percent, while its peer group average has been 170 percent.

Summary
American Century Target Maturities Trust 2020 is a very straightforward portfolio of zero-coupon U.S. Treasury securities that pay no current income (interest is accreted) and has a maturity date of approximately 2020. Due to the nature of zero-coupon, long-term bonds, the portfolio is extremely volatile and almost always finishes either in the very top or very bottom quartile of bond performance. However, risk-adjusted returns have been excellent.

Profile

minimum initial investment $2,500	*IRA accounts available* . . . . yes
subsequent minimum investment . . . $50	*IRA minimum investment* $1,000
available in all 50 states . . . . yes	*date of inception* . . . . Dec. 1989
telephone exchanges . . . . yes	*dividend/income paid* . . . . annually
number of funds in family 87	*average credit quality* . . . . AAA

Franklin U.S. Government Securities Series-Class A

777 Mariners Island Boulevard
San Mateo, CA 94404
800-342-5236
www.franklin-templeton.com

total return	★★★
risk reduction	★★★★★
management	★★★★
current income	★★★★
expense control	★★★★★
symbol FKUSX	21 points
up-market performance	excellent
down-market performance	poor
predictability of returns	excellent

Total Return   ★★★

Over the past five years, Franklin U.S. Government Securities Series-Class A has taken $10,000 and turned it into $14,030 ($11,910 over three years and $19,670 over the past 10 years). This translates into an annualized return of 7 percent over the past five years, 6 percent over the past three years, and 7 percent for the decade. Over the past five years, this fund has outperformed 44 percent of all mutual funds; within its general category it has done better than 91 percent of its peers. Government bond funds have averaged 6 percent annually over these same five years (all periods ending March 31, 2000).

During the past five years, a $10,000 initial investment became $8,135 after taxes, assuming a 39.6 percent income tax bracket (state and federal combined) and a capital gains rate of 28 percent. This means that investors in this fund were able to preserve 58 percent of their total returns. Compared to other fixed-income funds, this fund's tax savings are considered to be very good.

Risk/Volatility   ★★★★★

Over the past five years, Franklin Securities has been safer than 90 percent of all government bond funds. Over the past decade, the fund has had one negative year, while the Lehman Brothers Aggregate Bond Index had two (off 3 percent in 1994 and 1 percent in 1999). The fund has underperformed the Lehman Brothers Aggregate Bond Index five times and the Lehman Brothers Government Bond Index five times in the last 10 years.

	last 5 years		last 10 years	
worst year	1%	1999	-3%	1994
best year	17%	1995	17%	1995

In the past, Franklin Securities Series has done better than 95 percent of its peer group in up markets but outperformed only 15 percent of its competition in down markets. Consistency, or predictability, of returns for Franklin Securities can be described as excellent. This fund's risk-related return is very good.

Management   ★★★★
There are 21,500 fixed-income securities in this $8 billion portfolio. The average government bond fund today is $190 million in size. Close to 97 percent of the fund's holdings are in bonds. The average maturity of the bonds in this account is 22 years; the weighted coupon rate averages 7.3 percent. The portfolio's fixed-income holdings can be categorized as long-term, high-quality debt.

A team has managed this fund for the past 11 years. Management only invests in U.S. Government securities, almost exclusively in mortgage-backed securities; the top 20 holdings of the fund are all in GNMAs. Lead manager Jack Lemein prefers GNMAs because they have federal backing but pay more than Treasuries. Additionally, GNMAs tend to prepay principal at a slower rate than other agency issues. There are 78 funds besides U.S. Government Securities within the Franklin Templeton family. Overall, the fund family's risk-adjusted performance can be described as good.

Current Income   ★★★★
Over the past year, Franklin Securities Series had a 12-month yield of 6.5 percent. During this same 12-month period, the typical government bond fund had a yield that averaged 5.5 percent.

Expenses   ★★★★★
Franklin Securities Series' expense ratio is .7 percent; it has averaged .6 percent annually over the past three calendar years. The average expense ratio for the 600 funds in this category is 1.1 percent. This fund's turnover rate over the past year has been 25 percent, while its peer group average has been 170 percent.

Summary
Franklin U.S. Government Securities Series-Class A has had good risk-adjusted returns over the past 3, 5, and 10 years. This is perhaps the best-known government securities fund in the United States. The vast majority of the fund is invested in GNMAs. The fund has done extremely well in up markets but has not done well when the bond market sinks. Still, the portfolio has been safer than 90 percent of its peer group. Expense control and low turnover have been superb.

Profile

minimum initial investment $1,000	IRA accounts available .... yes
subsequent minimum investment ... $50	IRA minimum investment $250
available in all 50 states .... yes	date of inception .... May 1970
telephone exchanges .... yes	dividend/income paid .... monthly
number of funds in family 79	average credit quality .... AAA

Principal Government Securities Income A
P.O. Box 10423
Des Moines, IA 50306
800-451-5447
www.principal.com

total return	★★★
risk reduction	★★★★
management	★★★★
current income	★★★★★
expense control	★★★★★
symbol PRGVX	21 points
up-market performance	excellent
down-market performance	fair
predictability of returns	very good

Total Return   ★★★

Over the past five years, Principal Government Securities Income A has taken $10,000 and turned it into $14,030 ($12,250 over three years and $21,590 over the past 10 years). This translates into an annualized return of 7 percent over the past five years, 7 percent over the past three years, and 8 percent for the decade. Over the past five years, this fund has outperformed 44 percent of all mutual funds; within its general category it has done better than 93 percent of its peers. Government bond funds have averaged 6 percent annually over these same five years (all periods ending March 31, 2000).

During the past five years, a $10,000 initial investment became $8,560 after taxes, assuming a 39.6 percent income tax bracket (state and federal combined) and a capital gains rate of 28 percent. This means that investors in this fund were able to preserve 61 percent of their total returns. Compared to other fixed-income funds, this fund's tax savings are considered to be very good.

Risk/Volatility   ★★★★

Over the past five years, Principal Income has been safer than 40 percent of all government bond funds. Over the past decade, the fund has had one negative year, while the Lehman Brothers Aggregate Bond Index had two (off 3 percent in 1994 and 1 percent in 1999). The fund has underperformed the Lehman Brothers Aggregate Bond Index four times and the Lehman Brothers Government Bond Index four times in the last 10 years.

	last 5 years		last 10 years	
worst year	0%	1999	-5%	1994
best year	19%	1995	19%	1995

In the past, Principal Income has done better than 85 percent of its peer group in up markets and outperformed 30 percent of its competition in down markets. Consistency, or predictability, of returns for Principal Income can be described as very good. This fund's risk-related return is also very good.

Management   ★★★★
There are 290 fixed-income securities in this $270 billion portfolio. The average government bond fund today is $190 million in size. Close to 97 percent of the fund's holdings are in bonds. The average maturity of the bonds in this account is 25 years; the weighted coupon rate averages 6.7 percent. The portfolio's fixed-income holdings can be categorized as very high-quality, long-term debt.

Martin Schafer has managed this fund for the past 15 years. The vast majority of the fund's holdings are in GNMAs. Management favors seasoned discount mortgage-backed securities because they provide appreciation when they are prepaid. There are 55 funds besides Government Securities Income within the Principal family. Overall, the fund family's risk-adjusted performance can be described as good.

Current Income   ★★★★★
Over the past year, Principal Income had a 12-month yield of 6.2 percent. During this same 12-month period, the typical government bond fund had a yield that averaged 5.5 percent.

Expenses   ★★★★★
Principal Income's expense ratio is .9 percent; it has averaged .9 percent annually over the past three calendar years. The average expense ratio for the 600 funds in this category is 1.1 percent. This fund's turnover rate over the past year has been 15 percent, while its peer group average has been 170 percent.

Summary
Principal Government Securities Income A is the choice for the conservative investor interested in the greatest amount of current income. The fund's GNMA holdings possess no surprises; management scores highly in virtually every category. Part of the fund's success has been due to its efforts to keep expenses and turnover low.

Profile

minimum initial investment $1,000	IRA accounts available .... yes
subsequent minimum investment .. $100	IRA minimum investment $500
available in all 50 states .... yes	date of inception .... May 1985
telephone exchanges .... yes	dividend/income paid .... monthly
number of funds in family 56	average credit quality .... AAA

State Street Research Government Income A

One Financial Center
Boston, MA 02111
800-882-0052
www.ssrfunds.com

total return	★★★
risk reduction	★★★★
management	★★★★
current income	★★★★★
expense control	★★★
symbol SSGIX	19 points
up-market performance	good
down-market performance	very good
predictability of returns	very good

Total Return   ★★★

Over the past five years, State Street Research Government Income A has taken $10,000 and turned it into $14,030 ($11,910 over three years and $21,590 over the past 10 years). This translates into an annualized return of 7 percent over the past five years, 6 percent over the past three years, and 8 percent for the decade. Over the past five years, this fund has outperformed 47 percent of all mutual funds; within its general category it has done better than 86 percent of its peers. Government bond funds have averaged 6 percent annually over these same five years (all periods ending March 31, 2000).

During the past five years, a $10,000 initial investment became $8,980 after taxes, assuming a 39.6 percent income tax bracket (state and federal combined) and a capital gains rate of 28 percent. This means that investors in this fund were able to preserve 64 percent of their total returns. Compared to other fixed-income funds, this fund's tax savings are considered to be excellent.

Risk/Volatility   ★★★★

Over the past five years, State Street Income has been safer than 60 percent of all government bond funds. Over the past decade, the fund has had two negative years, while the Lehman Brothers Aggregate Bond Index also had two (off 3 percent in 1994 and 1 percent in 1999). The fund has underperformed the Lehman Brothers Aggregate Bond Index six times and the Lehman Brothers Government Bond Index five times in the last 10 years.

	last 5 years		last 10 years	
worst year	-2%	1999	-3%	1994
best year	18%	1995	18%	1995

In the past, State Street Income has done better than 50 percent of its peer group in up markets and outperformed 80 percent of its competition in down markets. Consistency, or predictability, of returns for State Street Income can be described as very good. This fund's risk-related return is good.

Management   ★★★★
There are 85 fixed-income securities in this $650 million portfolio. The average gov-
ernment bond fund today is $190 million in size. Close to 90 percent of the fund's
holdings are in bonds. The average maturity of the bonds in this account is eight
years; the weighted coupon rate averages 8 percent. The portfolio's fixed-income
holdings can be categorized as intermediate-term, very high-quality debt.

John Kallis has managed this fund for the past 14 years. Virtually all of the
fund's top 20 largest holdings are in U.S. Treasury Bonds, FNMAs, or GNMAs.
Management has been able to enhance returns by investing a small portion of its
assets in commercial mortgages and foreign bonds. There are 92 funds besides
Government Income within the State Street Research family. Overall, the fund
family's risk-adjusted performance can be described as good.

Current Income   ★★★★★
Over the past year, State Street Income had a 12-month yield of 6.2 percent. During
this same 12-month period, the typical government bond fund had a yield that averaged 5.5 percent.

Expenses   ★★★
State Street Income's expense ratio is 1.1 percent; it has also averaged 1.1 percent
annually over the past three calendar years. The average expense ratio for the 600
funds in this category is 1.1 percent. This fund's turnover rate over the past year
has been 160 percent, while its peer group average has been 170 percent.

Summary
State Street Research Government Income A has had good risk-adjusted returns
over the past 3, 5, and 10 years. The fund really shines when it comes to current
income, providing some of the very highest yields in the industry—a difficult feat
when one considers the average maturity of the portfolio's holdings. Compared to
other government bond funds, this State Street offering has excellent after-tax
returns.

Profile
minimum initial investment . . . . $2,500   *IRA accounts available* . . . . yes
subsequent minimum investment . . . $50   *IRA minimum investment* $2,000
available in all 50 states . . . . yes   *date of inception* . . . . March 1987
telephone exchanges . . . . yes   *dividend/income paid* . . . . monthly
number of funds in family 93   *average credit quality* . . . . AAA

Vanguard Long-Term U.S. Treasury
Vanguard Financial Center
P.O. Box 2600
Valley Forge, PA 19482
800-662-7447
www.vanguard.com

total return	★★★★
risk reduction	★
management	★★★
current income	★★★★
expense control	★★★★★
symbol VUSTX	17 points
up-market performance	fair
down-market performance	excellent
predictability of returns	good

Total Return   ★★★★

Over the past five years, Vanguard Long-Term U.S. Treasury has taken $10,000 and turned it into $15,390 ($12,950 over three years and $23,670 over the past 10 years). This translates into an annualized return of 9 percent over the past five years, 9 percent over the past three years, and 9 percent for the decade. Over the past five years, this fund has outperformed 49 percent of all mutual funds; within its general category it has done better than 86 percent of its peers. Government bond funds have averaged 6 percent annually over these same five years (all periods ending March 31, 2000).

During the past five years, a $10,000 initial investment grew to $10,155 after taxes, assuming a 39.6 percent income tax bracket (state and federal combined) and a capital gains rate of 28 percent. This means that investors in this fund were able to preserve 66 percent of their total returns. Compared to other fixed-income funds, this fund's tax savings are considered to be excellent.

Risk/Volatility   ★

Over the past five years, Vanguard Long-Term has only been safer than 25 percent of all government bond funds. Over the past decade, the fund has had three negative years, while the Lehman Brothers Aggregate Bond Index had two (off 3 percent in 1994 and 1 percent in 1999). The fund has underperformed the Lehman Brothers Aggregate Bond Index four times and the Lehman Brothers Government Bond Index four times in the last 10 years.

	last 5 years		last 10 years	
worst year	-9%	1999	-9%	1999
best year	30%	1995	30%	1995

In the past, Vanguard Long-Term has done better than 30 percent of its peer group in up markets and outperformed 85 percent of its competition in down markets.

Consistency, or predictability, of returns for Vanguard Long-Term can be described as good. This fund's risk-related return is also good.

Management ★★★
There are 22 fixed-income securities in this $1.2 billion portfolio. The average government bond fund today is $190 million in size. Close to 100 percent of the fund's holdings are in bonds. The vast majority of the holdings are in government-backed GNMAs. The average maturity of the bonds in this account is 10 years; the weighted coupon rate averages 7.5 percent. The portfolio's fixed-income holdings can be categorized as intermediate-term, high-quality debt.

Ian MacKinnon and Robert Auwaerter have managed this fund for the past 10 years. Management takes a conservative approach and avoids any kind of dramatic interest-rate bet. There are 77 funds besides Long-Term U.S. Treasury within the Vanguard family. Overall, the fund family's risk-adjusted performance can be described as very good.

Current Income ★★★★
Over the past year, Vanguard Long-Term had a 12-month yield of 6 percent. During this same 12-month period, the typical government bond fund had a yield that averaged 5.5 percent.

Expenses ★★★★★
Vanguard Long-Term's expense ratio is .3 percent; it has averaged .3 percent annually over the past three calendar years. The average expense ratio for the 600 funds in this category is 1.1 percent. This fund's turnover rate over the past year has been 20 percent, while its peer group average has been 170 percent.

Summary
Vanguard Long-Term U.S. Treasury has had very attractive risk-adjusted returns over the past 3, 5, and 10 years. Bear market performance has been spectacular, and so has been management's control over expenses. Tax minimization has also been some of the best in its entire category. This is just one of several Vanguard offerings that are highly recommended in this edition, and previous editions, of the book.

Profile
minimum initial investment $3,000	*IRA accounts available* .... yes
subsequent minimum investment .. $100	*IRA minimum investment* $1,000
available in all 50 states .... yes	*date of inception* .... May 1986
telephone exchanges .... yes	*dividend/income paid* .... monthly
number of funds in family 78	*average credit quality* .... AAA

Growth Funds

These funds generally seek capital appreciation, with current income as a distant secondary concern. Growth funds typically invest in U.S. common stocks, while avoiding speculative issues and aggressive trading techniques. The goal of most of these funds is long-term growth. The approaches used to attain this appreciation can vary significantly among growth funds.

Over the past 15 years, U.S. stocks have outperformed both corporate and government bonds. From 1985 through 1999, common stocks have averaged 18.9 percent compounded per year, compared to 10.5 percent for corporate bonds and 11.0 percent for government bonds. A $10,000 investment in stocks, as measured by the S & P 500, grew to over $134,740 over the past 15 years; a similar initial investment in corporate bonds grew to $44,640.

Looking at a longer time frame, common stocks have also fared quite well. A dollar invested in stocks at the beginning of 1950 grew to $589 by the end of 1999. This translates into an average compound return of 13.6 percent per year. Over the past 50 years, the worst year for common stocks was 1974, when a loss of 26 percent was suffered. One year later, these same stocks posted a gain of 37 percent. The best year so far has been 1954, when growth stocks posted a gain of 53 percent.

Growth stocks have outperformed bonds in every single decade. If President George Washington had invested $1 in common stocks with an average return of 12 percent, his investment would be worth over $406 billion today. If George had been a bit lucky and averaged 14 percent on his stock portfolio, his portfolio would be large enough to pay our national debt five times over!

To give you an idea as to the likelihood of making money in common stocks, look at the table below. It covers 129 years and shows the odds of making money (a positive return) over each of several different time periods.

Standard & Poor's Composite 500 Stock Index
Various periods, 1871–1997 (dividends not included)

Length of Period	Total Number of Periods	Rose	Declined	Unchanged	Percentage Opportunity for Profit (not including dividends)
1 year	129	84	45	1	65%
5 years	125	100	25	1	80%
10 years	120	108	12	0	90%
15 years	116	107	9	0	92%
20 years	110	107	3	0	97%
25 years	105	104	1	0	99%
30 years	100	100	0	0	100%

Twenty-one hundred funds make up the growth category. Total market capitalization of this category is $1.4 trillion. The standard deviation for this group is 27.4 percent; beta (stock market-related risk) is 0.9, 10 percent less than that of the overall market, as measured by the S & P 500. The typical portfolio of a growth fund is divided up as follows: 90 percent U.S. stocks, 5 percent foreign stocks, and the balance in money market instruments. Turnover rate is 101 percent per year. The yield on growth funds averages about 0.3 percent annually. Fund expenses for this group average 1.5 percent per year.

Volatility (standard deviation) in today's markets is unprecedented. As the S & P 500 chart below shows, nearly half of the past year's 104 trading days (through May 31, 2000) saw changes of 1 percent. Nearly one-quarter of the days saw changes greater than 2 percent. Finally, all but six (98 out of 104) trading days experienced at least a 1 percent change between the intraday low and high.

Percentage of Time S & P 500 Had 1-2% Daily Changes (1990–2000)

		% of trading days with changes of + or -			
Year	S & P 500	1%	2%	1% intraday	2% intraday
1990	- 3.2%	29.6	5.1	60.1	14.7
1991	30.6%	23.3	3.6	50.2	7.1
1992	7.7%	11.0	0.0	28.0	0.8
1993	10.0%	6.7	0.4	14.6	1.6
1994	1.3%	10.7	0.8	27.0	1.6
1995	37.4%	5.2	0.0	17.9	1.2
1996	23.1%	15.0	1.2	39.4	4.4
1997	33.4%	32.0	5.9	70.8.	15.1
1998	28.6%	31.4	9.1	69.1	22.2
1999	21.1%	36.5	9.1	77.0	21.0
2000 *	-2.8%	48.1	22.1	94.2	44.2

* through May 31, 2000

Over the past three years, growth funds have had an average compound return of 28.3 percent per year; the annual return for the past five years has been 24.6 percent. For the past decade, growth funds have averaged 17.5 percent annually and 16.7 percent per year for the past 15 years (all periods ending May 31, 2000).

Growth Funds

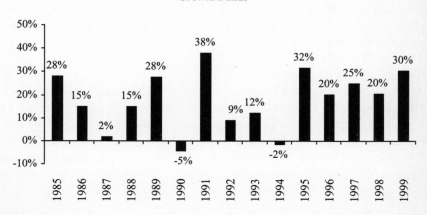

AIM Summit I

11 Greenway Plaza, Suite 1919
Houston, TX 77046
800-959-4246
www.aimfunds.com

total return	★★★★
risk reduction	★★★★★
management	★★★★★
tax minimization	★★★★★
expense control	★★★★★
symbol SMMIX	24 points
up-market performance	excellent
down-market performance	good
predictability of returns	excellent

Total Return   ★★★★

Over the past five years, AIM Summit I has taken $10,000 and turned it into
$41,620 ($28,630 over three years and $73,050 over the past 10 years). This trans-
lates into an annualized return of 33 percent over the past five years, 42 percent
over the past three years, and 22 percent for the decade. Over the past five years,
this fund has outperformed 96 percent of all mutual funds; within its general category it has done better than 86 percent of its peers. Growth funds have averaged 25
percent annually over these same five years (all periods ending March 31, 2000).

Risk/Volatility   ★★★★★

Over the past five years, Summit has been safer than 30 percent of all growth
funds. Over the past decade, the fund has had one negative year, while the S & P
500 has also had one (off 3 percent in 1990). The fund has underperformed the S
& P 500 six times in the last 10 years.

	last 5 years		last 10 years	
worst year	20%	1996	-3%	1994
best year	51%	1999	51%	1999

In the past, Summit has done better than 90 percent of its peer group in up
markets and outperformed 50 percent of its competition in down markets.
Consistency, or predictability, of returns for Summit can be described as excellent.
This fund's risk-related return is also excellent.

Management   ★★★★★

There are 135 stocks in this $3.3 billion portfolio. The average growth fund today
is $700 million in size. Close to 97 percent of the fund's holdings are in stocks. The
stocks in this portfolio have an average price-earnings (p/e) ratio of 36 and a
median market capitalization of $73 billion. Technology stocks represent over 50
percent of the fund's holdings, followed by financials (10 percent) and retail trade
(7 percent). The portfolio's equity holdings can be categorized as large-cap and

growth-oriented issues. The fund has a correlation of just roughly 55 percent to the S & P 500 (versus 85 percent for growth funds in general).

A team has managed this fund for the past five years. Management is interested in three kinds of stocks: core (long-term growth), small-cap emerging growth, and value (equities selling at a discount relative to the market). Most of the time, two-thirds of the portfolio is devoted to growth with the remaining third earmarked for value plays. As with other members of the AIM family, a bottom-up approach is used to select specific securities. There are 152 funds besides Summit within the AIM family. Overall, the fund family's risk-adjusted performance can be described as very good.

Tax Minimization ★★★★★
During the past five years, a $10,000 initial investment grew to $37,870 after taxes, assuming a 39.6 percent income tax bracket (state and federal combined) and a capital gains rate of 28 percent. This means that investors in this fund were able to preserve 91 percent of their total returns. Compared to other equity funds, this fund's tax savings are considered to be excellent.

Expenses ★★★★★
Summit's expense ratio is .7 percent; it has also averaged .7 percent annually over the past three calendar years. The average expense ratio for the 2,100 funds in this category is 1.5 percent. This fund's turnover rate over the past year has been 80 percent, while its peer group average has been 100 percent.

Summary
AIM Summit I turns in a near-perfect score, receiving 24 out of a possible 25 points. Few funds in the book can match this record, regardless of category. This is a solid choice across the board. There are a small number of growth funds that have turned in better results over the past three and five years, but not at this comparatively low risk level. This is a highly recommended choice for the tax-conscious investor who is looking for domestic growth.

Profile

minimum initial investment $50	*IRA accounts available* . . . . yes
subsequent minimum investment . . . $50	*IRA minimum investment* $50
available in all 50 states . . . . yes	*date of inception* . . . . Nov. 1982
telephone exchanges . . . . yes	*dividend/income paid* . . . . annually
number of funds in family 153	*largest sector weighting* . . . technology

Alliance Premier Growth B

P.O. Box 1520
Secaucus, NJ 07096
800-227-4618
www.alliancecapital.com

total return	★★★★
risk reduction	★★★★
management	★★★
tax minimization	★★★★★
expense control	★
symbol APGBX	17 points
up-market performance	very good
down-market performance	poor
predictability of returns	excellent

Total Return   ★★★★

Over the past five years, Alliance Premier Growth B has taken $10,000 and turned it into $43,200 ($26,860 over three years). This translates into an annualized return of 34 percent over the past five years and 39 percent over the past three years. Over the past five years, this fund has outperformed 96 percent of all mutual funds; within its general category it has done better than 81 percent of its peers. Growth funds have averaged 25 percent annually over these same five years (all periods ending March 31, 2000).

Risk/Volatility   ★★★★

Over the past five years, Premier Growth has been safer than 30 percent of all growth funds. Since its inception, the fund has had one negative year, while the S & P 500 has also had one (off 3 percent in 1990). The fund has underperformed the S & P 500 three times since the fund's inception.

	last 5 years		since inception	
worst year	23%	1996	-6%	1994
best year	48%	1998	48%	1998

In the past, Premier Growth has done better than 70 percent of its peer group in up markets and outperformed 20 percent of its competition in down markets. Consistency, or predictability, of returns for Premier Growth can be described as excellent. This fund's risk-related return is also excellent.

Management   ★★★

There are 70 stocks in this $10.3 billion portfolio. The average growth fund today is $700 million in size. Close to 100 percent of the fund's holdings are in stocks. The stocks in this portfolio have an average price-earnings (p/e) ratio of 38 and a median market capitalization of $101 billion. Technology stocks represent close to one-third of the fund's holdings, followed by financials (18 percent) and retail trade stocks (16 percent). The portfolio's equity holdings can be categorized as large-cap and growth-oriented issues. The fund has a correlation of roughly 90 percent to the S & P 500 (versus 85 percent for growth funds in general).

Alfred Harrison has managed this fund for the past nine years. Management looks for growth outside the traditional sectors, looking at stocks from transportation and cyclicals, as well as the more popular technology and health care. Harrison is particularly attracted to stocks of undervalued companies with strong earnings and a competitive position. There are 156 funds besides Premier Growth within the Alliance Capital family. Overall, the fund family's risk-adjusted performance can be described as very good.

Tax Minimization   ★★★★★
During the past five years, a $10,000 initial investment grew to $40,180 after taxes, assuming a 39.6 percent income tax bracket (state and federal combined) and a capital gains rate of 28 percent. This means that investors in this fund were able to preserve 93 percent of their total returns. Compared to other equity funds, this fund's tax savings are considered to be excellent.

Expenses   ★
Premier Growth's expense ratio is 2.2 percent; it has averaged 2.2 percent annually over the past three calendar years. The average expense ratio for the 2,100 funds in this category is 1.5 percent. This fund's turnover rate over the past year has been 75 percent, while its peer group average has been 100 percent.

Summary
Alliance Premier Growth B receives high marks in all important categories, but its overall score is punished due to its high expenses, which are the highest of its peer group in this book. Nevertheless, the fund turns in impressive return figures (which take into account expenses and turnover) and very good risk reduction. The fund's strongest suit is tax minimization, which is some of the highest in a group of over 2,100 members.

Profile
minimum initial investment $250	*IRA accounts available* . . . . yes
subsequent minimum investment . . . $50	*IRA minimum investment* $250
available in all 50 states . . . . yes	*date of inception* . . . . Sept. 1992
telephone exchanges . . . . yes	*dividend/income paid* . . . . annually
number of funds in family 157	*largest sector weighting* . . . technology

Federated Growth Strategies Trust A

Federated Investors Tower
Pittsburgh, PA 15222
800-341-7400
www.federatedinvestors.com

total return	★★★★
risk reduction	★★★★
management	★★★★
tax minimization	★★★★
expense control	★★★★
symbol FGSAX	20 points
up-market performance	excellent
down-market performance	poor
predictability of returns	very good

Total Return   ★★★★

Over the past five years, Federated Growth Strategies Trust A has taken $10,000 and turned it into $44,840 ($29,240 over three years and $67,275 over the past 10 years). This translates into an annualized return of 35 percent over the past five years, 43 percent over the past three years, and 21 percent for the decade. Over the past five years, this fund has outperformed 97 percent of all mutual funds; within its general category it has done better than 88 percent of its peers. Growth funds have averaged 25 percent annually over these same five years (all periods ending March 31, 2000).

Risk/Volatility   ★★★★

Over the past five years, Growth Strategies has been safer than 85 percent of all growth funds. Over the past decade, the fund has had two negative years, while the S & P 500 has had one (off 3 percent in 1990). The fund has underperformed the S & P 500 five times in the last 10 years.

	last 5 years		last 10 years	
worst year	16%	1998	-12%	1994
best year	71%	1999	71%	1999

In the past, Growth Strategies has done better than 95 percent of its peer group in up markets and outperformed 20 percent of its competition in down markets. Consistency, or predictability, of returns for Growth Strategies can be described as very good. This fund's risk-related return is excellent.

Management   ★★★★

There are 115 stocks in this $1.4 billion portfolio. The average growth fund today is $700 million in size. Close to 98 percent of the fund's holdings are in stocks. The stocks in this portfolio have an average price-earnings (p/e) ratio of 42 and a median market capitalization of $49 billion. Technology represents over 40 percent of the fund's holdings, followed by nondurables (10 percent) and health care (9 percent). The portfolio's equity holdings can be categorized as large-cap and a blend of growth and value stocks. The fund has a correlation of just roughly 75 percent to the S & P 500 (versus 85 percent for growth funds in general).

James Grefenstette has managed this fund since 1994; Salvatore Esposito became comanager in 1997. Management uses a bottom-up approach to security selection, favoring mid- to large-cap issues that are expected to have better-than-average growth rates over the next one and five years. Earnings and price momentum as well as "shareholder friendly companies" are core criteria for prospective holdings. There are 148 funds besides Growth Strategies within the Federated family. Overall, the fund family's risk-adjusted performance can be described as very good.

Tax Minimization   ★★★★
During the past five years, a $10,000 initial investment grew to $38,560 after taxes, assuming a 39.6 percent income tax bracket (state and federal combined) and a capital gains rate of 28 percent. This means that investors in this fund were able to preserve 86 percent of their total returns. Compared to other equity funds, this fund's tax savings are considered to be very good.

Expenses   ★★★★
Growth Strategies' expense ratio is 1.2 percent; it has averaged 1.2 percent annually over the past three calendar years. The average expense ratio for the 2,100 funds in this category is 1.5 percent. This fund's turnover rate over the past year has been 115 percent, while its peer group average has been 100 percent.

Summary
Federated Growth Strategies Trust A does not deviate wildly from the S & P 500. Management scores very well in every single category. The fund has outperformed close to 90 percent of its peers. Bear market performance has only been ok in the past, but patient investors will be happy with this portfolio. This is a solid growth fund that is a member of a fund family with a large number of other top-rated funds.

Profile
minimum initial investment $1,500
subsequent minimum investment . . $100
available in all 50 states . . . . yes
telephone exchanges . . . . yes
number of funds in family 149

IRA accounts available . . . . yes
IRA minimum investment $250
date of inception . . . . Aug. 1984
dividend/income paid . . . . annually
largest sector weighting . . . technology

Harbor Capital Appreciation
One SeaGate
Toledo, OH 43666
800-422-1050
www.harborfunds.com

total return	★★★★
risk reduction	★★★★★
management	★★★★★
tax minimization	★★★★★
expense control	★★★★★
symbol HACAX	24 points
up-market performance	excellent
down-market performance	poor
predictability of returns	excellent

Total Return   ★★★★

Over the past five years, Harbor Capital Appreciation has taken $10,000 and turned it into $44,840 ($29,860 over three years and $93,130 over the past 10 years). This translates into an annualized return of 35 percent over the past five years, 44 percent over the past three years, and 25 percent for the decade. Over the past five years, this fund has outperformed 96 percent of all mutual funds; within its general category it has done better than 87 percent of its peers. Growth funds have averaged 25 percent annually over these same five years (all periods ending March 31, 2000).

Risk/Volatility   ★★★★★

Over the past five years, Capital Appreciation has been safer than 40 percent of all growth funds. Over the past decade, the fund has had one negative year, while the S & P 500 has also had one (off 3 percent in 1990). The fund has underperformed the S & P 500 twice in the last 10 years.

	last 5 years		last 10 years	
worst year	20%	1996	-2%	1990
best year	46%	1999	55%	1991

In the past, Capital Appreciation has done better than 90 percent of its peer group in up markets and outperformed 20 percent of its competition in down markets. Consistency, or predictability, of returns for Capital Appreciation can be described as excellent. This fund's risk-related return is also excellent.

Management   ★★★★★

There are 60 stocks in this $9.5 billion portfolio. The average growth fund today is $700 million in size. Close to 96 percent of the fund's holdings are in stocks. The stocks in this portfolio have an average price-earnings (p/e) ratio of 44 and a median market capitalization of $127 billion. Technology represents over 40 percent of the fund's holdings, followed by financials (12 percent) and health care (11 percent). The portfolio's equity holdings can be categorized as large-cap and growth-oriented issues. The fund has a correlation of roughly 75 percent to the S & P 500 (versus 85 percent for growth funds in general).

Spiros Segalas has managed this fund for the past 11 years. Segalas usually meets with a company's management before he will purchase their stock. Using a bottom-up approach, he prefers corporations that have great sales growth, strong balance sheets, and high returns on equity and assets. There are seven funds besides Capital Appreciation within the Harbor family. Overall, the fund family's risk-adjusted performance can be described as good.

Tax Minimization ★★★★★

During the past five years, a $10,000 initial investment grew to $42,150 after taxes, assuming a 39.6 percent income tax bracket (state and federal combined) and a capital gains rate of 28 percent. This means that investors in this fund were able to preserve 94 percent of their total returns. Compared to other equity funds, this fund's tax savings are considered to be excellent.

Expenses ★★★★★

Capital Appreciation's expense ratio is .7 percent; it has averaged .7 percent annually over the past three calendar years. The average expense ratio for the 2,100 funds in this category is 1.5 percent. This fund's turnover rate over the past year has been 70 percent, while its peer group average has been 100 percent.

Summary

Harbor Capital Appreciation receives an almost perfect score, 24 out of 25 possible points. Its only "non-excellent" rating is performance, which still receives a "superior" mark. In fact, the fund's performance places it ahead of 87 percent of its competition with a risk level that is dramatically below its peer group. Risk and expense ratios are very low and tax efficiency is extremely high. This is part of a relatively small fund family that has a couple of other offerings worth considering.

Profile

minimum initial investment $2,000	*IRA accounts available* .... yes
subsequent minimum investment .. $500	*IRA minimum investment* $500
available in all 50 states .... yes	*date of inception* .... Dec. 1987
telephone exchanges .... yes	*dividend/income paid* .... annually
number of funds in family 8	*largest sector weighting* ... technology

Janus Enterprise
100 Fillmore Street, Suite 300
Denver, CO 80206
800-525-8983
www.janusfunds.com

total return	★★★★
risk reduction	★★★★
management	★★★★
tax minimization	★★★★★
expense control	★★★★
symbol JAENX	21 points
up-market performance	excellent
down-market performance	good
predictability of returns	very good

Total Return   ★★★★
Over the past five years, Janus Enterprise has taken $10,000 and turned it into
$51,890 ($42,520 over three years). This translates into an annualized return of 39
percent over the past five years and 62 percent over the past three years. Over the
past five years, this fund has outperformed 98 percent of all mutual funds; within
its general category it has done better than 90 percent of its peers. Growth funds
have averaged 25 percent annually over these same five years (all periods ending
March 31, 2000).

Risk/Volatility   ★★★★
Over the past five years, Enterprise has been safer than 65 percent of all growth
funds. Since its inception, the fund has had no negative years, while the S & P 500
has had one (off 3 percent in 1990). The fund has underperformed the S & P 500
three times since the fund's inception.

	last 5 years		since inception	
worst year	11%	1997	9%	1994
best year	122%	1999	122%	1999

In the past, Enterprise has done better than 95 percent of its peer group in up
markets and outperformed 60 percent of its competition in down markets.
Consistency, or predictability, of returns for Janus Enterprise can be described as
very good. This fund's risk-related return is excellent.

Management   ★★★★
There are 55 stocks in this $8.8 billion portfolio. The average growth fund today is
$700 million in size. Close to 97 percent of the fund's holdings are in stocks. The
stocks in this portfolio have an average price-earnings (p/e) ratio of 51 and a
median market capitalization of $8 billion. Technology represents close to 40 per-
cent of the fund's holdings, followed by nondurables (16 percent) and services (14
percent). The portfolio's equity holdings can be categorized as large-cap and

growth-oriented issues. The fund has a correlation of just roughly 25 percent to the S & P 500 (versus 85 percent for growth funds in general).

James Goff has managed this fund for the past nine years. He primarily invests in companies whose market cap is between $1–$10 billion. Fundamental analysis using a bottom-up approach is how stocks are screened. Management targets companies that have an annual growth rate of at least 20 percent and are likely to dominate their market because of their unique product or service. There are 21 funds besides Enterprise within the Janus family. Overall, the fund family's risk-adjusted performance can be described as excellent.

Tax Minimization ★★★★★

During the past five years, a $10,000 initial investment grew to $47,740 after taxes, assuming a 39.6 percent income tax bracket (state and federal combined) and a capital gains rate of 28 percent. This means that investors in this fund were able to preserve 92 percent of their total returns. Compared to other equity funds, this fund's tax savings are considered to be excellent.

Expenses ★★★★

Janus Enterprise's expense ratio is 1 percent; it has also averaged 1 percent annually over the past three calendar years. The average expense ratio for the 2,100 funds in this category is 1.5 percent. This fund's turnover rate over the past year has been 95 percent, while its peer group average has been 100 percent.

Summary

Janus Enterprise performs very well in every category except tax minimization, an area where it really shines (with a 92 tax efficiency rating). Like a number of other Janus offerings, this fund will frequently concentrate on a relatively small number of equities that can represent a large percentage of the overall portfolio. Such concentration has certainly paid off in the past for Janus, across the board. This fund, as well as several other Janus portfolios, continue to be highly recommended.

Profile

minimum initial investment $2,500	*IRA accounts available* .... yes
subsequent minimum investment .. $100	*IRA minimum investment* $500
available in all 50 states .... yes	*date of inception* .... Sept. 1992
telephone exchanges .... yes	*dividend/income paid* .... annually
number of funds in family 22	*largest sector weighting* ..... services

Janus Mercury
100 Fillmore Street, Suite 300
Denver, CO 80206
800-525-8983
www.janusfunds.com

total return	★★★★★
risk reduction	★★★★★
management	★★★★★
tax minimization	★★★★
expense control	★★★★★
symbol JAMRX	24 points
up-market performance	excellent
down-market performance	excellent
predictability of returns	excellent

Total Return   ★★★★★
Over the past five years, Janus Mercury has taken $10,000 and turned it into
$57,735 ($41,735 over three years). This translates into an annualized return of 42
percent over the past five years and 61 percent over the past three years. Over the
past five years, this fund has outperformed 99 percent of all mutual funds; within
its general category it has done better than 96 percent of its peers. Growth funds
have averaged 25 percent annually over these same five years (all periods ending
March 31, 2000).

Risk/Volatility   ★★★★★
Over the past five years, Mercury has been safer than 40 percent of all growth
funds. Since its inception, the fund has had no negative years, while the S & P 500
has had one (off 3 percent in 1990). The fund has underperformed the S & P 500
three times since the fund's inception.

	last 5 years		since inception	
worst year	12%	1997	12%	1997
best year	96%	1999	96%	1999

In the past, Mercury has done better than 97 percent of its peer group in up
markets and outperformed 95 percent of its competition in down markets.
Consistency, or predictability, of returns for Janus Mercury can be described as
excellent. This fund's risk-related return is also excellent.

Management   ★★★★★
There are 55 stocks in this $17 billion portfolio. The average growth fund today is
$700 million in size. Close to 95 percent of the fund's holdings are in stocks. The
stocks in this portfolio have an average price-earnings (p/e) ratio of 43 and a median
market capitalization of $46 billion. Technology represents roughly 35 percent of
the fund's holdings, followed by nondurables (9 percent) and industrial cyclicals (9
percent). The portfolio's equity holdings can be categorized as large-cap and

growth-oriented issues. The fund has a correlation of just roughly 50 percent to the S & P 500 (versus 85 percent for growth funds in general).

Warren Lammert III has managed this fund for the past eight years. He has the flexibility to invest in any company, of any size, anywhere in the world. Management looks for companies whose products are difficult to imitate in quality or scope. High valuations do not bother Lammert, provided the company's growth rate and fundamentals meet expectations. There are 21 funds besides Mercury within the Janus family. Overall, the fund family's risk-adjusted performance can be described as excellent.

Tax Minimization   ★★★★
During the past five years, a $10,000 initial investment grew to $51,380 after taxes, assuming a 39.6 percent income tax bracket (state and federal combined) and a capital gains rate of 28 percent. This means that investors in this fund were able to preserve 89 percent of their total returns. Compared to other equity funds, this fund's tax savings are considered to be very good.

Expenses   ★★★★★
Mercury's expense ratio is .9 percent; it has also averaged .9 percent annually over the past three calendar years. The average expense ratio for the 2,100 funds in this category is 1.5 percent. This fund's turnover rate over the past year has been 85 percent, while its peer group average has been 100 percent.

Summary
Janus Mercury, as well as the Janus fund family in general, has risk-adjusted returns that are excellent. This particular Janus offering ranks as the second-best performer in its entire category (which is comprised of 2,100 other funds). Not only have the returns been amazing, but the portfolio's risk level is exceedingly low for its group. This fund has an overall score of 24 out of 25 possible points, plus it is one of the very few funds whose up- and down- market performance, as well as predictability of returns, have been superb.

Profile
minimum initial investment $2,500	*IRA accounts available* .... yes
subsequent minimum investment .. $100	*IRA minimum investment* $500
available in all 50 states .... yes	*date of inception* .... May 1993
telephone exchanges .... yes	*dividend/income paid* .... annually
number of funds in family 22	*largest sector weighting* ... technology

Marshall Mid-Cap Growth Y

1000 North Water Street
Milwaukee, WI 53202
800-236-8560
www.marshallfunds.com

total return	★★★★
risk reduction	★★★★
management	★★★★
tax minimization	★★★★
expense control	★★★
symbol MRMSX	19 points
up-market performance	very good
down-market performance	poor
predictability of returns	very good

Total Return   ★★★★

Over the past five years, Marshall Mid-Cap Growth Y has taken $10,000 and turned it into $41,616 ($30,486 over three years). This translates into an annualized return of 33 percent over the past five years and 45 percent over the past three years. Over the past five years, this fund has outperformed 92 percent of all mutual funds; within its general category it has done better than 80 percent of its peers. Growth funds have averaged 25 percent annually over these same five years (all periods ending March 31, 2000).

Risk/Volatility   ★★★★

Over the past five years, Mid-Cap Growth has been safer than 40 percent of all growth funds. Since its inception, the fund has had one negative year, while the S & P 500 has also had one (off 3 percent in 1990). The fund has underperformed the S & P 500 five times since the fund's inception.

	last 5 years		since inception	
worst year	16%	1998	-6%	1994
best year	61%	1999	61%	1999

In the past, Mid-Cap Growth has done better than 85 percent of its peer group in up markets but outperformed just 10 percent of its competition in down markets. Consistency, or predictability, of returns for Mid-Cap Growth can be described as very good. This fund's risk-related return is excellent.

Management   ★★★★

There are 65 stocks in this $330 million portfolio. The average growth fund today is $700 million in size. Close to 95 percent of the fund's holdings are in stocks. The stocks in this portfolio have an average price-earnings (p/e) ratio of 42 and a median market capitalization of $7 billion. Technology represents close to 40 percent of the fund's holdings, followed by services (35 percent) and financials (10 percent). The portfolio's equity holdings can be categorized as mid-cap and growth-oriented issues. The fund has a correlation of approximately 70 percent to the S & P 500 (versus 85 percent for growth funds in general).

Steven Hayward has managed this fund for the past seven years. Management focuses on companies that are expected to have annual growth rates of at least 20 percent. Companies selected demonstrate significant changes in the area(s) of new products, services, distribution, and/or restructuring. There are 18 funds besides Mid-Cap Growth within the Marshall family. Overall, the fund family's risk-adjusted performance can be described as very good.

Tax Minimization   ★★★★
During the past five years, a $10,000 initial investment grew to $37,040 after taxes, assuming a 39.6 percent income tax bracket (state and federal combined) and a capital gains rate of 28 percent. This means that investors in this fund were able to preserve 89 percent of their total returns. Compared to other equity funds, this fund's tax savings are considered to be very good.

Expenses   ★★★
Marshall Mid-Cap Growth Y's expense ratio is 1.2 percent; it has averaged 1.2 percent annually over the past three calendar years. The average expense ratio for the 2,100 funds in this category is 1.5 percent. This fund's turnover rate over the past year has been 170 percent, while its peer group average has been 100 percent.

Summary
Marshall Mid-Cap Growth Y is consistently good in every single category. The fund has outperformed 80 percent of its peer group but has not done particularly well during bear markets. Tax minimization has been quite good. This equity offering is just one of several very good Marshall offerings that should be strongly considered by investors.

Profile
minimum initial investment $1,000	*IRA accounts available* .... yes
subsequent minimum investment ... $50	*IRA minimum investment* $1,000
available in all 50 states .... yes	*date of inception* .... Sept. 1993
telephone exchanges .... yes	*dividend/income paid* .... quarterly
number of funds in family 19	*largest sector weighting* ... technology

Nicholas-Applegate Growth Equity A

P.O. Box 82169
San Diego, CA 92138
800-551-8643
www.prudential.com

total return	★★★★
risk reduction	★★★
management	★★★
tax minimization	★★★★
expense control	★★
symbol NAPGX	16 points
up-market performance	excellent
down-market performance	poor
predictability of returns	good

Total Return   ★★★★

Over the past five years, Nicholas-Applegate Growth Equity A has taken $10,000 and turned it into $46,530 ($35,120 over three years and $85,940 over the past 10 years). This translates into an annualized return of 36 percent over the past five years, 52 percent over the past three years, and 24 percent for the decade. Over the past five years, this fund has outperformed 88 percent of all mutual funds; within its general category it has done better than 70 percent of its peers. Growth funds have averaged 25 percent annually over these same five years (all periods ending March 31, 2000).

Risk/Volatility   ★★★

Over the past five years, Growth Equity has been safer than 40 percent of all growth funds. Over the past decade, the fund has had two negative years, while the S & P 500 has had one (off 3 percent in 1990). The fund has underperformed the S & P 500 six times in the last 10 years.

	last 5 years		last 10 years	
worst year	13%	1998	-10%	1990
best year	98%	1999	98%	1999

In the past, Growth Equity has done better than 98 percent of its peer group in up markets and outperformed 20 percent of its competition in down markets. Consistency, or predictability, of returns for Growth Equity can be described as good. This fund's risk-related return is excellent.

Management   ★★★

There are 95 stocks in this $450 million portfolio. The average growth fund today is $700 million in size. Close to 100 percent of the fund's holdings are in stocks. The stocks in this portfolio have an average price-earnings (p/e) ratio of 54 and a median market capitalization of $14 billion. Technology represents over 60 percent of the fund's holdings, followed by services (9 percent) and health care (7 percent).

The portfolio's equity holdings can be categorized as mid-cap and growth-oriented issues. The fund has a correlation of just roughly 25 percent to the S & P 500 (versus 85 percent for growth funds in general).

A team has managed this fund for the past five years; William Chenoweth has been the lead manager since 1998. Most of the time, 90 percent of the holdings will be in stocks that fall within the cap rates of the Russell Midcap Growth Index. Management selects stocks that fall within the following guidelines: positive corporate change that improves its fundamentals, sustainability of growth acceleration, and investor recognition of a positive corporate change. Securities are sold when the agent for change no longer exists or better opportunities present themselves. There are 184 funds besides Growth Equity within the Prudential family. Overall, the fund family's risk-adjusted performance can be described as good.

Tax Minimization ★★★★
During the past five years, a $10,000 initial investment grew to $39,550 after taxes, assuming a 39.6 percent income tax bracket (state and federal combined) and a capital gains rate of 28 percent. This means that investors in this fund were able to preserve 85 percent of their total returns. Compared to other equity funds, this fund's tax savings are considered to be very good.

Expenses ★★
Growth Equity's expense ratio is 1.4 percent; it has also averaged 1.4 percent annually over the past three calendar years. The average expense ratio for the 2,100 funds in this category is 1.5 percent. This fund's turnover rate over the past year has been 170 percent, while its peer group average has been 100 percent.

Summary
Nicholas-Applegate Growth Equity A is a fund that performs with flying colors during bull markets but can be quite disappointing during down markets. Still, the fund has outperformed 70 percent of its peer group and has been safer than about 40 percent of its category. Total return and tax minimization are the fund's two strongest areas.

Profile
minimum initial investment $1,000	*IRA accounts available* .... yes
subsequent minimum investment .. $100	*IRA minimum investment* $1
available in all 50 states .... yes	*date of inception* .... Apr. 1987
telephone exchanges .... yes	*dividend/income paid* .... annually
number of funds in family 185	*largest sector weighting* ... technology

Reynolds Blue Chip Growth
80 East Sir Francis Drake Boulevard
Larkspur, CA 94939
800-773-9665
www.reynoldsfunds.com

total return	★★★★
risk reduction	★★★★★
management	★★★★
tax minimization	★★★★★
expense control	★★★★
symbol RBCGX	22 points
up-market performance	excellent
down-market performance	excellent
predictability of returns	excellent

Total Return ★★★★
Over the past five years, Reynolds Blue Chip Growth has taken $10,000 and turned it into $51,890 ($31,765 over three years and $73,050 over the past 10 years). This translates into an annualized return of 39 percent over the past five years, 47 percent over the past three years, and 22 percent for the decade. Over the past five years, this fund has outperformed 98 percent of all mutual funds; within its general category it has done better than 93 percent of its peers. Growth funds have averaged 25 percent annually over these same five years (all periods ending March 31, 2000).

Risk/Volatility ★★★★★
Over the past five years, Blue Chip has been safer than 50 percent of all growth funds. Over the past decade, the fund has had two negative years, while the S & P 500 has had one (off 3 percent in 1990). The fund has underperformed the S & P 500 five times in the last 10 years.

	last 5 years		last 10 years	
worst year	28%	1996	-5%	1993
best year	54%	1998	54%	1998

In the past, Blue Chip has done better than 90 percent of its peer group in up markets and outperformed 90 percent of its competition in down markets. Consistency, or predictability, of returns for Blue Chip can be described as excellent. This fund's risk-related return is also excellent.

Management ★★★★
There are 250 stocks in this $675 million portfolio. The average growth fund today is $700 million in size. Close to 99 percent of the fund's holdings are in stocks. The stocks in this portfolio have an average price-earnings (p/e) ratio of 43 and a median market capitalization of $110 billion. Technology represents just over 50 percent of the fund's holdings, followed by health care (12 percent) and nondurables (10 percent). The portfolio's equity holdings can be categorized as

large-cap and growth-oriented issues. The fund has a correlation of 85 percent to the S & P 500 (versus 85 percent for growth funds in general).

Frederick Reynolds has managed this fund for the past 13 years. Management favors a buy-and-hold strategy, looking for stocks whose earnings are likely to out-perform the S & P 500. Sectors are first identified and chosen based on their like-lihood of doing better than the overall economy. There are two funds besides Blue Chip within the Reynolds family. Overall, the fund family's risk-adjusted perfor-mance can be described as excellent.

Tax Minimization ★★★★★
During the past five years, a $10,000 initial investment grew to $51,370 after taxes, assuming a 39.6 percent income tax bracket (state and federal combined) and a capital gains rate of 28 percent. This means that investors in this fund were able to preserve 99 percent of their total returns. Compared to other equity funds, this fund's tax savings are considered to be excellent.

Expenses ★★★★
Blue Chips expense ratio is 1.4 percent; it has averaged 1.4 percent annually over the past three calendar years. The average expense ratio for the 2,100 funds in this category is 1.5 percent. This fund's turnover rate over the past year has been 35 percent, while its peer group average has been 100 percent.

Summary
Reynolds Blue Chip Growth has ranked in the top quintile of performance during four of the past five years. The fund scores very well or excellent in every single category. It is also one of the few portfolios, regardless of category, that receives the highest possible rating for up- and down-market performance as well as con-sistency. This growth offering is part of a very small family of funds whose other members should be strongly considered.

Profile
minimum initial investment $1,000	*IRA accounts available* .... yes
subsequent minimum investment .. $100	*IRA minimum investment* $100
available in all 50 states .... yes	*date of inception* .... Aug. 1988
telephone exchanges .... yes	*dividend/income paid* .... annually
number of funds in family 3	*largest sector weighting* ... technology

Spectra

1 World Trade Center, Suite 9333
New York, NY 10048
800-711-6141
www.algerfunds.com

total return	★★★★★
risk reduction	★★★★
management	★★★
tax minimization	★★★
expense control	★
symbol SPECX	16 points
up-market performance	very good
down-market performance	very good
predictability of returns	excellent

Total Return   ★★★★★

Over the past five years, Spectra has taken $10,000 and turned it into $57,735 ($35,820 over three years and $148,840 over the past 10 years). This translates into an annualized return of 42 percent over the past five years, 53 percent over the past three years, and 31 percent for the decade. Over the past five years, this fund has outperformed 99 percent of all mutual funds; within its general category it has done better than 97 percent of its peers. Growth funds have averaged 25 percent annually over these same five years (all periods ending March 31, 2000).

Risk/Volatility   ★★★★

Over the past five years, Spectra has been safer than 20 percent of all growth funds. Over the past decade, the fund has had no negative years, while the S & P 500 has had one (off 3 percent in 1990). The fund has underperformed the S & P 500 twice in the last 10 years.

	last 5 years		last 10 years	
worst year	19%	1996	3%	1990
best year	72%	1999	72%	1999

In the past, Spectra has done better than 80 percent of its peer group in up markets and outperformed 80 percent of its competition in down markets. Consistency, or predictability, of returns for Spectra can be described as excellent. This fund's risk-related return is also excellent.

Management   ★★★

There are 67 stocks in this $1.1 billion portfolio. The average growth fund today is $700 million in size. Close to 100 percent of the fund's holdings are in stocks. The stocks in this portfolio have an average price-earnings (p/e) ratio of 55 and a median market capitalization of $32 billion. Technology represents close to 60 percent of the fund's holdings, followed by nondurables (9 percent) and industrial cyclicals (7 percent). The portfolio's equity holdings can be categorized as large-cap and

growth-oriented issues. The fund has a correlation of just roughly 45 percent to the S & P 500 (versus 85 percent for growth funds in general).

David Alger has managed this fund since 1974; David Hyun became comanager in 1998. Management, along with a large team of analysts, looks for investments in a somewhat unique and refreshing manner—they closely scrutinize trade journals, attend industry trade shows, and engage in conversations with company's management, customers, and suppliers. The process starts with a universe of 1,400 corporations with an emphasis on high unit-growth and lifecycle change. There are 19 funds besides Spectra within the Alger family. Overall, the fund family's risk-adjusted performance can be described as excellent.

Tax Minimization ★★★
During the past five years, a $10,000 initial investment grew to $50,810 after taxes, assuming a 39.6 percent income tax bracket (state and federal combined) and a capital gains rate of 28 percent. This means that investors in this fund were able to preserve 88 percent of their total returns. Compared to other equity funds, this fund's tax savings are considered to be very good.

Expenses ★
Spectra's expense ratio is 1.9 percent; it has averaged 2 percent annually over the past three calendar years. The average expense ratio for the 2,100 funds in this category is 1.5 percent. This fund's turnover rate over the past year has been 190 percent, while its peer group average has been 100 percent.

Summary
Spectra has scored in the top one or two quintiles over seven of the past seven calendar years (ending December 31, 1999). This fund is part of the Alger group, a management company who got on, and understood, the technology revolution early. More importantly, the group is known for their savvy security selection that often goes "against the Street" (until the herd wakes up). This kind of research has paid off handsomely for the company consistently. Expenses are on the high side, as is turnover, but who cares with raw returns like these. Tax efficiency is also quite good.

Profile
minimum initial investment $1,000	*IRA accounts available* .... yes
subsequent minimum investment .. $100	*IRA minimum investment* $250
available in all 50 states .... yes	*date of inception* .... July 1969
telephone exchanges .... yes	*dividend/income paid* .... annually
number of funds in family 20	*largest sector weighting* ... technology

Strong Growth
P.O. Box 2936
Milwaukee, WI 53201
800-368-1030
www.strongfunds.com

total return	★★★★
risk reduction	★★★
management	★★★★
tax minimization	★★★★★
expense control	★★
symbol SGROX	18 points
up-market performance	excellent
down-market performance	good
predictability of returns	very good

Total Return   ★★★★
Over the past five years, Strong Growth has taken $10,000 and turned it into $50,050 ($33,750 over three years). This translates into an annualized return of 38 percent over the past five years and 50 percent over the past three years. Over the past five years, this fund has outperformed 98 percent of all mutual funds; within its general category it has done better than 94 percent of its peers. Growth funds have averaged 25 percent annually over these same five years (all periods ending March 31, 2000).

Risk/Volatility   ★★★
Over the past five years, Strong has been safer than 20 percent of all growth funds. Since its inception, the fund has had no negative years, while the S & P 500 has had one (off 3 percent in 1990). The fund has underperformed the S & P 500 three times since the fund's inception.

	last 5 years		since inception	
worst year	19%	1997	17%	1994
best year	75%	1999	75%	1999

In the past, Strong has done better than 95 percent of its peer group in up markets and outperformed 60 percent of its competition in down markets. Consistency, or predictability, of returns for Strong can be described as very good. This fund's risk-related return is excellent.

Management   ★★★★
There are 110 stocks in this $4.2 billion portfolio. The average growth fund today is $700 million in size. Close to 94 percent of the fund's holdings are in stocks. The stocks in this portfolio have an average price-earnings (p/e) ratio of 56 and a median market capitalization of $22 billion. Technology represents close to 65 percent of the fund's holdings, followed by services (14 percent) and health (9 percent). The portfolio's equity holdings can be categorized as large-cap and

growth-oriented issues. The fund has a correlation of 35 percent to the S & P 500 (versus 85 percent for growth funds in general).

Ronald Ognar has managed this fund for the past seven years. Management typically buys stocks whose companies are expected to have above-average sales and earnings growth. A bottom-up approach is used to find the fastest-growing corporations. At the first sign of trouble a stock is unloaded. There are 40 funds besides Growth within the Strong family. Overall, the fund family's risk-adjusted performance can be described as very good.

Tax Minimization   ★★★★★
During the past five years, a $10,000 initial investment grew to $46,550 after taxes, assuming a 39.6 percent income tax bracket (state and federal combined) and a capital gains rate of 28 percent. This means that investors in this fund were able to preserve 93 percent of their total returns. Compared to other equity funds, this fund's tax savings are considered to be excellent.

Expenses   ★★
Strong's expense ratio is 1.2 percent; it has averaged 1.3 percent annually over the past three calendar years. The average expense ratio for the 2,100 funds in this category is 1.5 percent. This fund's turnover rate over the past year has been 320 percent, while its peer group average has been 100 percent.

Summary
Strong Growth has had exceptional risk-adjusted returns over the past three and five years. The fund has an incredibly high turnover rate, but frequent trading has not hurt these very good returns. Tax minimization has also been exceptional. This large fund family has a number of other portfolios that will appeal to investors of all risk levels.

Profile
minimum initial investment $2,500	*IRA accounts available* .... yes
subsequent minimum investment ... $50	*IRA minimum investment* $250
available in all 50 states .... yes	*date of inception* .... Dec. 1993
telephone exchanges .... yes	*dividend/income paid* .... quarterly
number of funds in family 41	*largest sector weighting* ... technology

Van Kampen Emerging Growth A

One Parkview Plaza
Oakbrook Terrace, IL 60181
800-421-5666
www.vankampen.com

total return	★★★★★
risk reduction	★★★
management	★★★★
tax minimization	★★★★★
expense control	★★★★
symbol ACEGX	21 points
up-market performance	excellent
down-market performance	excellent
predictability of returns	very good

Total Return   ★★★★★

Over the past five years, Van Kampen Emerging Growth A has taken $10,000 and turned it into $66,340 ($45,740 over three years and $148,840 over the past 10 years). This translates into an annualized return of 46 percent over the past five years, 66 percent over the past three years, and 31 percent for the decade. Over the past five years, this fund has outperformed 99 percent of all mutual funds; within its general category it has done better than 98 percent of its peers. Growth funds have averaged 25 percent annually over these same five years (all periods ending March 31, 2000).

Risk/Volatility   ★★★

Over the past five years, Emerging Growth has been safer than 6 percent of all growth funds. Over the past decade, the fund has had one negative year, while the S & P 500 has also had one (off 3 percent in 1990). The fund has underperformed the S & P 500 three times in the last 10 years.

	last 5 years		last 10 years	
worst year	18%	1996	-7%	1994
best year	104%	1999	104%	1999

In the past, Emerging Growth has done better than 95 percent of its peer group in up markets and outperformed 90 percent of its competition in down markets. Consistency, or predictability, of returns for Emerging Growth can be described as very good. This fund's risk-related return is excellent.

Management   ★★★★

There are 130 stocks in this $9 billion portfolio. The average growth fund today is $700 million in size. Close to 92 percent of the fund's holdings are in stocks. The stocks in this portfolio have an average price-earnings (p/e) ratio of 64 and a median market capitalization of $42 billion. Technology represents 70 percent of the fund's holdings, followed by health care (4 percent) and utilities (3 percent).

The portfolio's equity holdings can be categorized as large-cap and growth-oriented issues. The fund has a correlation of just roughly 30 percent to the S & P 500 (versus 85 percent for growth funds in general).

A team has managed this fund for the past eight years. Management does not restrict a stock based on its size. Fundamentals are stressed, and companies whose growth rates are in excess of 20 percent annually are emphasized. The managers also prefer corporations with improving profit margins and favorable earnings estimates. Stocks are sold when either valuations or earnings decline. There are 121 funds besides Emerging Growth within the Van Kampen family. Overall, the fund family's risk-adjusted performance can be described as good.

Tax Minimization   ★★★★★
During the past five years, a $10,000 initial investment grew to $61,695 after taxes, assuming a 39.6 percent income tax bracket (state and federal combined) and a capital gains rate of 28 percent. This means that investors in this fund were able to preserve 93 percent of their total returns. Compared to other equity funds, this fund's tax savings are considered to be excellent.

Expenses   ★★★★
Emerging Growth's expense ratio is 1 percent; it has also averaged 1 percent annually over the past three calendar years. The average expense ratio for the 2,100 funds in this category is 1.5 percent. This fund's turnover rate over the past year has been 120 percent, while its peer group average has been 100 percent.

Summary
Van Kampen Emerging Growth A has ranked in the top one or two quintiles of performance for five of the past six years. The fund is also the number one performer in its entire category for the past three and five years. Tax efficiency has also been very impressive. If you are looking for the best performance in the area of domestic growth with reasonable risk, this is it.

Profile

minimum initial investment $1,000	*IRA accounts available* .... yes
subsequent minimum investment ... $25	*IRA minimum investment* $500
available in all 50 states .... yes	*date of inception* .... Oct. 1970
telephone exchanges .... yes	*dividend/income paid* .... annually
number of funds in family 122	*largest sector weighting* ... technology

White Oak Growth Stock

P.O. Box 419441
Kansas City, MO 64141
888-462-5386
www.oakassociates.com

total return	★★★★★
risk reduction	★★★★★
management	★★★★★
tax minimization	★★★★★
expense control	★★★★★
symbol WOGSX	25 points
up-market performance	excellent
down-market performance	poor
predictability of returns	excellent

Total Return   ★★★★★

Over the past five years, White Oak Growth Stock has taken $10,000 and turned it into $57,735 ($32,420 over three years). This translates into an annualized return of 42 percent over the past five years and 48 percent over the past three years. Over the past five years, this fund has outperformed 98 percent of all mutual funds; within its general category it has done better than 95 percent of its peers. Growth funds have averaged 25 percent annually over these same five years (all periods ending March 31, 2000).

Risk/Volatility   ★★★★★

Over the past five years, White Oak has been safer than 20 percent of all growth funds. Since its inception, the fund has had one negative year, while the S & P 500 has also had one (off 3 percent in 1990). The fund has underperformed the S & P 500 twice since the fund's inception.

	last 5 years		since inception	
worst year	24%	1997	0%	1993
best year	53%	1995	53%	1995

In the past, White Oak has done better than 95 percent of its peer group in up markets and outperformed just 10 percent of its competition in down markets. Consistency, or predictability, of returns for White Oak can be described as excellent. This fund's risk-related return is also excellent.

Management   ★★★★★

There are 25 stocks in this $3 billion portfolio. The average growth fund today is $700 million in size. Close to 97 percent of the fund's holdings are in stocks. The stocks in this portfolio have an average price-earnings (p/e) ratio of 42 and a median market capitalization of $117 billion. Technology represents over 45 percent of the fund's holdings, followed by financial stocks (22 percent) and health care (18 percent). The portfolio's equity holdings can be categorized as large-cap and growth-oriented issues. The fund has a correlation of just roughly 75 percent to the S & P 500 (versus 85 percent for growth funds in general).

James Oelschlager has managed this fund for the past eight years. Management prefers to make portfolio changes very slowly and likes to concentrate the vast majority of the fund in 25 or less issues. There are two funds besides Growth Stock within the Oak Associates family. Overall, the fund family's risk-adjusted performance can be described as excellent.

Tax Minimization ★★★★★
During the past five years, a $10,000 initial investment grew to $57,735 after taxes, assuming a 39.6 percent income tax bracket (state and federal combined) and a capital gains rate of 28 percent. This means that investors in this fund were able to preserve 100 percent of their total returns. Compared to other equity funds, this fund's tax savings are considered to be excellent.

Expenses ★★★★★
White Oak Growth Stock's expense ratio is 1 percent; it has also averaged 1 percent annually over the past three calendar years. The average expense ratio for the 2,100 funds in this category is 1.5 percent. This fund's turnover rate over the past year has been 5 percent, while its peer group average has been 100 percent.

Summary
White Oak Growth Stock has ranked in the top quintile of performance for six of the past seven years. This is quite a feat of return and consistency. The fund scores a perfect score (25 out of a possible 25 points). Only a couple of funds, in any category, receive a perfect score. This is a rare achievement when you consider that there are over 2,100 growth funds and well over 13,000 mutual funds in general. Management is to be commended.

Profile

minimum initial investment $2,000	*IRA accounts available* .... yes
subsequent minimum investment ... $50	*IRA minimum investment* $2,000
available in all 50 states .... yes	*date of inception* .... Aug. 1992
telephone exchanges .... yes	*dividend/income paid* .... annually
number of funds in family 3	*largest sector weighting* ... technology

Growth and Income Funds

These funds attempt to produce both capital appreciation and current income, with priority given to appreciation potential in the stocks purchased. Growth and income fund portfolios include seasoned, well-established firms that pay comparatively high cash dividends. But do not let this category's name mislead you. The average growth and "income" fund has an annual yield of just 0.7 percent, versus 0.3 percent for the typical growth fund. The goal of these funds is to provide long-term growth without excessive volatility in share price. Portfolio composition is almost always exclusively U.S. stocks, with an emphasis on technology, financial, industrial cyclical, health, energy, retail, and consumer staples stocks.

Over the past 50 years (ending December 31, 1999), common stocks have outperformed inflation, on average, 74 percent of the time over 1-year periods, 83 percent of the time over 5-year periods, 85 percent of the time over 10-year periods, 92 percent of the time over 15-year periods, and 100 percent of the time over any given 20-year period of time. Over the same period, high-quality, long-term corporate bonds have outperformed inflation, on average, 62 percent of the time over 1-year periods, 63 percent of the time over 5-year periods, 61 percent of the time over 10-year periods, 72 percent of the time over 15-year periods, and 68 percent over any given 20-year period of time.

Growth & Income Funds

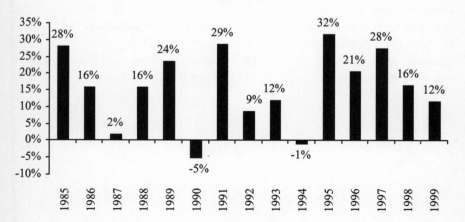

Eight hundred and seventy-five funds make up the growth and income category. Total market capitalization of this category is $900 billion. Another category, "equity-income" funds, has been combined with growth and income. Equity-income funds have had a standard deviation of 17.9 percent, an average annual dividend yield of 1.5 percent, a 65 percent turnover rate, and an average annual expense ratio of 1.4 percent. Combining equity-income and growth and income funds for this section, there are a total of 1,100 possible candidates. Total market capitalization of these two categories combined is $1.02 trillion.

Over the past three and five years, growth and income funds have had an average compound return of 19.3 and 20.4 percent per year respectively (versus 13.2 and 16.1 percent for equity-income funds). These funds have averaged 14.9 percent annually over the last 10 years and 14.3 percent annually for the past 15 years (versus 13.0 and 13.4 percent for equity-income). The standard deviation for growth and income funds has been 20.7 percent over the past three years (compared to 17.9 for equity-income and 27.4 percent for growth funds). This means that growth and income funds have been 14 percent more predictable than world stock funds but have been about 14 percent less predictable than pure equity-income funds.

AIM Charter A
11 Greenway Plaza, Suite 1919
Houston, TX 77046
800-959-4246
www.aimfunds.com

total return	★★★★
risk reduction	★★★★
management	★★★★
tax minimization	★★★★
expense control	★★
symbol CHTRX	18 points
up-market performance	excellent
down-market performance	poor
predictability of returns	very good

Total Return   ★★★★
Over the past five years, AIM Charter A has taken $10,000 and turned it into
$34,360 ($23,000 over three years and $60,340 over the past ten years). This trans-
lates into an annualized return of 28 percent over the past five years, 32 percent over
the past three years, and 20 percent for the decade. Over the past five years, this fund
has outperformed 91 percent of all mutual funds; within its general category it has
done better than 89 percent of its peers. Growth and income funds have averaged 19
percent annually over these same five years (all periods ending March 31, 2000).

Risk/Volatility   ★★★★
Over the past five years, Charter has been safer than 40 percent of all growth and
income funds. Over the past decade, the fund has had one negative year, while the
S & P 500 has also had one (off 3 percent in 1990). The fund has underperformed
the S & P 500 seven times in the last 10 years.

	last 5 years		last 10 years	
worst year	20%	1996	-4%	1994
best year	36%	1995	38%	1991

In the past, Charter has done better than 97 percent of its peer group in up
markets and outperformed 25 percent of its competition in down markets.
Consistency, or predictability, of returns for Charter can be described as very good.
This fund's risk-related return is also very good.

Management   ★★★★
There are 75 stocks in this $8.7 billion portfolio. The average growth and income fund
today is $930 million in size. Close to 93 percent of the fund's holdings are in stocks.
The stocks in this portfolio have an average price-earnings (p/e) ratio of 37 and a
median market capitalization of $114 billion. Technology represents over one-third of
the fund's holdings, followed by financial stocks (19 percent) and health care (13 per-

cent). The portfolio's equity holdings can be categorized as large-cap issues and a blend of growth and value stocks. The fund has a correlation of approximately 90 percent to the S & P 500 (versus 95 percent for growth and income funds in general).

Lanny Sachnowitz has managed this fund for 10 years; Monika Degan came on board as comanager in early 2000. In general, management likes to invest two-thirds of the fund's assets in income-producing securities, including convertibles. The comanagers look for seasoned companies with above-average earnings and dividends. There are 152 funds besides Charter within the AIM family. Overall, the fund family's risk-adjusted performance can be described as very good.

Tax Minimization   ★★★★
During the past five years, a $10,000 initial investment grew to $30,240 after taxes, assuming a 39.6 percent income tax bracket (state and federal combined) and a capital gains rate of 28 percent. This means that investors in this fund were able to preserve 88 percent of their total returns. Compared to other equity funds, this fund's tax savings are considered to be very good.

Expenses   ★★
Charter's expense ratio is 1.1 percent; it has also averaged 1.1 percent annually over the past three calendar years. The average expense ratio for the 1,100 funds in this category is 1.3 percent. This fund's turnover rate over the past year has been 105 percent, while its peer group average has been 65 percent.

Summary
AIM Charter A scores very well in every major category. The fund's expense ratio rating is punished a little bit because of the comparatively high turnover rate. The fund has outperformed 89 percent of its peers. Bull market performance has been great, but bear market returns have not been even average.

Profile

minimum initial investment $500	*IRA accounts available* .... yes
subsequent minimum investment ... $50	*IRA minimum investment* $250
available in all 50 states .... yes	*date of inception* .... Nov. 1968
telephone exchanges .... yes	*dividend/income paid* .... quarterly
number of funds in family 153	*largest sector weighting* ... technology

Citizens Index

230 Commerce Way, Suite 300
Portsmouth, NH 03801
800-223-7010
www.citizensfunds.com

total return	★★★★★
risk reduction	★★★★
management	★★★★
tax minimization	★★★★★
expense control	★★
symbol WAIDX	20 points
up-market performance	good
down-market performance	excellent
predictability of returns	very good

Total Return   ★★★★★

Over the past five years, Citizens Index has taken $10,000 and turned it into $38,580 ($25,155 over three years). This translates into an annualized return of 31 percent over the past five years and 36 percent over the past three years. Over the past five years, this fund has outperformed 100 percent of all mutual funds; within its general category it has done better than 100 percent of its peers. Growth and income funds have averaged 19 percent annually over these same five years (all periods ending March 31, 2000).

Risk/Volatility   ★★★★

Over the past five years, Citizens Index has been safer than 70 percent of all growth and income funds. Since its inception, the fund has had no negative years, while the S & P 500 has had one (off 3 percent in 1990). The fund has outperformed the S & P 500 every year since the fund's inception.

	last 5 years		since inception	
worst year	23%	1996	23%	1996
best year	43%	1998	43%	1998

In the past, Citizens Index has done better than 65 percent of its peer group in up markets and outperformed 90 percent of its competition in down markets. Consistency, or predictability, of returns for Citizens Index can be described as very good. This fund's risk-related return is excellent.

Management   ★★★★

There are 290 stocks in this $800 million portfolio. The average growth and income fund today is $930 million in size. Close to 100 percent of the fund's holdings are in stocks. The stocks in this portfolio have an average price-earnings (p/e) ratio of 45 and a median market capitalization of $95 billion. Technology represents just over 50 percent of the fund's holdings, followed by services (18 percent) and financials (10 percent). The portfolio's equity holdings can be categorized as large-cap and growth-oriented issues. The fund has a correlation of close to 95 percent to the S & P 500 (versus 95 percent for growth and income funds in general).

Sophia Collier has managed this fund for the past five years. Management invests in a proprietary index of 300 companies that are believed to represent the best of their respective industry groups. Roughly 200 of the 300 companies come from the S & P 500; the remaining 100 issues are smaller stocks that are included for industry diversification. Management conducts annual "socially conscious" reviews of each company in the portfolio, evaluating records on the environment, workplace issues, and community involvement. There are four funds besides Index within the Citizens family. Overall, the fund family's risk-adjusted performance can be described as excellent.

Tax Minimization ★★★★★
During the past five years, a $10,000 initial investment grew to $31,720 after taxes, assuming a 39.6 percent income tax bracket (state and federal combined) and a capital gains rate of 28 percent. This means that investors in this fund were able to preserve 96 percent of their total returns. Compared to other equity funds, this fund's tax savings are considered to be excellent.

Expenses ★★
Citizens Index's expense ratio is 1.6 percent; it has also averaged 1.6 percent annually over the past three calendar years. The average expense ratio for the 1,100 funds in this category is 1.3 percent. This fund's turnover rate over the past year has been 15 percent, while its peer group average has been 65 percent.

Summary
Citizens Index is a hybrid; the fund invests most of its assets in S & P 500 stocks with the remainder in smaller cap issues—but will only select companies that are socially conscious (for example, no tobacco, nuclear power plants, weapons makers, etc.). Total return and tax minimization have been outstanding and so has bear market performance. Expenses are a little on the high side, but this is largely offset by a very low turnover rate (which is a hidden charge and not included in a fund's expense ratio).

Profile

minimum initial investment $2,500	*IRA accounts available* .... yes
subsequent minimum investment ... $50	*IRA minimum investment* $1,000
available in all 50 states .... yes	*date of inception* .... March 1995
telephone exchanges .... yes	*dividend/income paid* .... annually
number of funds in family 5	*largest sector weighting* ... technology

Domini Social Equity
11 West 25th Street, 7th Floor
New York, NY 10010
800-762-6814
www.domini.com

total return	★★★★
risk reduction	★★★★
management	★★★★
tax minimization	★★★★★
expense control	★★★★★
symbol DSEFX	22 points
up-market performance	good
down-market performance	very good
predictability of returns	very good

Total Return   ★★★★
Over the past five years, Domini Social Equity has taken $10,000 and turned it into $34,360 ($21,970 over three years). This translates into an annualized return of 28 percent over the past five years and 30 percent over the past three years. Over the past five years, this fund has outperformed 90 percent of all mutual funds; within its general category it has done better than 87 percent of its peers. Growth and income funds have averaged 19 percent annually over these same five years (all periods ending March 31, 2000).

Risk/Volatility   ★★★★
Over the past five years, Social Equity has been safer than 40 percent of all growth and income funds. Since its inception, the fund has had one negative year, while the S & P 500 has also had one (off 3 percent in 1990). The fund has underperformed the S & P 500 four times since the fund's inception.

	last 5 years		since inception	
worst year	22%	1996	0%	1994
best year	36%	1997	36%	1997

In the past, Social Equity has done better than 50 percent of its peer group in up markets and outperformed 75 percent of its competition in down markets. Consistency, or predictability, of returns for Social Equity can be described as very good. This fund's risk-related return is very good.

Management   ★★★★
There are 400 stocks in this $1.6 billion portfolio. The average growth and income fund today is $930 million in size. Close to 100 percent of the fund's holdings are in stocks. The stocks in this portfolio have an average price-earnings (p/e) ratio of 37 and a median market capitalization of $145 billion. Technology represents 47 percent of the fund's holdings, followed by financial stocks (13 percent) and nondurables (11 percent). The portfolio's equity holdings can be categorized as large-cap issues and

a blend of growth and value stocks. The fund has a correlation of 97 percent to the S & P 500 (versus 95 percent for growth and income funds in general).

John O'Toole has managed this fund for the past seven years. Management invests in a proprietary index of 400 stocks that strongly mimic the S & P 500. The fund does not invest in companies involved in gambling, alcohol, tobacco, nuclear power, or weapons. The managers do like companies that are concerned about their employees. Social Equity is the only fund within the Domini family.

Tax Minimization ★★★★★
During the past five years, a $10,000 initial investment grew to $33,670 after taxes, assuming a 39.6 percent income tax bracket (state and federal combined) and a capital gains rate of 28 percent. This means that investors in this fund were able to preserve 98 percent of their total returns. Compared to other equity funds, this fund's tax savings are considered to be excellent

Expenses ★★★★★
Social Equity's expense ratio is 1 percent; it has also averaged 1 percent annually over the past three calendar years. The average expense ratio for the 1,100 funds in this category is 1.3 percent. This fund's turnover rate over the past year has been 8 percent, while its peer group average has been 65 percent.

Summary
Domini Social Equity is one of only two socially conscious funds in the book. Despite the industry groups that are excluded, the fund has still managed to turn in some very good results over the past three and five years. This growth and income offering has an extremely impressive 98 percent tax efficiency, making it number two in its entire category. This is a very good choice; unfortunately, this is a one-fund "family."

Profile
minimum initial investment $1,000
subsequent minimum investment ... $50
available in all 50 states .... yes
telephone exchanges .... yes
number of funds in family 1

IRA accounts available .... yes
IRA minimum investment $250
date of inception .... June 1991
dividend/income paid ... semi-annually
largest sector weighting ... technology

Dreyfus Disciplined Stock
144 Glenn Curtis Boulevard
Uniondale, NY 11556
800-373-9387
www.dreyfus.com

total return	★★★★
risk reduction	★★★★
management	★★★★
tax minimization	★★★★★
expense control	★★★★
symbol DDSTX	21 points
up-market performance	very good
down-market performance	poor
predictability of returns	very good

Total Return   ★★★★
Over the past five years, Dreyfus Disciplined Stock has taken $10,000 and turned it into $31,760 ($20,480 over three years and $57,3300 over the past 10 years). This translates into an annualized return of 26 percent over the past five years, 27 percent over the past three years, and 19 percent for the decade. Over the past five years, this fund has outperformed 88 percent of all mutual funds; within its general category it has done better than 78 percent of its peers. Growth and income funds have averaged 19 percent annually over these same five years (all periods ending March 31, 2000).

Risk/Volatility   ★★★★
Over the past five years, Disciplined Stock has been safer than 50 percent of all growth and income funds. Over the past decade, the fund has had one negative year, while the S & P 500 has also had one (off 3 percent in 1990). The fund has underperformed the S & P 500 six times in the last 10 years.

	last 5 years		last 10 years	
worst year	18%	1999	-1%	1994
best year	37%	1995	37%	1995

In the past, Disciplined Stock has done better than 80 percent of its peer group in up markets and outperformed 40 percent of its competition in down markets. Consistency, or predictability, of returns for Disciplined Stock can be described as very good. This fund's risk-related return is also very good.

Management   ★★★★
There are 150 stocks in this $3.6 billion portfolio. The average growth and income fund today is $930 million in size. Close to 99 percent of the fund's holdings are in stocks. The stocks in this portfolio have an average price-earnings (p/e) ratio of 33 and a median market capitalization of $115 billion. Technology represents 28 percent of the fund's holdings, followed by financial stocks (15 percent) and industrial cyclicals

(13 percent). The portfolio's equity holdings can be categorized as large-cap issues and a blend of growth and value stocks. The fund has a correlation of 98 percent to the S & P 500 (versus 95 percent for growth and income funds in general).

Bert Mullins has managed this fund for the past 14 years. Management uses a computer program to initially analyze over 2,000 stocks based on relative value and momentum. Value measurements include p/e and price-to-book ratios; momentum screens look at the direction of earnings estimates versus actual earnings. There are 238 funds besides Disciplined Stock within the Dreyfus family. Overall, the fund family's risk-adjusted performance can be described as very good.

Tax Minimization ★★★★★
During the past five years, a $10,000 initial investment grew to $29,220 after taxes, assuming a 39.6 percent income tax bracket (state and federal combined) and a capital gains rate of 28 percent. This means that investors in this fund were able to preserve 92 percent of their total returns. Compared to other equity funds, this fund's tax savings are considered to be excellent.

Expenses ★★★★
Dreyfus Disciplined Stock's expense ratio is 1 percent; it has also averaged 1 percent annually over the past three calendar years. The average expense ratio for the 1,100 funds in this category is 1.3 percent. This fund's turnover rate over the past year has been 50 percent, while its peer group average has been 65 percent.

Summary
Dreyfus Disciplined Stock turns in very good performance and excellent tax efficiency. The fund's only weak point has been bear market performance, but patient investors will find this of no concern. This large fund family has a huge number of other offerings that are also quite good. This is one of the more highly regarded mutual fund families.

Profile
minimum initial investment $2,500	*IRA accounts available* .... yes
subsequent minimum investment .. $100	*IRA minimum investment* $750
available in all 50 states .... yes	*date of inception* .... Dec. 1987
telephone exchanges .... yes	*dividend/income paid*....... quarterly
number of funds in family 239	*largest sector weighting* ... technology

Fidelity
82 Devonshire Street
Boston, MA 02109
800-544-8888
www.fidelity.com

total return	★★★★
risk reduction	★★★★
management	★★★★
tax minimization	★★★★
expense control	★★★★★
symbol FFIDX	21 points
up-market performance	excellent
down-market performance	fair
predictability of returns	very good

Total Return   ★★★★
Over the past five years, Fidelity has taken $10,000 and turned it into $33,040
($21,970 over three years and $55,670 over the past 10 years). This translates into
an annualized return of 27 percent over the past five years, 30 percent over the past
three years, and 19 percent for the decade. Over the past five years, this fund has
outperformed 91 percent of all mutual funds; within its general category it has done
better than 90 percent of its peers. Growth and income funds have averaged 19 percent annually over these same five years (all periods ending March 31, 2000).

Risk/Volatility   ★★★★
Over the past five years, Fidelity has been safer than 85 percent of all growth and
income funds. Over the past decade, the fund has had one negative year, while the
S & P 500 has also had one (off 3 percent in 1990). The fund has underperformed
the S & P 500 five times in the last 10 years.

	last 5 years		last 10 years	
worst year	20%	1996	-5%	1990
best year	33%	1995	33%	1995

In the past, Fidelity has done better than 90 percent of its peer group in up
markets and outperformed 30 percent of its competition in down markets.
Consistency, or predictability, of returns for Fidelity can be described as very good.
This fund's risk-related return is also very good.

Management   ★★★★
There are 190 stocks in this $16 billion portfolio. The average growth and income
fund today is $930 million in size. Close to 95 percent of the fund's holdings are in
stocks. The stocks in this portfolio have an average price-earnings (p/e) ratio of 33
and a median market capitalization of $85 billion. Technology represents close to
one-fourth of the fund's holdings, followed by industrial cyclical stocks (15 percent)
and nondurables (14 percent). The portfolio's equity holdings can be categorized as

large-cap and a blend of growth and value stocks. The fund has a correlation of 93 percent to the S & P 500 (versus 95 percent for growth and income funds in general).

Beth Terrana has managed this fund for the past eight years. Management believes it is increasingly difficult for companies to improve earnings through unit growth alone. Therefore, the fund prefers to invest in companies that are going through a turnaround or restructuring or are low-cost producers. There are 141 funds besides this growth and income fund within the Fidelity family. Overall, the fund family's risk-adjusted performance can be described as good.

Tax Minimization   ★★★
During the past five years, a $10,000 initial investment grew to $29,070 after taxes, assuming a 39.6 percent income tax bracket (state and federal combined) and a capital gains rate of 28 percent. This means that investors in this fund were able to preserve 88 percent of their total returns. Compared to other equity funds, this fund's tax savings are considered to be very good.

Expenses   ★★★★★
Fidelity's expense ratio is .6 percent; it has also averaged .6 percent annually over the past three calendar years. The average expense ratio for the 1,100 funds in this category is 1.3 percent. This fund's turnover rate over the past year has been 70 percent, while its peer group average has been 65 percent.

Summary
Fidelity is solid across the board. Bull market returns have been fantastic. Management has also done a particularly good job of keeping overhead low. It is difficult to beat the research and other kinds of expertise that are found at this powerhouse. Fidelity is the best known fund family and this is one of their flagship funds.

Profile
minimum initial investment $2,500	*IRA accounts available* .... yes
subsequent minimum investment .. $250	*IRA minimum investment* $500
available in all 50 states .... yes	*date of inception* .... Apr. 1930
telephone exchanges .... yes	*dividend/income paid* .... quarterly
number of funds in family 142	*largest sector weighting* ... technology

Gateway

400 TechneCenter Drive, Suite 220
Milford, OH 45150
800-354-6339
www.gatewayfund.com

total return	★
risk reduction	★★★★★
management	★★★
tax minimization	★★★★★
expense control	★★★★★
symbol GATEX	19 points
up-market performance	fair
down-market performance	excellent
predictability of returns	excellent

Total Return ★

Over the past five years, Gateway has taken $10,000 and turned it into $17,620 ($14,430 over three years and $27,440 over the past 10 years). This translates into an annualized return of 12 percent over the past five years, 13 percent over the past three years, and 11 percent for the decade. Over the past five years, this fund has outperformed 55 percent of all mutual funds; within its general category it has done better than 15 percent of its peers. Growth and income funds have averaged 19 percent annually over these same five years (all periods ending March 31, 2000).

Risk/Volatility ★★★★★

Over the past five years, Gateway has been safer than 99 percent of all growth and income funds. Over the past decade, the fund has had no negative years, while the S & P 500 has had one (off 3 percent in 1990). The fund has underperformed the S & P 500 eight times in the last 10 years.

	last 5 years		last 10 years	
worst year	11%	1996	5%	1992
best year	13%	1999	18%	1991

In the past, Gateway has done better than 40 percent of its peer group in up markets and outperformed 97 percent of its competition in down markets. Consistency, or predictability, of returns for Gateway can be described as excellent. This fund's risk-related return is very good.

Management ★★★

There are 225 stocks in this $1 billion portfolio. The average growth and income fund today is $930 million in size. Close to 99 percent of the fund's holdings are in stocks. The stocks in this portfolio have an average price-earnings (p/e) ratio of 37 and a median market capitalization of $150 billion. Technology represents one-third of the fund's holdings, followed by industrial cyclical stocks (14 percent) and finance equities (11 percent). The portfolio's equity holdings can be categorized as large-cap and a blend of growth and value stocks. The fund has a correlation of 75 percent to the S & P 500 (versus 95 percent for growth and income funds in general).

J. Patrick Rogers has managed this fund for the past six years. Management's objective is to get annual returns that range from 10–14 percent with a strong emphasis on the lowest risk possible. The portfolio is very similar to the S & P 500, but current income is increased by having the managers sell covered calls on the entire holdings. Such option selling certainly limits upside potential, but it also decreases downside risk. There are two funds besides this growth and income fund within the Gateway family. Overall, the fund family's risk-adjusted performance can be described as fair.

Tax Minimization ★★★★★
During the past five years, a $10,000 initial investment grew to $16,390 after taxes, assuming a 39.6 percent income tax bracket (state and federal combined) and a capital gains rate of 28 percent. This means that investors in this fund were able to preserve 93 percent of their total returns. Compared to other equity funds, this fund's tax savings are considered to be excellent.

Expenses ★★★★★
Gateway's expense ratio is 1 percent; it has also averaged 1 percent annually over the past three calendar years. The average expense ratio for the 1,100 funds in this category is 1.3 percent. This fund's turnover rate over the past year has been 10 percent, while its peer group average has been 65 percent.

Summary
Gateway is the only fund in its group to extensively use options as a way to provide high current income (which is largely reinvested) as well as reducing risk. This makes this fund somewhat of a niche play. It is the lowest risk growth and income fund to appear in the book but deserves similar kudos for its control of expenses and tax minimization. Not many funds do well in down markets, and this is one of the few that conservative equity investors will feel secure owning.

Profile
minimum initial investment $1,000	*IRA accounts available* .... yes
subsequent minimum investment .. $100	*IRA minimum investment* $500
available in all 50 states .... yes	*date of inception* .... Dec. 1977
telephone exchanges .... yes	*dividend/income paid* .... quarterly
number of funds in family 3	*largest sector weighting* ... technology

IPS Millennium
625 South Gay Street, Suite 630
Knoxville, TN 37902
800-249-6927
www.ipsfunds.com

total return	★★★★★
risk reduction	★★
management	★★★★
tax minimization	★★★★★
expense control	★★
symbol IPSMX	18 points
up-market performance	excellent
down-market performance	excellent
predictability of returns	very good

Total Return   ★★★★★
Over the past five years, IPS Millennium has taken $10,000 and turned it into
$64,100 ($45,740 over three years). This translates into an annualized return of 45
percent over the past five years and 66 percent over the past three years. Over the
past five years, this fund has outperformed 99 percent of all mutual funds; within
its general category it has done better than 99 percent of its peers. Growth and
income funds have averaged 19 percent annually over these same five years (all
periods ending March 31, 2000).

Risk/Volatility   ★★
Over the past five years, IPS has been safer than 60 percent of all growth and
income funds. Since its inception, the fund has had no negative years, while the
S & P 500 has had one (off 3 percent in 1990). The fund has underperformed the
S & P 500 once since the fund's inception.

	last 5 years		since inception	
worst year	21%	1997	21%	1997
best year	119%	1999	119%	1999

In the past, IPS has done better than 99 percent of its peer group in up mar-
kets and outperformed 95 percent of its competition in down markets.
Consistency, or predictability, of returns for IPS can be described as very good.
This fund's risk-related return is excellent.

Management   ★★★★
There are 70 stocks in this $325 million portfolio. The average growth and income
fund today is $930 million in size. Close to 84 percent of the fund's holdings are
in stocks. The stocks in this portfolio have an average price-earnings (p/e) ratio of
47 and a median market capitalization of $21 billion. Technology represents over
two-thirds of the fund's holdings, followed by utilities (17 percent) and services
(10 percent). The portfolio's equity holdings can be categorized as large-cap and

growth-oriented issues. The fund has a correlation of 45 percent to the S & P 500 (versus 95 percent for large-cap growth funds in general).

Robert Loest has managed this fund for the past five years. Management looks for companies that are fundamentally undervalued and have above-average growth prospects. There is one other fund besides Millennium within the IPS family. Overall, the fund family's risk-adjusted performance can be described as excellent.

Tax Minimization   ★★★★★
During the past five years, a $10,000 initial investment grew to $64,100 after taxes, assuming a 39.6 percent income tax bracket (state and federal combined) and a capital gains rate of 28 percent. This means that investors in this fund were able to preserve 100 percent of their total returns. Compared to other equity funds, this fund's tax savings are considered to be excellent.

Expenses   ★★
IPS's expense ratio is 1.4 percent; it has also averaged 1.4 percent annually over the past three calendar years. The average expense ratio for the 1,100 funds in this category is 1.3 percent. This fund's turnover rate over the past year has been 85 percent, while its peer group average has been 65 percent.

Summary
IPS Millennium is the number one performing growth and income fund in the book. It has easily beaten all of its competitors over the past three and five years. Tax minimization has also been outstanding. The fund has ranked in the top quartile of performance for four of the past five years. Amazingly, the fund has also been safer than 60 percent of its peers. There are only two funds in the IPS family; hopefully they will add more offerings.

Profile
minimum initial investment $1,000	*IRA accounts available* .... yes
subsequent minimum investment .. $100	*IRA minimum investment* $1,000
available in all 50 states .... yes	*date of inception* .... Jan. 1995
telephone exchanges .... yes	*dividend/income paid* ... semi-annually
number of funds in family 2	*largest sector weighting* ... technology

Strong Total Return
P.O. Box 2936
Milwaukee, WI 53201
800-368-1030
www.strongfunds.com

total return	★★★★★
risk reduction	★★★
management	★★★★
tax minimization	★★★
expense control	★
symbol STRFX	16 points
up-market performance	excellent
down-market performance	very good
predictability of returns	good

Total Return   ★★★★★
Over the past five years, Strong Total Return has taken $10,000 and turned it into
$40,075 ($29,240 over three years and $67,220 over the past 10 years). This trans-
lates into an annualized return of 32 percent over the past five years, 43 percent
over the past three years, and 21 percent for the decade. Over the past five years,
this fund has outperformed 96 percent of all mutual funds; within its general category it has done better than 83 percent of its peers. Growth and income funds have
averaged 19 percent annually over these same five years (all periods ending March
31, 2000).

Risk/Volatility   ★★★
Over the past five years, Total Return has been safer than 70 percent of all growth
and income funds. Over the past decade, the fund has had two negative years, while
the S & P 500 has had one (off 3 percent in 1990). The fund has underperformed
the S & P 500 six times in the last 10 years.

	last 5 years		last 10 years	
worst year	14%	1996	-7%	1990
best year	60%	1999	60%	1999

In the past, Total Return has done better than 99 percent of its peer group in
up markets and outperformed 80 percent of its competition in down markets.
Consistency, or predictability, of returns for Total Return can be described as good.
This fund's risk-related return is excellent.

Management   ★★★★
There are 100 stocks in this $1.7 billion portfolio. The average growth and income
fund today is $930 million in size. Close to 95 percent of the fund's holdings are in
stocks. The stocks in this portfolio have an average price-earnings (p/e) ratio of 44
and a median market capitalization of $101 billion. Technology represents more than
40 percent of the fund's holdings, followed by financial stocks (9 percent) and retail

trade (9 percent). The portfolio's equity holdings can be categorized as large-cap and growth-oriented issues. The fund has a correlation of 65 percent to the S & P 500 (versus 95 percent for growth and income funds in general).

Ronald Ognar and Ian Rogers have managed this fund for the past seven years. Management uses a bottom-up approach and focuses on large companies. Roughly half of the portfolio is in securities with high yields and half in growth. There are 40 funds besides Total Return within the Strong family. Overall, the fund family's risk-adjusted performance can be described as very good.

Tax Minimization ★★★
During the past five years, a $10,000 initial investment grew to $33,660 after taxes, assuming a 39.6 percent income tax bracket (state and federal combined) and a capital gains rate of 28 percent. This means that investors in this fund were able to preserve 84 percent of their total returns. Compared to other equity funds, this fund's tax savings are considered to be good.

Expenses ★
Total Return's expense ratio is 1 percent; it has also averaged 1 percent annually over the past three calendar years. The average expense ratio for the 1,100 funds in this category is 1.3 percent. This fund's turnover rate over the past year has been 400 percent, while its peer group average has been 65 percent.

Summary
Strong Total Return ranks as the second-best performer in its category, which consists of over 1,100 candidates. Return is definitely the portfolio's strong suit, but the fund has managed to do a very good job in bear markets as well. The fund is an excellent choice for the no-nonsense growth and income equity investor who is simply concerned with the bottom line—risk and return.

Profile
minimum initial investment $2,500	*IRA accounts available* . . . . yes
subsequent minimum investment . . . $50	*IRA minimum investment* $250
available in all 50 states . . . . yes	*date of inception* . . . . Dec. 1981
telephone exchanges . . . . yes	*dividend/income paid* . . . . quarterly
number of funds in family 41	*largest sector weighting* . . . technology

Vanguard 500 Index
Vanguard Financial Center
P.O. Box 2600
Valley Forge, PA 19483
800-662-7447
www.vanguard.com

total return	★★★★
risk reduction	★★★★
management	★★★★★
tax minimization	★★★★★
expense control	★★★★★
symbol VFINX	23 points
up-market performance	excellent
down-market performance	very good
predictability of returns	very good

Total Return   ★★★★
Over the past five years, Vanguard 500 Index has taken $10,000 and turned it into $33,040 ($20,485 over three years and $55,575 over the past 10 years). This translates into an annualized return of 27 percent over the past five years, 27 percent over the past three years, and 19 percent for the decade. Over the past five years, this fund has outperformed 88 percent of all mutual funds; within its general category it has done better than 82 percent of its peers. Growth and income funds have averaged 19 percent annually over these same five years (all periods ending March 31, 2000).

Risk/Volatility   ★★★★
Over the past five years, 500 Index has been safer than 65 percent of all growth and income funds. Over the past decade, the fund has had one negative year, while the S & P 500 has also had one (off 3 percent in 1990). The fund has underperformed the S & P 500 eight times in the last 10 years.

	last 5 years		last 10 years	
worst year	21%	1999	-3%	1990
best year	37%	1995	37%	1995

In the past, 500 Index has done better than 95 percent of its peer group in up markets and outperformed 65 percent of its competition in down markets. Consistency, or predictability, of returns for Vanguard 500 Index can be described as very good. This fund's risk-related return is also very good.

Management   ★★★★★
There are 505 stocks in this $100 billion portfolio. The average growth and income fund today is $930 million in size. Close to 100 percent of the fund's holdings are in stocks. The stocks in this portfolio have an average price-earnings (p/e) ratio of 37 and a median market capitalization of $142 billion. Technology represents close to

40 percent of the fund's holdings, followed by financial stocks (12 percent) and industrial cyclicals (12 percent). The portfolio's equity holdings can be categorized as large-cap and a blend of growth and value stocks. The fund has a correlation of 99 percent to the S & P 500 (versus 95 percent for growth and income funds in general).

George Sauter has managed this fund for the past 14 years. Management seeks to duplicate the price and yield of the S & P 500 Index. The fund has tracked the return's of the index extremely closely since the portfolio's inception. There are 77 funds besides 500 Index within the Vanguard family. Overall, the fund family's risk-adjusted performance can be described as very good.

Tax Minimization   ★★★★★
During the past five years, a $10,000 initial investment grew to $31,720 after taxes, assuming a 39.6 percent income tax bracket (state and federal combined) and a capital gains rate of 28 percent. This means that investors in this fund were able to preserve 96 percent of their total returns. Compared to other equity funds, this fund's tax savings are considered to be excellent.

Expenses   ★★★★★
500 Index's expense ratio is .2 percent; it has also averaged .2 percent annually over the past three calendar years. The average expense ratio for the 1,100 funds in this category is 1.3 percent. This fund's turnover rate over the past year has been 6 percent, while its peer group average has been 65 percent.

Summary
Vanguard 500 Index speaks for itself. The fund, as well as the index it duplicates, has been in the top two quintiles of performance for each of the past six years. Only a modest percentage of growth or growth and income funds consistently outperform the S & P 500 Index. This is a somewhat passive approach to investing in stocks (somewhat because the S & P Corporation does make changes to the index regularly) that frequently outperforms active management. This fund has a tremendous appeal to a wide range of investors. It is a particularly appealing choice for those that question or doubt all of the hype about mutual fund investing.

Profile
minimum initial investment $3,000	*IRA accounts available* . . . . yes
subsequent minimum investment . . $100	*IRA minimum investment* $1,000
available in all 50 states . . . . yes	*date of inception* . . . . Aug. 1976
telephone exchanges . . . . no	*dividend/income paid* . . . . quarterly
number of funds in family 78	*largest sector weighting* . . . technology

Vanguard Tax-Managed Growth & Income

Vanguard Financial Center
P.O. Box 2600
Valley Forge, PA 19483
800-662-7447
www.vanguard.com

total return	★★★★
risk reduction	★★★★
management	★★★★★
tax minimization	★★★★★
expense control	★★★★★
symbol VTGIX	23 points
up-market performance	very good
down-market performance	good
predictability of returns	very good

Total Return   ★★★★

Over the past five years, Vanguard Tax-Managed Growth & Income has taken $10,000 and turned it into $33,040 ($20,480 over three years). This translates into an annualized return of 27 percent over the past five years and 27 percent over the past three years. Over the past five years, this fund has outperformed 88 percent of all mutual funds; within its general category it has done better than 83 percent of its peers. Growth and income funds have averaged 19 percent annually over these same five years (all periods ending March 31, 2000).

Risk/Volatility   ★★★★

Over the past five years, Tax-Managed has been safer than 60 percent of all growth and income funds. Since its inception, the fund has had no negative years, while the S & P 500 has had one (off 3 percent in 1990). The fund has underperformed the S & P 500 once since the fund's inception.

	last 5 years		since inception	
worst year	21%	1999	21%	1999
best year	38%	1995	38%	1995

In the past, Tax-Managed has done better than 80 percent of its peer group in up markets and outperformed 60 percent of its competition in down markets. Consistency, or predictability, of returns for Tax-Managed can be described as very good. This fund's risk-related return is also very good.

Management   ★★★★★

There are 505 stocks in this $2.3 billion portfolio. The average growth and income fund today is $930 million in size. Close to 100 percent of the fund's holdings are in stocks. The stocks in this portfolio have an average price-earnings (p/e) ratio of 35 and a median market capitalization of $99 billion. Technology represents close to 30 percent of the fund's holdings, followed by financial stocks (15 percent) and industrial cyclicals (13 percent). The portfolio's equity holdings can be categorized as large-cap and value-oriented issues. The fund has a correlation of 99 percent to the S & P 500 (versus 95 percent for growth and income funds in general).

George Sauter has managed this fund for the past seven years. The fund invests in almost every stock found in the S & P 500 Index in approximately the same proportions as the index. Stocks that are usually sold are those that have the highest cost basis, thereby resulting in the lowest tax consequence. Management also considers selling stocks that have declined in price, thereby creating a capital loss that can be used to offset other capital gains. There are 77 funds besides Tax-Managed within the Vanguard family. Overall, the fund family's risk-adjusted performance can be described as very good.

Tax Minimization ★★★★★
During the past five years, a $10,000 initial investment grew to $32,050 after taxes, assuming a 39.6 percent income tax bracket (state and federal combined) and a capital gains rate of 28 percent. This means that investors in this fund were able to preserve 97 percent of their total returns. Compared to other equity funds, this fund's tax savings are considered to be excellent.

Expenses ★★★★★
Tax-Manager's expense ratio is .2 percent; it has also averaged .2 percent annually over the past three calendar years. The average expense ratio for the 1,100 funds in this category is 1.3 percent. This fund's turnover rate over the past year has been 4 percent, while its peer group average has been 65 percent.

Summary
Vanguard Tax-Managed Growth & Income is managed by the same person who manages the Vanguard 500 Index Fund. These two portfolios are virtually identical except that this one has slightly greater tax efficiency. Like its virtual twin brother, this tax-managed offering is highly recommended.

Profile

minimum initial investment . . . $10,000	*IRA accounts available* . . . . no
subsequent minimum investment . . $100	*IRA minimum investment* . . . . n/a
available in all 50 states . . . . yes	*date of inception* . . . . Sept. 1994
telephone exchanges . . . . yes	*dividend/income paid* . . . . quarterly
number of funds in family 78	*largest sector weighting* . . . technology

High-Yield Bond Funds

Sometimes referred to as "junk bond" funds, high-yield bond funds invest in corporate bonds rated lower than BBB or BAA. The world of bonds is divided into two general categories: investment grade and high-yield. Investment grade, sometimes referred to as "bank quality," means that the bond issue has been rated AAA, AA, A, or BAA (or BBB if the rating service is Standard and Poor's instead of Moody's). Certain institutions and fiduciaries are forbidden to invest their clients' monies in anything less than investment grade. Everything less than bank quality is considered junk.

Yet the world of bonds is not black and white. There are several categories of high-yield bonds. Junk bond funds contain issues that range from BB to C; a rating less than C means that the bond is in default, and payment of interest and/or principal is in arrears. High-yield bond funds perform best during good economic times. Such issues should be avoided by traditional investors during recessionary periods, since the underlying corporations may have difficulty making interest and principal payments when business slows down. However, these bonds, like common stocks, can perform very well during the second half of a recession.

Although junk bonds may exhibit greater volatility than their investment-grade peers, they are safer when it comes to interest rate risk. Since junk issues have higher-yielding coupons and often shorter maturities than quality corporate bond funds, they fluctuate less in value when interest rates change. Thus, during expansionary periods in the economy when interest rates are rising, high-yield funds will generally drop less in value than high-quality corporate or government bond funds. Conversely, when interest rates are falling, government and corporate bonds will appreciate more in value than junk funds. High-yield bonds resemble equities at least as much as they do traditional bonds when it comes to economic cycles and certain important technical factors. Studies show that only 19 percent of the average junk fund's total return is explained by the up or down movement of the Lehman Brothers Government/Corporate Bond Index. To give an idea of how low this number is, 94 percent of a typical high-quality corporate bond fund's performance is explainable by movement in the same index. Indeed, even international bond funds have a higher correlation coefficient than junk, with 25 percent of their performance explained by the Lehman index.

The table below covers the five-year period ending May 31, 2000 and compares the total return of three well known bond indexes: Credit Suisse High Yield Index (bonds rated BBB or lower), the Lehman Aggregate Bond Index (securities from the Lehman Government/Corporate, Mortgage-Backed Securities, and Asset-Backed Indexes), and the Lehman Government Bond Index (all publicly traded domestic debt of the U.S. Government).

index	1 year	3 years	5 years	10 years
high-yield	0.7%	4.5%	7.9%	11.2%
aggregate	1.9%	6.7%	7.1%	8.0%
government	2.5%	7.0%	7.2%	8.0%

The high end of the junk bond market, those debentures rated BA and BB, have been able to withstand the general beating the junk bond market incurred during the late 1980s and early 1990s. Moderate and conservative investors who want high-yield bonds as part of their portfolio should focus on funds that have a high percentage of their assets in higher-rated bonds, BB or better.

According to Salomon Brothers, the people who are responsible for the Lehman Brothers corporate and government bond indices used in this book, junk bond defaults averaged only 0.8 percent from 1980 to 1984. This rate almost tripled from 1985 to 1989 as defaults averaged 2.2 percent per year. Then, in 1990, defaults surged to 4.6 percent. Analysis based on historical data did not predict this huge increase in defaults. Bear in mind that BB-rated junk bonds can be expected to perform closer to high-quality bonds than will lower-rated junk. During 1990, for example, BB-rated bonds declined only slightly in price and actually delivered positive returns, whereas bonds rated CCC declined over 30 percent. During the mid-1990s, the default risk for the entire category had fallen to about 1.5 percent per year (well under 1 percent in the case of high-yield bond funds). From the mid-1990s through the first quarter of 2000, default rates increased to over 3.0 percent per year.

Over the past three and five years, high-yield corporate bond funds have had an average compound total return of 4.3 percent and 7.6 percent, respectively. The annual return for the past 10 years has been 10.2 percent, and 9.3 percent for the last 15 years (all figures as of May 31, 2000). The standard deviation for high-yield bond funds has been 8 percent over the past three years. This means that these

High-Yield Bond Funds

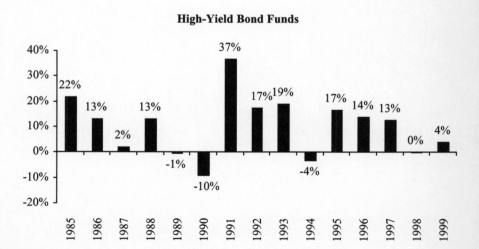

funds have been less volatile than any equity fund category but have experienced over twice the return variances of other types of domestic bond funds. Turnover has averaged 105 percent. Three hundred and thirty funds make up the high-yield category. Total market capitalization of this category is $100 billion.

The majority of investors believe that the track record of high-yield bonds has been mixed, particularly in recent years. There was a crash in this market in 1990, but the overall track record has been quite good. These bond funds were up 13.4 percent in 1987, the year of the stock market crash. As the junk bond scare started in 1989, the fund category was still able to show a 12.8 percent return for the calendar year. The following year the group showed a negative return of 9.5 percent.

The 1990 loss was caused by regulatory agencies putting pressure on the insurance industry, formerly the largest owner of this investment category. This, together with the demise of Drexel Burnham, the largest issuer of junk bonds, caused high-yield bonds to suffer their biggest loss in recent memory. And yet the very next year, 1991, high-yield bond funds did better than ever before, up over 36.7 percent. The following two years were also quite good—up 17.5 percent in 1992 and up 19.0 percent in 1993. The following year, 1994, these funds fell 3.6 percent, followed by a gain of 13.9 percent in 1996, 13 percent in 1997, a loss of 0.4 percent in 1998, and a gain of 4.1 percent in 1999.

Fidelity Advisor High-Yield T

82 Devonshire Street
Boston, MA 02109
800-522-7297
www.fidelity.com

total return	★★★★★
risk reduction	★★★
management	★★★★
current income	★★★
expense control	★★★★★
symbol FAHYX	20 points
up-market performance	excellent
down-market performance	poor
predictability of returns	very good

Total Return   ★★★★★

Over the past five years, Fidelity Advisor High-Yield T has taken $10,000 and turned it into $16,105 ($12,250 over three years and $33,950 over the past 10 years). This translates into an annualized return of 10 percent over the past five years, 7 percent over the past three years, and 13 percent for the decade. Over the past five years, this fund has outperformed 57 percent of all mutual funds; within its general category it has done better than 88 percent of its peers. High-yield bond funds have averaged 8 percent annually over these same five years (all periods ending March 31, 2000).

During the past five years, a $10,000 initial investment became $9,660 after taxes, assuming a 39.6 percent income tax bracket (state and federal combined) and a capital gains rate of 28 percent. This means that investors in this fund were able to preserve 60 percent of their total returns. Compared to other fixed-income funds, this fund's tax savings are considered to be excellent.

Risk/Volatility   ★★★

Over the past five years, Fidelity Advisor has been safer than 30 percent of all high-yield bond funds. Over the past decade, the fund has had two negative years, while the Lehman Brothers Aggregate Bond Index has also had two (off 3 percent in 1994 and 1 percent in 1999); the Credit Suisse High-Yield Bond Index fell twice (off 6 percent in 1990 and 1 percent in 1994). The fund has underperformed the Lehman Brothers Aggregate Bond Index twice and the Credit Suisse High-Yield Bond Index three times in the last 10 years.

	last 5 years		last 10 years	
worst year	0%	1998	-2%	1994
best year	19%	1995	35%	1991

In the past, Fidelity Advisor High-Yield has done better than 95 percent of its peer group in up markets and outperformed 25 percent of its competition in down markets. Consistency, or predictability, of returns for Fidelity Advisor can be described as very good. This fund's risk-related return is also very good.

Management   ★★★★
There are 285 fixed-income securities in this $4.2 billion portfolio. The average high-yield bond fund today is $310 million in size. Close to 80 percent of the fund's holdings are in bonds. The average maturity of the bonds in this account is seven years; the weighted coupon rate averages 8.5 percent. The portfolio's fixed-income holdings can be categorized as intermediate-term, low-quality debt. Roughly 45 percent of the portfolio is in B-rated bonds with another 40 percent nonrated and 10 percent in BB-rated issues.

Margaret Eagle has managed this fund for the past 13 years. Management favors smaller issues that are discovered by the fund's huge research team. There are 44 funds besides High-Yield within the Fidelity Advisor family. Overall, the fund family's risk-adjusted performance can be described as good.

Current Income   ★★★
Over the past year, Fidelity Advisor had a 12-month yield of 8.3 percent. During this same 12-month period, the typical high-yield bond fund had a yield that averaged 9.2 percent.

Expenses   ★★★★★
Fidelity Advisor's expense ratio is 1 percent; it has averaged 1.1 percent annually over the past three calendar years. The average expense ratio for the 330 funds in this category is 1.3 percent. This fund's turnover rate over the past year has been 60 percent, while its peer group average has been 105 percent.

Summary
Fidelity Advisor High-Yield T ties as the number-one performer in its category for the past three and five years. Capital preservation has also been tops. Management is to be commended for keeping expenses low and turnover comparatively very low. Quite simply, this is a fantastic fund.

Profile

minimum initial investment $2,500	*IRA accounts available* .... yes
subsequent minimum investment .. $250	*IRA minimum investment* $500
available in all 50 states .... yes	*date of inception* .... Jan. 1987
telephone exchanges .... yes	*dividend/income paid* .... monthly
number of funds in family 45	*average credit quality*........... B

Invesco High-Yield

P.O Box 173706
Denver, CO 80217
800-525-8085
www.invesco.com

total return	★★★★★
risk reduction	★★★
management	★★★★
current income	★★★★
expense control	★★★
symbol FHYPX	19 points
up-market performance	very good
down-market performance	fair
predictability of returns	excellent

Total Return ★★★★★

Over the past five years, Invesco High-Yield has taken $10,000 and turned it into $16,105 ($12,250 over three years and $25,940 over the past 10 years). This translates into an annualized return of 10 percent over the past five years, 7 percent over the past three years, and 10 percent for the decade. Over the past five years, this fund has outperformed 59 percent of all mutual funds; within its general category it has done better than 94 percent of its peers. High-yield bond funds have averaged 8 percent annually over these same five years (all periods ending March 31, 2000).

During the past five years, a $10,000 initial investment became $9,020 after taxes, assuming a 39.6 percent income tax bracket (state and federal combined) and a capital gains rate of 28 percent. This means that investors in this fund were able to preserve 56 percent of their total returns. Compared to other fixed-income funds, this fund's tax savings are considered to be excellent.

Risk/Volatility ★★★

Over the past five years, Invesco High-Yield has been safer than 50 percent of all high-yield bond funds. Over the past decade, the fund has had two negative years, while the Lehman Brothers Aggregate Bond Index has also had two (off 3 percent in 1994 and 1 percent in 1999); the Credit Suisse High-Yield Bond Index fell twice (off 6 percent in 1990 and 1 percent in 1994). The fund has underperformed the Lehman Brothers Aggregate Bond Index four times and the Credit Suisse High-Yield Bond Index five times in the last 10 years.

	last 5 years		last 10 years	
worst year	0%	1998	-5%	1994
best year	18%	1995	24%	1991

In the past, Invesco has done better than 75 percent of its peer group in up markets and outperformed 40 percent of its competition in down markets. Consistency, or predictability, of returns for Invesco can be described as excellent. This fund's risk-related return is very good.

Management   ★★★★

There are 105 fixed-income securities in this $700 million portfolio. The average high-yield bond fund today is $310 million in size. Close to 95 percent of the fund's holdings are in bonds. The average maturity of the bonds in this account is seven years; the weighted coupon rate averages 6.5 percent. The portfolio's fixed-income holdings can be categorized as intermediate-term, low-quality debt. Close to 85 percent of the fund's holdings are in B-rated issues, 8 percent is non-rated, and 5 percent is BB rated.

Jerry Paul has managed this fund for the past seven years. Management looks for companies that are expected to make fundamental improvements. Paul is particularly attracted to corporations that he believes will benefit handsomely from any kind of merger or acquisition. There are 19 funds besides High-Yield within the Invesco family. Overall, the fund family's risk-adjusted performance can be described as very good.

Current Income   ★★★★

Over the past year, Invesco had a 12-month yield of 9.7 percent. During this same 12-month period, the typical high-yield bond fund had a yield that averaged 9.2 percent.

Expenses   ★★★

Invesco's expense ratio is 1 percent; it has also averaged 1 percent annually over the past three calendar years. The average expense ratio for the 330 funds in this category is 1.3 percent. This fund's turnover rate over the past year has been 150 percent, while its peer group average has been 105 percent.

Summary

Invesco High-Yield ties for the best-performer in its category for the past three and five years. Compared to other fixed-income portfolios, this fund's tax efficiency is considered to be excellent. This fund is designed for the investor interested in maximizing current income as well as total return (appreciation of principal). Invesco is a medium-sized fund family that is well respected in the industry; there are a number of other Invesco offerings that investors will find appealing.

Profile

minimum initial investment $1,000	*IRA accounts available* .... yes
subsequent minimum investment ... $50	*IRA minimum investment* $250
available in all 50 states .... yes	*date of inception* .... March 1984
telephone exchanges .... yes	*dividend/income paid* .... monthly
number of funds in family 20	*average credit quality* .... B

Lord Abbett Bond-Debenture A

General Motors Building
767 Fifth Avenue
New York, NY 10153
800-201-6984
www.lordabbett.com

total return	★★★★
risk reduction	★★★★★
management	★★★★★
current income	★★★
expense control	★★★★★
symbol LBNDX	22 points
up-market performance	very good
down-market performance	very good
predictability of returns	excellent

Total Return   ★★★★

Over the past five years, Lord Abbett Bond-Debenture A has taken $10,000 and turned it into $15,390 ($12,250 over three years and $25,940 over the past 10 years). This translates into an annualized return of 9 percent over the past five years, 7 percent over the past three years, and 10 percent for the decade. Over the past five years, this fund has outperformed 54 percent of all mutual funds; within its general category it has done better than 71 percent of its peers. High-yield bond funds have averaged 8 percent annually over these same five years (all periods ending March 31, 2000).

During the past five years, a $10,000 initial investment became $8,920 after taxes, assuming a 39.6 percent income tax bracket (state and federal combined) and a capital gains rate of 28 percent. This means that investors in this fund were able to preserve 58 percent of their total returns. Compared to other fixed-income funds, this fund's tax savings are considered to be excellent.

Risk/Volatility   ★★★★★

Over the past five years, Bond-Debenture has been safer than 90 percent of all high-yield bond funds. Over the past decade, the fund has had two negative years, while the Lehman Brothers Aggregate Bond Index has also had two (off 3 percent in 1994 and 1 percent in 1999); the Credit Suisse High-Yield Bond Index fell twice (off 6 percent in 1990 and 1 percent in 1994). The fund has underperformed the Lehman Brothers Aggregate Bond Index four times and the Credit Suisse High-Yield Bond Index six times in the last 10 years.

	last 5 years		last 10 years	
worst year	4%	1999	-8%	1990
best year	18%	1995	38%	1991

In the past, Bond-Debenture has done better than 80 percent of its peer group in up markets and outperformed 80 percent of its competition in down markets.

Consistency, or predictability, of returns for Bond-Debenture can be described as excellent. This fund's risk-related return is very good.

Management   ★★★★★
There are 305 fixed-income securities in this $3.8 billion portfolio. The average high-yield bond fund today is $310 million in size. Close to 92 percent of the fund's holdings are in bonds. The average maturity of the bonds in this account is nine years; the weighted coupon rate averages 7.3 percent. The portfolio's fixed-income holdings can be categorized as intermediate-term, low-quality debt. Just under half of the fund is in B-rated issues, another 20 percent is in BB-rated bonds, and 15 percent is in AAA-rated debt instruments.

Christopher Towle has managed this fund for the past nine years. Management must keep at least one-fifth of its assets in very high quality securities, and 10 percent or less is in defaulted bonds. The fund stays away from the newer companies, preferring to select those seasoned firms that have stable growth and cash flow. There are 89 funds besides Bond-Debenture within the Lord Abbett family. Overall, the fund family's risk-adjusted performance can be described as good.

Current Income   ★★★
Over the past year, Bond-Debenture had a 12-month yield of 8.5 percent. During this same 12-month period, the typical high-yield bond fund had a yield that averaged 9.2 percent.

Expenses   ★★★★★
Bond-Debenture's expense ratio is .9 percent; it has also averaged .9 percent annually over the past three calendar years. The average expense ratio for the 330 funds in this category is 1.3 percent. This fund's turnover rate over the past year has been 85 percent, while its peer group average has been 105 percent.

Summary
Lord Abbett Bond-Debenture A is the perfect way for risk-wary investors to get involved in the lower-rated debt market. For its category, this is the lowest-risk offering in the book. Management is rated as superb, keeping expenses low and portfolio risk at a minimum. Tax minimization is also rated as tops.

Profile
minimum initial investment $1,000	*IRA accounts available* .... yes
subsequent minimum investment $1	*IRA minimum investment* $250
available in all 50 states .... yes	*date of inception* .... April 1971
telephone exchanges .... yes	*dividend/income paid* .... monthly
number of funds in family 90	*average credit quality* .... BB

MainStay Hi-Yield Corporate B

260 Cherry Hill Road
Parsippany, NJ 07054
800-624-6782
www.mainstayfunds.com

total return	★★★★★
risk reduction	★★★★
management	★★★★
current income	★★★★★
expense control	★
symbol MKHCX	19 points
up-market performance	excellent
down-market performance	fair
predictability of returns	excellent

Total Return   ★★★★★

Over the past five years, MainStay Hi-Yield Corporate B has taken $10,000 and turned it into $16,105 ($12,250 over three years and $31,060 over the past 10 years). This translates into an annualized return of 10 percent over the past five years, 7 percent over the past three years, and 12 percent for the decade. Over the past five years, this fund has outperformed 60 percent of all mutual funds; within its general category it has done better than 93 percent of its peers. High-yield bond funds have averaged 8 percent annually over these same five years (all periods ending March 31, 2000).

During the past five years, a $10,000 initial investment became $9,660 after taxes, assuming a 39.6 percent income tax bracket (state and federal combined) and a capital gains rate of 28 percent. This means that investors in this fund were able to preserve 60 percent of their total returns. Compared to other fixed-income funds, this fund's tax savings are considered to be excellent.

Risk/Volatility   ★★★★

Over the past five years, MainStay has been safer than 95 percent of all high-yield bond funds. Over the past decade, the fund has had one negative year, while the Lehman Brothers Aggregate Bond Index has had two (off 3 percent in 1994 and 1 percent in 1999); the Credit Suisse High-Yield Bond Index fell twice (off 6 percent in 1990 and 1 percent in 1994). The fund has underperformed the Lehman Brothers Aggregate Bond Index twice and the Credit Suisse High-Yield Bond Index three times in the last 10 years.

	last 5 years		last 10 years	
worst year	1%	1998	-8%	1990
best year	20%	1995	32%	1991

In the past, MainStay has done better than 96 percent of its peer group in up markets and outperformed 40 percent of its competition in down markets.

Consistency, or predictability, of returns for MainStay can be described as excellent. This fund's risk-related return is very good.

Management   ★★★★
There are 300 fixed-income securities in this $3.7 billion portfolio. The average high-yield bond fund today is $310 million in size. Close to 75 percent of the fund's holdings are in bonds. The average maturity of the bonds in this account is eight years; the weighted coupon rate averages 7.9 percent. The portfolio's fixed-income holdings can be categorized as intermediate-term, low-quality debt. Two-thirds of the assets are in B-rated issues, followed by 15 percent in BB and 15 percent in issues rated below B.

    Steven Tananbaum and Don Morgan have managed this fund for the past seven years. Management prefers companies that have dominant franchises and strong financials. The fund invests in domestic and foreign debt, most of which is rated from BBB to B. During defensive periods the portfolio can invest more than a quarter of its assets in U.S. government securities. There are 81 funds besides Hi-Yield Corporate within the MainStay family. Overall, the fund family's risk-adjusted performance can be described as good.

Current Income   ★★★★★
Over the past year, MainStay had a 12-month yield of 10.8 percent. During this same 12-month period, the typical high-yield bond fund had a yield that averaged 9.2 percent.

Expenses   ★
MainStay's expense ratio is 1.8 percent; it has averaged 1.7 percent annually over the past three calendar years. The average expense ratio for the 330 funds in this category is 1.3 percent. This fund's turnover rate over the past year has been 125 percent, while its peer group average has been 105 percent.

Summary
MainStay Hi-Yield Corporate B has had exceptional risk-adjusted returns for the past five and 10 years. Raw returns have been quite good and current income has been extremely high. Overall tax minimization for the fund has been outstanding compared to the fund's peer group. This portfolio has outperformed 93 percent of its category while maintaining a below-average risk level.

Profile

minimum initial investment $500	*IRA accounts available* . . . . yes
subsequent minimum investment . . . $50	*IRA minimum investment* $500
available in all 50 states . . . . yes	*date of inception* . . . . May 1986
telephone exchanges . . . . yes	*dividend/income paid* . . . . monthly
number of funds in family 82	*average credit quality* . . . . B

MFS High-Income A

P.O. Box 2281
Boston, MA 02107
800-637-2929
www.mfs.com

total return	★★★★
risk reduction	★★★★
management	★★★★
current income	★★★★
expense control	★★★
symbol MHITX	19 points
up-market performance	excellent
down-market performance	fair
predictability of returns	excellent

Total Return   ★★★★

Over the past five years, MFS High-Income A has taken $10,000 and turned it into $15,390 ($12,250 over three years and $28,390 over the past 10 years). This translates into an annualized return of 9 percent over the past five years, 7 percent over the past three years, and 11 percent for the decade. Over the past five years, this fund has outperformed 55 percent of all mutual funds; within its general category it has done better than 78 percent of its peers. High-yield bond funds have averaged 8 percent annually over these same five years (all periods ending March 31, 2000).

During the past five years, a $10,000 initial investment became $9,080 after taxes, assuming a 39.6 percent income tax bracket (state and federal combined) and a capital gains rate of 28 percent. This means that investors in this fund were able to preserve 59 percent of their total returns. Compared to other fixed-income funds, this fund's tax savings are considered to be excellent.

Risk/Volatility   ★★★★

Over the past five years, MFS has been safer than 75 percent of all high-yield bond funds. Over the past decade, the fund has had two negative years, while the Lehman Brothers Aggregate Bond Index has also had two (off 3 percent in 1994 and 1 percent in 1999); the Credit Suisse High-Yield Bond Index fell twice (off 6 percent in 1990 and 1 percent in 1994). The fund has underperformed the Lehman Brothers Aggregate Bond Index and the Credit Suisse High-Yield Bond Index three times in the last 10 years.

	last 5 years		last 10 years	
worst year	1%	1998	-17%	1990
best year	17%	1995	49%	1991

In the past, MFS has done better than 90 percent of its peer group in up markets and outperformed 40 percent of its competition in down markets. Consistency, or predictability, of returns for MFS can be described as excellent. This fund's risk-related return is very good.

Management   ★★★★
There are 290 fixed-income securities in this $1.4 billion portfolio. The average high-yield bond fund today is $310 million in size. Close to 92 percent of the fund's holdings are in bonds. The average maturity of the bonds in this account is eight years; the weighted coupon rate averages 9.2 percent. The portfolio's fixed-income holdings can be categorized as intermediate-term, low-quality debt. Over 75 percent of the fund's assets are in B-rated issues, with another 10 percent rated BB and roughly 5 percent in nonrated bonds.

Robert Manning has managed this fund for the past seven years. Management has the flexibility to invest up to a quarter of the portfolio in equities and may also invest up to half its assets in foreign securities. Part of management's success has been its ability to underweight sectors that have not performed well in recent years. The fund has also done a particularly good job of individual security selection. There are 137 funds besides High-Income within the MFS family. Overall, the fund family's risk-adjusted performance can be described as good.

Current Income   ★★★★
Over the past year, MFS had a 12-month yield of 9.8 percent. During this same 12-month period, the typical high-yield bond fund had a yield that averaged 9.2 percent.

Expenses   ★★★
MFS's expense ratio is 1 percent; it has also averaged 1 percent annually over the past three calendar years. The average expense ratio for the 330 funds in this category is 1.3 percent. This fund's turnover rate over the past year has been 135 percent, while its peer group average has been 105 percent.

Summary
MFS High-Income A is one of the best high-yield bond funds. Management scores very well in every category. The fund has done extremely well during bull bond markets but has only done a fair job during debt market downturns. Despite such performance, the fund is still considered safer than three-fourths of its peer group.

Profile

minimum initial investment $1,000	*IRA accounts available* .... yes
subsequent minimum investment ... $50	*IRA minimum investment* $250
available in all 50 states .... yes	*date of inception* .... Jan. 1978
telephone exchanges .... yes	*dividend/income paid* .... monthly
number of funds in family 138	*average credit quality* .... B

Metals and Natural Resources Funds

These funds purchase metals in one or more of the following forms: bullion, South African gold stocks, and non–South African mining stocks. The United States, Canada, and Australia are the three major stock-issuing producers of metals outside of South Africa. Metals funds, also referred to as gold funds, often own minor positions in other precious metals stocks, such as silver and platinum.

The proportion and type of metal held by a fund can have a great impact on its performance and volatility. Outright ownership of gold bullion is almost always less volatile than owning stock in a gold mining company. Thus, much greater gains or losses occur in metals funds that purchase only gold stocks, compared to funds that hold high levels of bullion, coins, and stock. Silver, incidentally, has nearly twice the volatility of gold, yet has not enjoyed any greater returns over the long term.

Gold, or metals, funds can do well during periods of political uncertainty and inflationary concerns. Over the past several hundred years, gold and silver have served as hedges against inflation. Most readers will be surprised to learn that, historically, both metals have outperformed inflation by less than one percent annually.

Metals funds are the third riskiest category of mutual funds described in this book (technology stocks are number one and aggressive growth stocks are number two), with a standard deviation of 36—about 10 percent lower than the standard deviation of aggressive growth funds. And yet, although this is certainly a high-risk investment when viewed on its own, ownership of a metals fund can actually reduce a portfolio's overall risk level and often enhance its total return. Why? Because gold usually has a negative correlation to other investments. When the other investments go down in value, gold will often go up. Thus, a portfolio made up strictly of government bonds will actually exhibit more risk and less return than one made up of 90 percent government and 10 percent metals funds.

There are 40 metals funds; total market capitalization is less than $2 billion. Turnover has averaged 115 percent. The p/e ratio for metals funds is 31, while dividend yield is a little less than 0.5 percent. Over the past three years, these funds have averaged -20.6 percent per year, -12.5 percent for the last five years, -6.7 percent for the past decade, and -2.4 percent for the last 15 years.

Natural resources funds invest in the stocks of companies that deal in the ownership, production, transmission, transportation, refinement, and/or storage of oil, natural gas, and timber. These funds also invest in companies that either own or are involved in real estate.

There are 65 natural resources funds; total market capitalization is under $5 billion. This group has had a standard deviation of 30 percent over the past three years. Beta, or market-related risk, has been 0.8 percent, but do not let this low number fool you. As you can see by the standard deviation, few equity categories are riskier. Turnover has averaged 125 percent. The p/e ratio for natural resources funds is 34; dividend yield is 0.5 percent. Over the past 3 years, these funds have averaged 2.4 percent, 9.4 percent for the past 5 years, 7.7 percent for the last 10 years, and 9.5 percent for the past 15 years.

Metals and natural resources funds should be avoided by anyone who cannot tolerate wide price swings in any single part of his portfolio. These funds are designed as an integral part of a diversified portfolio, for investors who look at the overall return of their holdings. Despite the potential benefits of diversification, metals funds are still not recommended for the vast majority of investors. The track record for metals funds is simply terrible except for an occasional great year (for example, +81.1 percent in 1993) and variations of return are frequently wild.

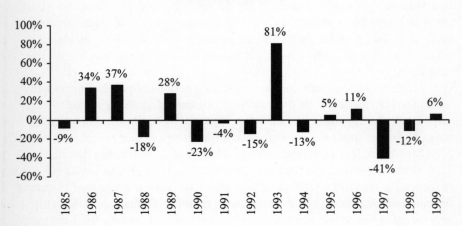

Precious Metals Funds

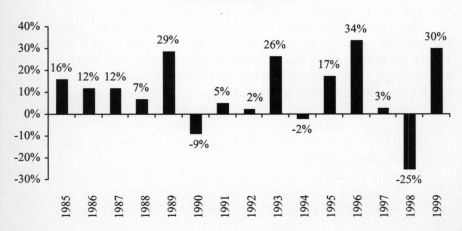

Natural Resources Funds

Franklin Gold A
777 Mariners Island Boulevard
San Mateo, CA 94403
800-342-5236
www.franklin-templeton.com

total return	★★★
risk reduction	★★★★
management	★★★★
tax minimization	★★★★★
expense control	★★★★★
symbol FKRCX	21 points
up-market performance	excellent
down-market performance	good
predictability of returns	poor

Total Return ★★★
Over the past five years, Franklin Gold A has taken $10,000 and turned it into $6,590 ($6,815 over three years and $7,370 over the past 10 years). This translates into an annualized return of -8 percent over the past five years, -12 percent over the past three years, and -3 percent for the decade. Over the past five years, this fund has done better than 77 percent of its peers. Metals and natural resources funds have averaged negative returns over these same five years (all periods ending March 31, 2000).

Risk/Volatility ★★★★
Over the past five years, Franklin Gold has been safer than 90 percent of all metals and natural resources funds. Over the past decade, the fund has had six negative years, while the S & P 500 has had one (off 3 percent in 1990). The fund has underperformed the S & P 500 eight times in the last 10 years.

	last 5 years		last 10 years	
worst year	-36%	1997	-36%	1997
best year	25%	1999	74%	1993

In the past, Franklin Gold has done better than 95 percent of its peer group in up markets and outperformed 55 percent of its competition in down markets. Consistency, or predictability, of returns for Franklin Gold can be described as poor. This fund's risk-related return is very good.

Management ★★★★
There are 35 stocks in this $200 million portfolio. The average metals and natural resources fund today is $68 million in size. Close to 99 percent of the fund's holdings are in stocks. The stocks in this portfolio have an average price-earnings (p/e) ratio of 37 and a median market capitalization of $4.8 billion. The portfolio's equity holdings can be categorized as mid-cap and value-oriented issues. Close to two-thirds of the portfolio is in industrial cyclical stocks. The fund has a correlation of

just roughly 15 percent to the S & P 500 (versus 10 percent for precious metals funds in general).

Martin Wiskemann has managed this fund for almost 20 years; Steve Land came on board as comanager in 1999. Management always invests at least 65 percent of its portfolio in companies involved with precious metals or their operations. Management diversification is largely based on a company's mine-life expectancy: long-life mines (greater than 20 years of reserves), medium-life mines (those with 10–20 years of reserves), platinum-mining, strategic metals mines, as well as mining finance firms. There are 78 funds besides Gold within the Franklin Templeton family. Overall, the fund family's risk-adjusted performance can be described as good.

Tax Minimization   ★★★★★
During the past five years, a $10,000 initial investment shrunk to $6,590 after taxes, assuming a 39.6 percent income tax bracket (state and federal combined) and a capital gains rate of 28 percent. This means that investors in this fund were able to preserve 100 percent of their total losses. Compared to other equity funds, this fund's tax savings are considered to be excellent.

Expenses   ★★★★★
Franklin's expense ratio is 1.3 percent; it has averaged 1.2 percent annually over the past three calendar years. The average expense ratio for the 105 funds in this category is 1.9 percent. This fund's turnover rate over the past year has been 4 percent, while its peer group average has been 120 percent.

Summary
Franklin Gold A is the only gold fund recommended in the book. Returns have been quite negative over the past several years, but the fund was up 25 percent in 1999 and 74 percent in 1993. Metals funds are not recommended for the vast majority of investors, but for those who somehow believe they should include this kind of diversification, this fund is the number one choice. The fund family includes a large number of other top-ranking funds and is particularly highly thought of in the area of fixed-income and international securities.

Profile
minimum initial investment $1,000	IRA accounts available . . . . yes
subsequent minimum investment $50	IRA minimum investment $250
available in all 50 states . . . . yes	date of inception . . . . . : . . . . May 1969
telephone exchanges . . . . yes	dividend/income paid . . . . annually
number of funds in family 79	largest sector weighting industrial cyclicals

Vanguard Energy

Vanguard Financial Center
P.O. Box 2600
Valley Forge, PA 19482
800-662-7447
www.vanguard.com

total return	★★★★★
risk reduction	★★★★★
management	★★★★★
tax minimization	★★★★
expense control	★★★★★
symbol VGENX	24 points
up-market performance	fair
down-market performance	good
predictability of returns	excellent

Total Return ★★★★★

Over the past five years, Vanguard Energy has taken $10,000 and turned it into $19,250 ($12,950 over three years and $25,940 over the past 10 years). This translates into an annualized return of 14 percent over the past five years, 9 percent over the past three years, and 10 percent for the decade. Over the past five years, this fund has outperformed 57 percent of all mutual funds; within its general category it has done better than 82 percent of its peers. Metals and natural resources funds have averaged negative returns over these same five years (all periods ending March 31, 2000).

Risk/Volatility ★★★★★

Over the past five years, Vanguard Energy has been safer than 65 percent of all metals and natural resources funds. Over the past decade, the fund has had three negative years, while the S & P 500 has had one (off 3 percent in 1990). The fund has underperformed the S & P 500 seven times in the last 10 years.

	last 5 years		last 10 years	
worst year	-21%	1998	-21%	1998
best year	34%	1996	34%	1996

In the past, Vanguard has done better than 35 percent of its peer group in up markets and outperformed 50 percent of its competition in down markets. Consistency, or predictability, of returns for Vanguard can be described as excellent. This fund's risk-related return is poor.

Management ★★★★★

There are 55 stocks in this $980 million portfolio. The average metals and natural resources fund today is $68 million in size. Close to 95 percent of the fund's holdings are in stocks. The stocks in this portfolio have an average price-earnings (p/e) ratio of 39 and a median market capitalization of $24 billion. Energy represents close to 70 percent of the fund's holdings, followed by industrial cyclicals (15 percent) and utilities (2 percent). The portfolio's equity holdings can be categorized as large-cap issues with a blend of growth and value stocks. The fund has a correlation of just 27 percent to the S & P 500 (versus 28 percent for energy and natural resources funds in general).

Ernst von Metzsch has managed this fund for the past 17 years. There are 77 funds besides Energy within the Vanguard family. Overall, the fund family's risk-adjusted performance can be described as very good.

Tax Minimization ★★★★

During the past five years, a $10,000 initial investment grew to $17,100 after taxes, assuming a 39.6 percent income tax bracket (state and federal combined) and a capital gains rate of 28 percent. This means that investors in this fund were able to preserve 89 percent of their total returns. Compared to other equity funds, this fund's tax savings are considered to be very good.

Expenses ★★★★★

Energy's expense ratio is .4 percent; it has also averaged .4 percent annually over the past three calendar years. The average expense ratio for the 105 funds in this category is 1.9 percent. This fund's turnover rate over the past year has been 19 percent, while its peer group average has been 120 percent.

Summary

Vanguard Energy realizes that it is difficult to find consistent growth in this sector so value is emphasized. Management seeks broad diversification within the energy group that includes domestic as well as foreign equities. The fund invests in producers, refiners, pipeline, tankers, and other related energy companies. This is the only fund recommended in its category. The fund receives an almost perfect score, 24 out of 25 possible points. Prospective investors should be extremely patient since this sector's performance is largely tied to oil and gas prices.

Profile

minimum initial investment $3,000	*IRA accounts available* . . . . yes
subsequent minimum investment . . $100	*IRA minimum investment* $1,000
available in all 50 states . . . . yes	*date of inception* . . . . May 1984
telephone exchanges . . . . yes	*dividend/income paid* . . . . annually
number of funds in family 78	*largest sector weighting* . . . . . . energy

Money Market Funds

Money market funds invest in securities that mature in less than one year. They are made up of one or more of the following instruments: Treasury bills, certificates of deposit, commercial paper, repurchase agreements, Euro-dollar CDs, and notes. There are four different categories of money market funds: all-purpose, government-backed, federally tax-free, and doubly tax-exempt.

All-purpose funds are the most popular and make up the bulk of the money market universe. Fully taxable, they are composed of securities such as CDs, commercial paper, and T-bills.

Government-backed money market funds invest only in short-term paper, directly or indirectly backed by the U.S. government. These funds are technically safer than the all-purpose variety, but only one money market fund has ever defaulted (a fund set up by a bank for banks). The yield on government-backed funds is somewhat lower than that of its all-purpose peers.

Federally tax-free funds are made up of municipal notes. Investors in these funds do not have to pay federal income taxes on the interest earned. The before-tax yield on federally tax-free funds is certainly lower than that of all-purpose and government-backed funds, but the after-tax return can be greater for the moderate- or high-tax-bracket investor.

Double-tax-exempt funds invest in the municipal obligations of a specific state. You must be a resident of that state in order to avoid paying state income taxes on any interest earned. Nonresident investors will still receive a federal tax exemption.

All money market funds are safer than any other mutual fund or category of funds in this book. They have a perfect track record (if you exclude the one money market fund set up for banks)—investors can only make money in these interest-bearing accounts. The rate of return earned in a money market depends upon the average maturity of the fund's paper, the kinds of securities held, the quality rating of that paper, and how efficiently the fund is operated. A lean fund will almost always outperform a similar fund with high operating costs.

Investments such as United States Treasury bills and, for all practical purposes, money market funds, are often referred to as "risk-free." These kinds of investments are free from price swings and default risk because of their composition. However, as we have come to learn, there is more than one form of risk. Money market funds should never be considered as a medium- or long-term investment. The real return on this investment is poor. An investment's real return takes into account the effects of inflation and income taxes. During virtually every period of time, the after-tax, after-inflation return on all money market funds has been near zero or even negative.

Over the past 50 years, United States Treasury bills—an index often used as a substitute for money market funds—have outperformed inflation on average 80 percent of the time over 1-year periods, 80 percent of the time over 5-year periods, 78 percent of the time over 10-year periods, 92 percent of the time over 15-year periods, and 97 percent over any given 20-year period of time. These figures are not adjusted for income taxes. Money market funds have rarely, if ever, outperformed inflation on an after-tax basis when looking at 3-, 5-, 10-, 15-, or 20-year holding positions.

Investors often look back to the good old days of the early 1980s, when money market funds briefly averaged 18 percent, and wish such times would come again. Well, those were not good times. During the early 1980s the top tax bracket, state and federal combined, was 55 percent. If you began with an 18-percent return and deducted taxes, many taxpayers saw their 18-percent return knocked down to about 9 percent. This may look great, especially for a "risk-free" investment, but we are not through yet. During the partial year in which money market accounts paid 18 percent, inflation was 12 percent. Now, if you take the 9-percent return and subtract 12 percent for inflation; the real return was actually –3 percent for the year. So much for the good old days.

Money market funds are the best place to park your money while you are looking at other investment alternatives or if you will be using the money during the next year. These funds can provide the convenience of check writing and a yield that is highly competitive with interest rates in general. These incredibly safe funds should only be considered for short-term periods or for regular expenditures, the way you would use a savings or checking account.

Since money market funds only came into existence for the general public in the mid-1970s, Treasury bills are often used as a substitute by those who wish to analyze the performance of these funds over a long period of time. The results are instructive. Since the beginning of 1950, a dollar invested in T-bills grew to $12.30 by the end of 1999. By the end of 1999, you would have needed $7.12 to equal the purchasing power of $1 at the beginning of 1950.

To give you a better sense of the cumulative effects of inflation, consider what a $100,000 investment in a money market fund would have to yield at the beginning of 2000 to equal the same purchasing power as the interest (or yield) from a $100,000 investment in a money market fund 20 years ago (1981). At the beginning of 2000, for instance, a $100,000 account held since 1981 would need to generate $10,280 to equal the same purchasing power as a $100,000 account yielding approximately 5.3 percent in 1981 (the average interest rate for money market accounts that year). The reality, however, is that at the beginning of 2000, money market funds were yielding 5 percent ($5,000 a year versus the $10,280 that would be required to maintain purchasing power).

You may have avoided stock investing in the past because "stocks are too risky." Yet it all depends upon how you define risk. As an example, in 1969 a $100,000 CD generated enough interest ($7,900) to buy a new, "fully loaded" Cadillac ($5,936) plus take a week-long cruise. As of the beginning of 1997, that same $100,000 CD would not generate enough income (CD rates were 4.95 percent) to buy one-eighth of the Cadillac ($4,950 versus $43,000 for the cost of a 1997 Cadillac Hardtop Sedan De Ville).

As a risk-reduction tool, the addition of a money market fund may be a worthwhile strategy. For the period between 1960 and 1996, a 50–50 mix of stocks and cash delivered 79 percent of the S & P's return, with half the volatility. A more aggressive mix of 60 percent stocks and 40 percent cash yielded 84 percent of the S & P's gains, with just 60 percent of the risk (as measured by standard deviation).

Over the past three years, taxable money market funds have had an average compound return of 4.9 percent per year. The annual return for the past five years has been 5.0 percent; and 4.8 percent for the past 10 years (all periods ending March 31, 2000). During these same time periods, tax-free money market funds had the following average annual returns: 3 percent for the past 3- and 5-year period and 3.1 percent for the last 10 years. The standard deviation for money market funds is lower than any other mutual fund category. This means that these funds have had less return variances than any other group. Close to 1,300 funds make up the money market category. Total market capitalization of this category is over $1.2 trillion.

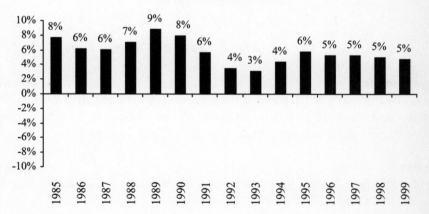

Taxable Money Market Funds

Fidelity Advisors Stable Value

82 Devonshire Street
Mail Zone F 9A
Boston, MA 02109
www.fidelity.com
800-526-0084

total return	★★★★★
risk reduction	★★★★★
management	★★★★★
expense control	★★★★★
symbol FTAAE	20 points

Total Return   ★★★★★

Over the past three years, Fidelity Advisor Stable Value has taken $10,000 and turned it into $11,851. This translates into an annualized return of 5.8 percent. Taxable money market funds have averaged 4.9 percent for the past three years (all periods ending March 31, 2000).

Risk/Volatility   ★★★★★

During the last three and five years, the fund's standard deviation has been .15 percent.

	last 3 years		last 10 years	
worst year	5.6%	1999	5.6%	1999
best year	6.0%	1997	6.0%	1997

Management   ★★★★★

The average maturity of the paper in the portfolio is approximately 2.9 years. The fund has been managed by Robert Middlebrook since 1996. The fund has outperformed its peer group average over the past 1, 3, 5, and 10 years.

Expenses   ★★★★★

The expense ratio for this $390 million fund is .03 percent. This means that for every $1,000 invested, $.30 goes to paying overhead.

Summary

Fidelity Advisor Stable Value is highly recommended. It has the lowest expense ratio of any money market fund.

Profile

minimum initial investment	$2,500	IRA accounts available	no
subsequent minimum investment	$100	IRA minimum investment	n/a
available in all 50 states	yes	date of inception	1988
telephone exchanges	yes	dividend/income paid	daily
number of funds in family	45		

Glenmede Government Cash

One Liberty Place
1650 Market Street, Suite 1200
Philadelphia, PA 19103
www.glenmede.com
800-442-8299

total return	★★★★★
risk reduction	★★★★★
management	★★★★★
expense control	★★★★★
symbol GTGXX	20 points

Total Return ★★★★★
Over the past five years, Glenmede Government Cash has taken $10,000 and turned it into $13,062 ($11,715 over three years). This translates into an annualized return of 5.4 percent over the past three years and 5.5 percent over the last five years. Government money market funds have averaged 4.9 percent for the past three and five years (all periods ending March 31, 2000).

Risk/Volatility ★★★★★
During the last three and five years, the fund's standard deviation has been .13 percent.

	last 5 years		last 10 years	
worst year	5.1%	1999	3.2%	1993
best year	5.9%	1995	8.3%	1990

Management ★★★★★
The average maturity of the paper in the portfolio is approximately 38 days. The fund has been managed by Mary Ann Wirts since 1996. The fund has outperformed its peer group average over the past 1, 3, 5, and 10 years.

Expenses ★★★★★
The expense ratio for this $390 million fund is .11 percent. This means that for every $1,000 invested, $1.10 goes to paying overhead.

Summary
Glenmede Government Cash is highly recommended.

Profile

minimum initial investment $25,000	*IRA accounts available* . . . . n/a
subsequent minimum investment . $1,000	*IRA minimum investment* . . . . n/a
available in all 50 states . . . . yes	*date of inception* 1988
telephone exchanges . . . . yes	*dividend/income paid* . . . . daily
number of funds in family 11	

Glenmede Tax-Exempt Cash

One Liberty Place
1650 Market St., Suite 1200
Philadelphia, PA 19103
www.glenmede.com
800-442-8299

total return	★★★★★
risk reduction	★★★★★
management	★★★★★
expense control	★★★★★
symbol GTCXX	20 points

Total Return   ★★★★★

Over the past five years, Glenmede Tax-Exempt Cash has taken $10,000 and turned it into $11,818 ($11,030 over three years). This translates into an annualized return of 3.3 percent over the past three and 3.4 percent over the last five years. Tax-free money market funds have averaged 2.9 percent for the past three years and 3.0 percent for the past five years (all periods ending March 31, 2000).

Risk/Volatility   ★★★★★

During the last three and five years, the fund's standard deviation has been .14 percent.

	last 5 years		last 10 years	
worst year	3.1%	1999	2.2%	1993
best year	3.8%	1995	5.9%	1990

Management   ★★★★★

The average maturity of the paper in the portfolio is approximately 37 days. The fund has been managed by May Ann Wirts since 1996. The fund has outperformed its peer group average over the past 1, 3, 5, and 10 years.

Expenses   ★★★★★

The expense ratio for this $420 million fund is .12 percent. This means that for every $1,000 invested, $1.20 goes to paying overhead.

Summary

Glenmede Tax-Exempt Cash is highly recommended.

Profile

minimum initial investment $25,000	*IRA accounts available* . . . . n/a
subsequent minimum investment . $1,000	*IRA minimum investment* . . . . n/a
available in all 50 states . . . . yes	*date of inception* 1988
telephone exchanges . . . . yes	*dividend/income paid* . . . . daily
number of funds in family 11	

Harris Insight Government Money N
103 Bellevue Parkway
WS-F103-04-07
Wilmington, DE 19809
www.harrisinsight.com
800-982-8782

total return	★★★★★
risk reduction	★★★★★
management	★★★★★
expense control	★★★★★
symbol HGCXX	20 points

Total Return   ★★★★★
Over the past five years, Harris Insight Government Money N has taken $10,000 and turned it into $12,999 ($11,692 over three years). This translates into an annualized return of 5.4 percent over the past three and five years. Government money market funds have averaged 4.9 percent for the past three and five years (all periods ending March 31, 2000).

Risk/Volatility   ★★★★★
During the last three and five years, the fund's standard deviation has been .13 percent.

	last 5 years		since inception	
worst year	5.0%	1999	5.0%	1990
best year	5.8%	1995	5.8%	1995

Management   ★★★★★
The average maturity of the paper in the portfolio is approximately 76 days. The fund has been comanaged by Randy T. Royther and Sanjay Patel since 1994. The fund has outperformed its peer group average over the past 1, 3, and 5 years.

Expenses   ★★★★★
The expense ratio for this $185 million fund is .19 percent. This means that for every $1,000 invested, $1.90 goes to paying overhead.

Summary
Harris Insight Government Money N is highly recommended.

Profile

minimum initial investment $1,000	*IRA accounts available* . . . . yes
subsequent minimum investment . . . $50	*IRA minimum investment* $250
available in all 50 states . . . . yes	*date of inception* 1994
telephone exchanges . . . . yes	*dividend/income paid* . . . . daily
number of funds in family 18	

Trust for Credit Unions Money Market
4900 Sears Tower
Chicago, IL 60606
800-621-2550

total return	★★★★★
risk reduction	★★★★★
management	★★★★★
expense control	★★★★★
symbol TCUXX	20 points

Total Return   ★★★★★
Over the past five years, Trust for Credit Unions (TCU) Money Market has taken $10,000 and turned it into $13,072 ($11,731 over three years). This translates into an annualized return of 5.5 percent over the past three and five years. Taxable money market funds have averaged 5.5 percent for the past three and five years (all periods ending March 31, 2000).

Risk/Volatility   ★★★★★
During the last three and five years, the fund's standard deviation has been .13 percent.

	last 5 years		last 10 years	
worst year	5.1%	1999	3.1%	1993
best year	5.9%	1995	8.3%	1990

Management   ★★★★★
The average maturity of the paper in the portfolio is approximately 18 days. The fund has been comanaged by Beinner, Dion, Clark, and McCarthy since 1988. The fund has outperformed its peer group average over the past 1, 3, 5, and 10 years.

Expenses   ★★★★★
The expense ratio for this $800 million fund is .13 percent. This means that for every $1,000 invested, $1.30 goes to paying overhead.

Summary
TCU Money Market is highly recommended. This fund is only available to credit union members.

Profile

minimum initial investment $1	IRA accounts available. . . . . no
subsequent minimum investment $1	IRA minimum investment . . . . n/a
available in all 50 states . . . . yes	date of inception. 1988
telephone exchanges. . . . . yes	dividend/income paid . . . . daily
number of funds in family . . . . n/a	

Vanguard Municipal Tax-Exempt Money Market

P.O. Box 2600
Valley Forge, PA 19482
800-635-1511
www.vanguard.com

total return	★★★★★
risk reduction	★★★★★
management	★★★★★
expense control	★★★★★
symbol VMSXX	20 points

Total Return ★★★★★
Over the past five years, Vanguard Municipal Tax-Exempt Money Market has taken $10,000 and turned it into $11,835 ($11,041 over three years). This translates into an annualized return of 3.4 percent over the past three and five years. Tax-Free money market funds have averaged 2.9 percent for the past three years and 3.0 percent for the past five years (all periods ending March 31, 2000).

Risk/Volatility ★★★★★
During the last three and five years, the fund's standard deviation has been .14 percent.

	last 5 years		last 10 years	
worst year	3.2%	1999	2.4%	1993
best year	3.8%	1995	5.8%	1990

Management ★★★★★
The average maturity of the paper in the portfolio is approximately 66 days. The fund has been managed by Pamela Wisehaupt Tynan since 1988. The fund has outperformed its peer group average over the past 1, 3, 5, and 10 years.

Expenses ★★★★★
The expense ratio for this $7.5 billion fund is .18 percent. This means that for every $1,000 invested, $1.80 goes to paying overhead.

Summary
Vanguard Municipal Tax-Exempt Money Market is highly recommended.

Profile
minimum initial investment $3,000
subsequent minimum investment . . $100
available in all 50 states . . . . yes
telephone exchanges . . . . yes
number of funds in family 78

IRA accounts available . . . . yes
IRA minimum investment $1,000
date of inception 1980
dividend/income paid . . . . daily

Wells Fargo Money Market Trust

525 Market St., 12th Floor
MAC 0103-121
San Francisco, CA 94105
800-222-8222
www.wellsfargo.com

total return	★★★★★
risk reduction	★★★★★
management	★★★★★
expense control	★★★★★
symbol SCCME	20 points

Total Return   ★★★★★

Over the past five years, Wells Fargo Money Market Trust has taken $10,000 and turned it into $13,067 ($11,730 over three years). This translates into an annualized return of 5.4 percent over the past three years and 5.5 percent for the last five years. Taxable money market funds have averaged 5.5 percent for the past three and five years (all periods ending March 31, 2000).

Risk/Volatility   ★★★★★

During the last three and five years, the fund's standard deviation has been .14 percent.

	last 5 years		last 9 years	
worst year	5.2%	1999	2.8%	1993
best year	5.8%	1995	5.8%	1995

Management   ★★★★★

The average maturity of the paper in the portfolio is approximately 78 days. The fund has been managed by Wells Fargo Investment Management since 1990. The fund has outperformed its peer group average over the past 1, 3, 5, and 9 years.

Expenses   ★★★★★

The expense ratio for this $550 million fund is .20 percent. This means that for every $1,000 invested, $2.00 goes to paying overhead.

Summary

Wells Fargo Money Market Trust is highly recommended.

Profile

minimum initial investment $1,000	*IRA accounts available* . . . . no
subsequent minimum investment . . $100	*IRA minimum investment* . . . . n/a
available in all 50 states . . . . yes	*date of inception* 1990
telephone exchanges . . . . yes	*dividend/income paid* . . . . daily
number of funds in family 61	

Municipal Bond Funds

Municipal bond funds invest in securities issued by municipalities, political subdivisions, and U.S. territories. The type of security issued is either a note or bond, both of which are interest-bearing instruments that are exempt from federal income taxes. There are three different categories of municipal bond funds: national, state-free, and high-yield.

National municipal bond funds are made up of debt instruments issued by a wide range of states. These funds are exempt from federal income taxes only. To determine what small percentage is also exempt from state income taxes, consult the fund's prospectus and look for the weighting of U.S. territory issues (U.S. Virgin Islands, Guam, Puerto Rico), District of Columbia items, and obligations from your state of residence.

State-free funds, sometimes referred to as "double tax-free funds," invest only in bonds and notes issued in a particular state. You must be a legal resident of that state in order to avoid paying state income taxes on the fund's return. For example, most California residents who are in a high tax bracket will only want to consider purchasing a municipal bond fund that has the name "California" in it. Residents of New York who purchase a California tax-free fund will escape federal income taxes but not state taxes.

High-yield tax-free funds invest in the same kinds of issues found in a national municipal bond fund but with one important difference. By seeking higher returns, high-yield funds look for lower-rated or nonrated notes and bonds. A municipality may decide not to obtain a rating for its issue because of the costs involved compared to the relatively small size of the bond or note being floated. Many nonrated issues are very safe. High-yield municipal bond funds are relatively new but should not be overlooked by the tax-conscious investor. These kinds of tax-free funds have demonstrated less volatility and higher return than their other tax-free counterparts.

Prospective investors need to compare tax-free bond yields to after-tax yields on corporate or government bond funds. To determine which of these three fund categories is best for you, use your marginal tax bracket, subtract this amount from one, and multiply the resulting figure by the taxable investment. For instance, suppose you were in the 35-percent bracket, state and federal combined. By subtracting this figure from 1, you are left with 0.65. Multiply 0.65 by the fully taxable yield you could get, let us say 9 percent. Sixty-five percent of 9 percent is 5.85 percent. The 5.85 percent represents what you get on a 9-percent investment after you have paid state and federal income taxes on it. This means that if you can get 5.85 percent or higher from a tax-free investment, take it.

Interest paid on tax-free investments is generally lower than interest paid on taxable investments like corporate bonds and bank CDs. But you should compare the yields on tax-free investments to taxable investments only after you have considered the municipal bond fund's tax-free advantage. The result will be the taxable equivalent yield—the yield you will have to get on a similar taxable investment to equal the tax-free yield. If the example above was not clear, look at the next table.

2000 Federal Income Tax Rates Plus Tax-Free Yields
Versus Equivalent Taxable Yields

if your taxable income is...		...then your marginal federal 2000 tax rate is...	and, for you a tax-free yield of:			
			3%	4%	5%	6%
single	joint		is equivalent to a taxable yield of:			
$0-26,250	$0-43,850	15.0%	3.5%	4.7%	5.9%	7.1%
26,251-63,550	43,851-105,950	28.0	4.2	5.6	6.9	8.3
63,551-132,600	105,951-161,450	31.0	4.3	5.8	7.2	8.7
132,601-288,350	161,451-288,350	36.0	4.7	6.3	7.8	9.4
over $288,350	over $288,350	39.6	5.0	6.6	8.3	9.9

As you can see from the table above, if you're in the 36-percent federal tax bracket, a taxable investment would have to yield 7.8 percent to give you the same after-tax income as a tax-free yield of 5.0 percent.

Municipal bond funds are not for investors who are in a low tax bracket. If such investors want to be in bonds, they would be better off in corporates or government issues. Furthermore, municipals should never be used in a retirement plan. There is only one way to make tax-free income taxable and that is to put it into a traditional IRA, pension, or profit-sharing plan. Everything that comes out of these plans is fully taxable by the federal government.

Over the past three and five years, the typical municipal bond fund has had an average compounded annual return of 4.1 and 4.8 percent respectively. They have averaged a total annual return (current yield plus bond appreciation or minus bond depreciation) of 6.3 percent over the past 10 years and 7.5 percent annually for the last 15 years. Municipal bond fund returns have been fairly stable over the past three years, having a standard deviation of 3 percent.

Nineteen hundred funds make up the municipal bond category. Total market capitalization of all municipal bond funds is $270 billion. Close to 98 percent of a typical municipal bond fund's portfolio is in tax-free bonds, with the balance in tax-free money market instruments. Close to 1,300 of the 1,900 municipal bond funds offered are single-state funds.

The typical municipal bond fund yields 4.6 percent in tax-free income each year. The average weighted maturity is 13 years. Expenses for this category are 1.0 percent each year.

As you read through the descriptions of the municipal bond funds selected, you will notice a paragraph in each describing the tax efficiency of the portfolio. This may surprise you, because municipal bonds are supposed to be tax-free. Keep in mind that only the income (current yield) from these instruments is free from federal income taxes (and often state income taxes, depending on the fund in question and your state of residence). Since bond funds generally have a high turnover rate (which triggers a potential capital gain or loss upon each sale of a security by the portfolio manager), there are capital gains considerations with municipal bonds.

Municipal Bond Funds

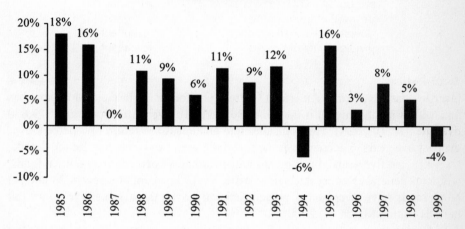

American Century California High-Yield Municipal
4500 Main Street
P.O. Box 419200
Kansas City, MO 64141
800-345-2021
www.americancentury.com

total return	★★★★★
risk reduction	★★★
management	★★★★
current income	★★★★
expense control	★★★★★
symbol BCHYX	21 points
up-market performance	good
down-market performance	excellent
predictability of returns	excellent

Total Return   ★★★★★
Over the past five years, American Century California High-Yield Municipal has taken $10,000 and turned it into $14,030 ($11,910 over three years and $19,670 over the past 10 years). This translates into an annualized return of 7 percent over the past five years, 6 percent over the past three years, and 7 percent for the decade. Over the past five years, this fund has outperformed 45 percent of all mutual funds; within its general category it has done better than 93 percent of its peers. Municipal bond funds have averaged 5 percent annually over these same five years (all periods ending March 31, 2000).

During the past five years, a $10,000 initial investment grew to $13,770 after taxes, assuming a 39.6 percent income tax bracket (state and federal combined) and a capital gains rate of 28 percent. This means that investors in this fund were able to preserve 98 percent of their total returns. Compared to other fixed-income funds, this fund's tax savings are considered to be excellent.

Risk/Volatility   ★★★
Over the past five years, California High-Yield has been safer than 96 percent of all municipal bond funds. Over the past decade, the fund has had two negative years, while the Lehman Brothers Aggregate Bond Index has also had two (off 3 percent in 1994 and 1 percent in 1999); the Lehman Brothers Municipal Bond Index also fell twice (off 5 percent in 1994 and 2 percent in 1999). The fund has underperformed the Lehman Brothers Aggregate Bond Index six times and the Lehman Brothers Municipal Bond Index four times in the last 10 years.

	last 5 years		last 10 years	
worst year	-3%	1999	-5%	1994
best year	18%	1995	18%	1995

In the past, California High-Yield has done better than 45 percent of its peer group in up markets and outperformed 96 percent of its competition in down markets.

Consistency, or predictability, of returns for California High-Yield can be described as excellent. This fund's risk-related return is good.

Management ★★★★
There are 160 fixed-income securities in this $300 million portfolio. The average municipal bond fund today is $150 million in size. Close to 100 percent of the fund's holdings are in bonds. The average maturity of the bonds in this account is 20 years; the weighted coupon rate averages 6.1 percent. The portfolio's fixed-income holdings can be categorized as long-term and intermediate-quality debt. Over half of the fund is invested in nonrated issues; another 20 percent is in AAA-rated paper followed by 15-percent in A rated bonds and 10 percent in BBB-rated debt instruments.

A team has managed this fund for the past 14 years. Lead manager Steven Permut has done a particularly good job of identifying individual securities. He avoids making interest rate bets. Management has been quite astute and accurate in a tricky marketplace—high-yield tax-free bonds. There are 86 funds besides California High-Yield within the American Century family. Overall, the fund family's risk-adjusted performance can be described as very good.

Current Income ★★★★
Over the past year, California High-Yield had a 12-month yield of 5.6 percent. During this same 12-month period, the typical municipal bond fund had a yield that averaged 4.4 percent.

Expenses ★★★★★
California High-Yield's expense ratio is .5 percent; it has also averaged .5 percent annually over the past three calendar years. The average expense ratio for the 1,900 funds in this category is 1.0 percent. This fund's turnover rate over the past year has been 55 percent, while its peer group average has been 40 percent.

Summary
American Century California High-Yield Municipal has ranked in the top quartile of performance for each of the past four years. The fund's risk-adjusted returns have been marvelous, whether you are looking at the past 3, 5, or 10 years. This is the number two performing municipal bond fund in the book and number one for California residents.

Profile
minimum initial investment $5,000	*IRA accounts available* .... no
subsequent minimum investment ... $50	*IRA minimum investment* .... n/a
available in all 50 states .... yes	*date of inception* .... Dec. 1986
telephone exchanges .... yes	*dividend/income paid* .... monthly
number of funds in family 87	*average credit quality* .... NR

American High-Income Municipal Bond

333 South Hope Street
Los Angeles, CA 90071
800-421-4120
www.americanfunds.com

total return	★★★★
risk reduction	★★★★★
management	★★★★★
current income	★★★★
expense control	★★★★★
symbol AMHIX	23 points
up-market performance	very good
down-market performance	poor
predictability of returns	excellent

Total Return   ★★★★

Over the past five years, American High-Income Municipal Bond has taken
$10,000 and turned it into $13,380 ($11,250 over three years). This translates into
an annualized return of 6 percent over the past five years and 4 percent over the
past three years. Over the past five years, this fund has outperformed 45 percent of
all mutual funds; within its general category it has done better than 99 percent of
its peers. Municipal bond funds have averaged 5 percent annually over these same
five years (all periods ending March 31, 2000).

During the past five years, a $10,000 initial investment grew to $12,980 after
taxes, assuming a 39.6 percent income tax bracket (state and federal combined) and
a capital gains rate of 28 percent. This means that investors in this fund were able
to preserve 97 percent of their total returns. Compared to other fixed-income funds,
this fund's tax savings are considered to be excellent.

Risk/Volatility   ★★★★★

Over the past five years, High-Income Municipal has been safer than 95 percent of
all municipal bond funds. Since its inception, the fund has had one negative year,
while the Lehman Brothers Aggregate Bond Index has had two (off 3 percent in
1994 and 1 percent in 1999); the Lehman Brothers Municipal Bond Index also fell
twice (off 5 percent in 1994 and 2 percent in 1999). The fund has underperformed
the Lehman Brothers Aggregate Bond Index twice and the Lehman Brothers
Municipal Bond Index twice since the fund's inception.

	last 5 years		since inception	
worst year	-2%	1999	-2%	1999
best year	19%	1995	19%	1995

In the past, High-Income Municipal has done better than 80 percent of its peer
group in up markets and outperformed 20 percent of its competition in down markets. Consistency, or predictability, of returns for High-Income Municipal can be
described as excellent. This fund's risk-related return is good.

Management ★★★★★

There are 290 fixed-income securities in this $550 million portfolio. The average municipal bond fund today is $150 million in size. Close to 97 percent of the fund's holdings are in bonds. The average maturity of the bonds in this account is 10 years; the weighted coupon rate averages 6.6 percent. The portfolio's fixed-income holdings can be categorized as long-term, medium-quality debt. Close to 40 percent of the portfolio is in BBB-rated paper, followed by 25 percent in BB, 15 percent in B, and 10 percent in AAA-rated debt instruments.

A team has managed this fund for the past six years. Management spreads its risk by investing in literally hundreds of different issues. The portfolio's diversification as to issuer and maturity have served it well. There are 28 funds besides High-Income Municipal within the American Funds family. Overall, the fund family's risk-adjusted performance can be described as very good.

Current Income ★★★★

Over the past year, High-Income Municipal had a 12-month yield of 5.5 percent. During this same 12-month period, the typical municipal bond fund had a yield that averaged 4.4 percent.

Expenses ★★★★★

High-Income Municipal's expense ratio is .8 percent; it has also averaged .8 percent annually over the past three calendar years. The average expense ratio for the 1,900 funds in this category is 1.0 percent. This fund's turnover rate over the past year has been 15 percent, while its peer group average has been 40 percent.

Summary

American High-Income Municipal Bond has had very good risk-adjusted returns over the past three years and superb results over the past five years. The fund has also outperformed 99 percent of its peer group. The fund's high-caliber management has done a super job when it comes to keeping overhead and turnover low; however, risk management is where this fund really shines—no small accomplishment when you consider the nature of the portfolio. Overall, this is the highest-rated tax-free bond fund in the book.

Profile

minimum initial investment $1,000	*IRA accounts available* .... yes
subsequent minimum investment ... $50	*IRA minimum investment* $250
available in all 50 states .... yes	*date of inception* .... Sept. 1994
telephone exchanges .... yes	*dividend/income paid* .... monthly
number of funds in family 29	*average credit quality* .... BBB

Franklin High Yield Tax-Free Income A

777 Mariners Island Boulevard
San Mateo, CA 94403
800-342-5236
www.franklin-templeton.com

total return	★★★★
risk reduction	★★★★
management	★★★★
current income	★★★★★
expense control	★★★★★
symbol FRHIX	22 points
up-market performance	very good
down-market performance	fair
predictability of returns	excellent

Total Return   ★★★★

Over the past five years, Franklin High Yield Tax-Free Income A has taken
$10,000 and turned it into $13,380 ($11,580 over three years and $19,670 over the
past 10 years). This translates into an annualized return of 6 percent over the past
five years, 5 percent over the past three years, and 7 percent for the decade. Over
the past five years, this fund has outperformed 42 percent of all mutual funds;
within its general category it has done better than 86 percent of its peers. Municipal
bond funds have averaged 5 percent annually over these same five years (all
periods ending March 31, 2000).

During the past five years, a $10,000 initial investment grew to $13,380 after
taxes, assuming a 39.6 percent income tax bracket (state and federal combined) and
a capital gains rate of 28 percent. This means that investors in this fund were able
to preserve 100 percent of their total returns. Compared to other fixed-income
funds, this fund's tax savings are considered to be excellent.

Risk/Volatility   ★★★★

Over the past five years, High Yield Tax-Free has been safer than 99 percent of all
municipal bond funds. Over the past decade, the fund has had two negative years,
while the Lehman Brothers Aggregate Bond Index has also had two (off 3 percent
in 1994 and 1 percent in 1999); the Lehman Brothers Municipal Bond Index also
fell twice (off 5 percent in 1994 and 2 percent in 1999). The fund has underperformed the Lehman Brothers Aggregate Bond Index five times and the Lehman
Brothers Municipal Bond Index four times in the last 10 years.

	last 5 years		last 10 years	
worst year	-3%	1999	-3%	1999
best year	16%	1995	16%	1995

In the past, High Yield Tax-Free has done better than 70 percent of its peer group
in up markets and outperformed 30 percent of its competition in down markets.

Consistency, or predictability, of returns for High Yield Tax-Free can be described as excellent. This fund's risk-related return is good.

Management ★★★★

There are 930 fixed-income securities in this $6.5 billion portfolio. The average municipal bond fund today is $150 million in size. Close to 99 percent of the fund's holdings are in bonds. The average maturity of the bonds in this account is 20 years; the weighted coupon rate averages 6.4 percent. The portfolio's fixed-income holdings can be categorized as long-term, medium-quality debt. Roughly a quarter of the fund is in AAA-rated issues, with another 20 percent in BBB and 25 percent in nonrated debt instruments.

Sheila Amoroso has managed this fund for the past 14 years. Management has been able to keep risk exposure very low by investing in close to 1,000 different issues. The fund's manager has one of the country's best bond research teams behind her. There are 78 funds besides High Yield Tax-Free within the Franklin Templeton family. Overall, the fund family's risk-adjusted performance can be described as good.

Current Income ★★★★★

Over the past year, High Yield Tax-Free had a 12-month yield of 6.1 percent. During this same 12-month period, the typical municipal bond fund had a yield that averaged 4.4 percent.

Expenses ★★★★★

High Yield Tax-Free's expense ratio is .6 percent; it has also averaged .6 percent annually over the past three calendar years. The average expense ratio for the 1,900 funds in this category is 1.0 percent. This fund's turnover rate over the past year has been 15 percent, while its peer group average has been 40 percent.

Summary

Franklin High Yield Tax-Free Income A has a lot to brag about. First, the fund has the highest possible ranking for risk-adjusted returns for the past 3, 5, and 10 years. Second, turnover and expenses are extremely low. Third, current income is quite high. Fourth, the portfolio has been safer than 99 percent of its peer group. This is a highly recommended fund.

Profile

minimum initial investment $1,000	*IRA accounts available* .... yes
subsequent minimum investment ... $50	*IRA minimum investment* $250
available in all 50 states .... yes	*date of inception* .... March 1986
telephone exchanges .... yes	*dividend/income paid* .... monthly
number of funds in family 79	*average credit quality* .... BBB

Franklin New York Tax-Free Income A

777 Mariners Island Boulevard
San Mateo, CA 94403
800-342-5236
www.franklin-templeton.com

total return	★★★★
risk reduction	★★★★★
management	★★★★★
current income	★★★★
expense control	★★★★★
symbol FNYTX	23 points
up-market performance	excellent
down-market performance	excellent
predictability of returns	excellent

Total Return   ★★★★

Over the past five years, Franklin New York Tax-Free Income A has taken $10,000 and turned it into $13,380 ($11,580 over three years and $19,670 over the past 10 years). This translates into an annualized return of 6 percent over the past five years, 5 percent over the past three years, and 7 percent for the decade. Over the past five years, this fund has outperformed 29 percent of all mutual funds; within its general category it has done better than 96 percent of its peers. Municipal bond funds have averaged 5 percent annually over these same five years (all periods ending March 31, 2000).

During the past five years, a $10,000 initial investment grew to $13,210 after taxes, assuming a 39.6 percent income tax bracket (state and federal combined) and a capital gains rate of 28 percent. This means that investors in this fund were able to preserve 99 percent of their total returns. Compared to other fixed-income funds, this fund's tax savings are considered to be excellent.

Risk/Volatility   ★★★★★

Over the past five years, New York Tax-Free has been safer than 95 percent of all municipal bond funds. Over the past decade, the fund has had two negative years, while the Lehman Brothers Aggregate Bond Index has also had two (off 3 percent in 1994 and 1 percent in 1999); the Lehman Brothers Municipal Bond Index also fell twice (off 5 percent in 1994 and 2 percent in 1999). The fund has underperformed the Lehman Brothers Aggregate Bond Index seven times and the Lehman Brothers Municipal Bond Index five times in the last 10 years.

	last 5 years		last 10 years	
worst year	-2%	1999	-4%	1994
best year	14%	1995	14%	1995

In the past, New York Tax-Free has done better than 97 percent of its peer group in up markets and outperformed 95 percent of its competition in down markets.

Consistency, or predictability, of returns for New York Tax-Free can be described as excellent. This fund's risk-related return is very good.

Management ★★★★★

There are 46 fixed-income securities in this $4.5 billion portfolio. The average municipal bond fund today is $150 million in size. Close to 100 percent of the fund's holdings are in bonds. The average maturity of the bonds in this account is 18 years; the weighted coupon rate averages 6.2 percent. The portfolio's fixed-income holdings can be categorized as long-term, high-quality debt. Over 45 percent of the fund is in AAA-rated bonds, followed by 20 percent in A-rated paper, 15 percent in BBB, and 15 percent in AA-rated debt instruments.

Sheila Amoroso and Mark Orsi have managed this fund for the past 11 years. Close to 97 percent of the portfolio is in New York tax-free bonds. The portfolio has a large amount of higher coupon paper that is less sensitive to interest rate changes. Management favors a buy-and-hold approach to investing. There are 78 funds besides New York Tax-Free within the Franklin Templeton family. Overall, the fund family's risk-adjusted performance can be described as good.

Current Income ★★★★

Over the past year, New York Tax-Free had a 12-month yield of 5.6 percent. During this same 12-month period, the typical municipal bond fund had a yield that averaged 4.4 percent.

Expenses ★★★★★

New York Tax-Free's expense ratio is .6 percent; it has also averaged .6 percent annually over the past three calendar years. The average expense ratio for the 1,900 funds in this category is 1.0 percent. This fund's turnover rate over the past year has been 10 percent, while its peer group average has been 40 percent.

Summary

Franklin New York Tax-Free Income A has had amazingly good risk-adjusted returns over the past 3, 5, and 10 years. The fund's expenses are quite low, and this helps give investors a comparatively high current income. This fund has been safer than 95 percent of its peers but has managed to outperform 96 percent of its category. This is the only New York municipal bond fund recommended in the book.

Profile

minimum initial investment $1,000	*IRA accounts available* .... no
subsequent minimum investment ... $50	*IRA minimum investment* .... n/a
available in all 50 states .... yes	*date of inception* .... Sept. 1982
telephone exchanges .... yes	*dividend/income paid* .... monthly
number of funds in family 79	*average credit quality* .... AA

Scudder Managed Municipal Bonds

Two International Place
Boston, MA 02110
800-225-2470
www.scudder.com

total return	★★★★
risk reduction	★★★
management	★★★★
current income	★★★★
expense control	★★★★★
symbol SCMBX	20 points
up-market performance	very good
down-market performance	excellent
predictability of returns	very good

Total Return ★★★★

Over the past five years, Scudder Managed Municipal Bonds has taken $10,000 and turned it into $13,380 ($11,580 over three years and $19,672 over the past 10 years). This translates into an annualized return of 6 percent over the past five years, 5 percent over the past three years, and 7 percent for the decade. Over the past five years, this fund has outperformed 39 percent of all mutual funds; within its general category it has done better than 94 percent of its peers. Municipal bond funds have averaged 5 percent annually over these same five years (all periods ending March 31, 2000).

During the past five years, a $10,000 initial investment grew to $13,250 after taxes, assuming a 39.6 percent income tax bracket (state and federal combined) and a capital gains rate of 28 percent. This means that investors in this fund were able to preserve 99 percent of their total returns. Compared to other fixed-income funds, this fund's tax savings are considered to be excellent.

Risk/Volatility ★★★

Over the past five years, Managed Municipal has been safer than 85 percent of all municipal bond funds. Over the past decade, the fund has had two negative years, while the Lehman Brothers Aggregate Bond Index has also had two (off 3 percent in 1994 and 1 percent in 1999); the Lehman Brothers Municipal Bond Index also fell twice (off 5 percent in 1994 and 2 percent in 1999). The fund has underperformed the Lehman Brothers Aggregate Bond Index seven times and the Lehman Brothers Municipal Bond Index five times in the last 10 years.

	last 5 years		last 10 years	
worst year	-2%	1999	-6%	1994
best year	17%	1995	17%	1995

In the past, Managed Municipal has done better than 75 percent of its peer group in up markets and outperformed 95 percent of its competition in down markets.

Consistency, or predictability, of returns for Managed Municipal can be described as very good. This fund's risk-related return is good.

Management   ★★★★
There are 150 fixed-income securities in this $400 million portfolio. The average municipal bond fund today is $150 million in size. Close to 100 percent of the fund's holdings are in bonds. The average maturity of the bonds in this account is 11 years; the weighted coupon rate averages 5.4 percent. The portfolio's fixed-income holdings can be categorized as long-term, high-quality debt. Close to 40 percent of the portfolio is rated AAA, followed by 25 percent in BBB, 20 percent nonrated, 10 percent AA, and 10 percent rated A.

Philip Condon has managed this fund for 14 years; Ashton Goodfield came on board as comanager three years ago. Management favors lower-rated bonds more than its peers, which has aided in the portfolio's performance. There are 38 funds besides Managed Municipal within the Scudder family. Overall, the fund family's risk-adjusted performance can be described as good.

Current Income   ★★★★
Over the past year, Managed Municipal had a 12-month yield of 5.3 percent. During this same 12-month period, the typical municipal bond fund had a yield that averaged 4.4 percent.

Expenses   ★★★★★
Managed Municipal's expense ratio is .6 percent; it has also averaged .6 percent annually over the past three calendar years. The average expense ratio for the 1,900 funds in this category is 1.0 percent. This fund's turnover rate over the past year has been 8 percent, while its peer group average has been 40 percent.

Summary
Scudder Managed Municipal Bonds has enjoyed excellent risk-adjusted returns over the past 3, 5, and 10 years. The fund has finished in the top quartile of performance for its category for each of the past five years. Expenses are low and so is turnover; these are two important elements for bond funds in general. The fund scores well in every department, but management has done a particularly commendable job when it comes to down-market performance.

Profile
minimum initial investment $2,500	*IRA accounts available* .... yes
subsequent minimum investment .. $100	*IRA minimum investment* $1,000
available in all 50 states .... yes	*date of inception* .... Oct. 1976
telephone exchanges .... yes	*dividend/income paid* .... monthly
number of funds in family 39	*average credit quality* .... AA

T. Rowe Price Tax-Free Income
100 East Pratt Street
Baltimore, MD 21202
800-638-5660
www.troweprice.com

total return	★★★★
risk reduction	★★★
management	★★★★
current income	★★★★
expense control	★★★★★
symbol PRTAX	20 points
up-market performance	excellent
down-market performance	poor
predictability of returns	very good

Total Return   ★★★★
Over the past five years, T. Rowe Price Tax-Free Income has taken $10,000 and turned it into $13,380 ($11,580 over three years and $19,670 over the past 10 years). This translates into an annualized return of 6 percent over the past five years, 5 percent over the past three years, and 7 percent for the decade. Over the past five years, this fund has outperformed 36 percent of all mutual funds; within its general category it has done better than 70 percent of its peers. Municipal bond funds have averaged 5 percent annually over these same five years (all periods ending March 31, 2000).

During the past five years, a $10,000 initial investment grew to $13,380 after taxes, assuming a 39.6 percent income tax bracket (state and federal combined) and a capital gains rate of 28 percent. This means that investors in this fund were able to preserve 100 percent of their total returns. Compared to other fixed-income funds, this fund's tax savings are considered to be excellent.

Risk/Volatility   ★★★
Over the past five years, Tax-Free Income has been safer than 70 percent of all municipal bond funds. Over the past decade, the fund has had two negative years, while the Lehman Brothers Aggregate Bond Index has also had two (off 3 percent in 1994 and 1 percent in 1999); the Lehman Brothers Municipal Bond Index also fell twice (off 5 percent in 1994 and 2 percent in 1999). The fund has underperformed the Lehman Brothers Aggregate Bond Index eight times and the Lehman Brothers Municipal Bond Index five times in the last 10 years.

	last 5 years		last 10 years	
worst year	-4%	1999	-5%	1994
best year	18%	1995	18%	1995

In the past, Tax-Free Income has done better than 95 percent of its peer group in up markets and outperformed 20 percent of its competition in down markets.

Consistency, or predictability, of returns for Tax-Free Income can be described as very good. This fund's risk-related return is good.

Management   ★★★★

There are 310 fixed-income securities in this $1.4 billion portfolio. The average municipal bond fund today is $150 million in size. Close to 95 percent of the fund's holdings are in bonds. The average maturity of the bonds in this account is 16 years; the weighted coupon rate averages 5.6 percent. The portfolio's fixed-income holdings can be categorized as long-term, high-quality debt. Over 55 percent of the portfolio is rated AAA, 25 percent AA, 10 percent A, and 5 percent BBB.

Mary Miller has managed this fund for the past five years. Management constantly monitors the portfolio's average duration, keeps expenses low, and maintains a high overall credit rating. There are 63 funds besides Tax-Free Income within the T. Rowe Price family. Overall, the fund family's risk-adjusted performance can be described as good.

Current Income   ★★★★

Over the past year, Tax-Free Income had a 12-month yield of 5.4 percent. During this same 12-month period, the typical municipal bond fund had a yield that averaged 4.4 percent.

Expenses   ★★★★★

Tax-Free Income's expense ratio is .6 percent; it has also averaged .6 percent annually over the past three calendar years. The average expense ratio for the 1,900 funds in this category is 1.0 percent. This fund's turnover rate over the past year has been 30 percent, while its peer group average has been 40 percent.

Summary

T. Rowe Price Tax-Free Income excels when it comes to consistency, low overhead, and bull market performance. Down-market returns have not been particularly good, but the fund has still managed to outperform 70 percent of its peers while being safer than close to three-quarters of its category.

Profile

minimum initial investment $2,500	*IRA accounts available* .... yes
subsequent minimum investment .. $100	*IRA minimum investment* $1,000
available in all 50 states .... yes	*date of inception* .... Oct. 1976
telephone exchanges .... yes	*dividend/income paid* .... monthly
number of funds in family 64	*average credit quality* .... AA

Van Kampen High-Yield Municipal A

One Parkview Plaza
Oakbrook Terrace, IL 60181
800-421-5666
www.vankampen.com

total return	★★★★
risk reduction	★★★★★
management	★★★★
current income	★★★★★
expense control	★★★★
symbol ACTHX	22 points
up-market performance	excellent
down-market performance	fair
predictability of returns	excellent

Total Return   ★★★★

Over the past five years, Van Kampen High-Yield Municipal A has taken $10,000 and turned it into $13,380 ($11,580 over three years and $19,670 over the past 10 years). This translates into an annualized return of 6 percent over the past five years, 5 percent over the past three years, and 7 percent for the decade. Over the past five years, this fund has outperformed 42 percent of all mutual funds; within its general category it has done better than 97 percent of its peers. Municipal bond funds have averaged 5 percent annually over these same five years (all periods ending March 31, 2000).

During the past five years, a $10,000 initial investment grew to $13,380 after taxes, assuming a 39.6 percent income tax bracket (state and federal combined) and a capital gains rate of 28 percent. This means that investors in this fund were able to preserve 100 percent of their total returns. Compared to other fixed-income funds, this fund's tax savings are considered to be excellent.

Risk/Volatility   ★★★★★

Over the past five years, High-Yield Municipal has been safer than 99 percent of all municipal bond funds. Over the past decade, the fund has had one negative year, while the Lehman Brothers Aggregate Bond Index has had two (off 3 percent in 1994 and 1 percent in 1999); the Lehman Brothers Municipal Bond Index also fell twice (off 5 percent in 1994 and 2 percent in 1999). The fund has underperformed the Lehman Brothers Aggregate Bond Index five times and the Lehman Brothers Municipal Bond Index four times in the last 10 years.

	last 5 years		last 10 years	
worst year	-2%	1999	-2%	1999
best year	14%	1995	14%	1995

In the past, High-Yield Municipal has done better than 90 percent of its peer group in up markets and outperformed 40 percent of its competition in down markets.

Consistency, or predictability, of returns for High-Yield Municipal can be described as excellent. This fund's risk-related return is very good.

Management   ★★★★

There are 730 fixed-income securities in this $1.5 billion portfolio. The average municipal bond fund today is $150 million in size. Close to 100 percent of the fund's holdings are in bonds. The average maturity of the bonds in this account is 21 years; the weighted coupon rate averages 7.2 percent. The portfolio's fixed-income holdings can be categorized as long-term and low-quality (or uncertain) debt. Close to 90 percent of the fund is invested in bonds that are not rated.

Wayne Godlin has managed this fund for the past 11 years. Management favors nonrated issues but believes that roughly 90 percent of these issues would be rated BB. Quality upgrades have outnumbered downgrades by a margin of close to five to one. The fund has done a particularly good job in going after smaller issues that are frequently priced better than the larger deals.

There are 121 funds besides High-Yield Municipal within the Van Kampen family. Overall, the fund family's risk-adjusted performance can be described as good.

Current Income   ★★★★★

Over the past year, High-Yield Municipal had a 12-month yield of 6.4 percent. During this same 12-month period, the typical municipal bond fund had a yield that averaged 4.4 percent.

Expenses   ★★★★

Van Kampen High-Yield Municipal A's expense ratio is .9 percent; it has also averaged .9 percent annually over the past three calendar years. The average expense ratio for the 1,900 funds in this category is 1.0 percent. This fund's turnover rate over the past year has been 20 percent, while its peer group average has been 40 percent.

Summary

Van Kampen High-Yield Municipal A has rated in the top half of its category's performance for each of the past six years; frequently it is in the top quartile. Despite its somewhat special holdings, the fund has been safer than 99 percent of its counterparts. Performance has been very good and predictability of returns has been excellent. This is one of the top-rated tax-free funds and is highly recommended.

Profile

minimum initial investment $500	*IRA accounts available* . . . . yes
subsequent minimum investment . . . $25	*IRA minimum investment* $500
available in all 50 states . . . . yes	*date of inception* . . . . Jan. 1986
telephone exchanges . . . . yes	*dividend/income paid* . . . . monthly
number of funds in family 122	*average credit quality* . . . . BB

Technology Funds

Consider the following statistics: the first desktop PC was introduced in 1984, the World Wide Web was invented in Switzerland in 1989, 46 million U.S. adults had Net access in 1997, 98 million U.S. adults had Net access in 1999, and the World Wide Web surpasses one billion unique pages in the year 2000. Just five years ago, it would have taken 47 minutes to download 1,000 pages; today this transmission takes just 40 seconds. Experts anticipate that by 2003 Internet commerce will become a $1 trillion industry, and that more than 600 million users will be online worldwide.

Around the world, consumers who are rapidly embracing existing hardware and software in areas such as electronics, information technology, and cellular technology are driving the burgeoning need for technology. Technologies once considered highly advanced are now seen as household essentials—with progressively lower prices as a result of mass marketing. Because of intense global competition, lack of pricing flexibility, and tight labor markets, corporations seeking to maintain their profit margins are increasingly investing in technology to enhance productivity.

The technology sector has emerged as one of the principal drivers of both the global economy and the U.S. stock markets, as it produced staggering returns in 1999. For example, the Pacific Stock Exchange Tech 100 Index gained 116 percent and the average technology mutual fund gained 136 percent in 1999.

However, technology stocks are also inherently more volatile and, consequently, riskier than the broad market as well as most, if not all, industry sectors. To demonstrate, let us examine standard deviation, the most common measure of performance volatility, or its tendency to move up or down. The higher the fund's standard deviation, the greater the fund's swings in performance. According to Morningstar, Inc., the standard deviation of returns for technology funds typically is roughly twice that of the S & P 500 Index.

Not all tech stocks are created equal. At the very basic level, Internet-related companies and general, non-Internet tech companies, such as those that make computers, chips, hard drives, or software, are at very different stages in their evolution. Internet companies are where regular technology companies were 10–15 years ago. The instability of Internet companies is what has made these stocks so volatile and so susceptible to momentum. As an example, Morgan Stanley's MOX Index of Internet stocks gained a staggering 514 percent between the end of 1998 and its peak on March 9, 2000, only to give up close to half of those gains over the next several weeks.

Technology stocks represent one of the fastest growing and largest contributors to the S & P 500 Index. At year-end 1999, technology stocks represented 30 percent of the S & P 500 Index and accounted for 80 percent of the Index's overall growth. As you can see below, 8 of the 10 largest contributors to the S & P 500's 1999 return were technology companies:

Largest Technology Contributors to the S & P 500's 1999 Return

company	% of S & P 500's return	rank (by size)
Microsoft	11.9%	1
Cisco	10.1%	2
Oracle	5.7%	5
Qualcomm	5.4%	6
Nortel Networks	4.9%	7
Sun Microsystems	4.2%	8
America Online	4.0%	9
Yahoo! Inc.	4.0%	10

Technology fund investing can be quite complex. Not only are there over 125 funds that are specifically in the technology sector, but there are hundreds more that are in other categories that are heavily technology oriented. According to Morningstar, Inc. data, of the 670 largest growth funds, 125 hold 50 percent or more in technology-related stocks. And this may not be the whole story. Just defining technology can be a challenging endeavor.

There are 150 funds in this $145 billion category. Since 1986, the technology sector has underperformed the S & P 500 in the following years: 1986 by 11.1 percent, 1987 by 5.7 percent, 1988 by 9.8 percent, 1989 by 10 percent, 1995 by 2.3 percent, 1996 by 5.9 percent, and 1997 by 22.2 percent. In 1999, techology stocks outperformed the S & P 500 by 109 percent.

The typical technology fund is divided as follows: 83 percent in technology stocks, 11 percent in service, and 2 percent in health stocks. The average technology fund is divided as follows: 86 percent in common stocks, 8 percent in foreign equities, and 6 percent in cash. The typical price-earnings (p/e) ratio for stocks in this category is 55.

Technology Funds

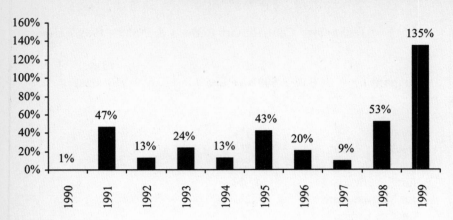

Alliance Technology A

P.O. Box 1520
Secaucus, NJ 07096
800-227-4618
www.alliancecapital.com

total return	★★★★
risk reduction	★★★★
management	★★★★
tax minimization	★★★★★
expense control	★★★★
symbol ALTFX	21 points
up-market performance	poor
down-market performance	good
predictability of returns	excellent

Total Return   ★★★★

Over the past five years, Alliance Technology A has taken $10,000 and turned it
into $55,730 ($40,200 over three years and $148,840 over the past 10 years). This
translates into an annualized return of 41 percent over the past five years, 59 percent over the past three years, and 31 percent for the decade. Over the past five
years, this fund has outperformed 99 percent of all mutual funds; within its general
category it has done better than 35 percent of its peers. Technology funds have
averaged 44 percent annually over these same five years (all periods ending March
31, 2000).

Risk/Volatility   ★★★★

Over the past five years, Technology has been safer than just 10 percent of all technology funds. Over the past decade, the fund has had one negative year, while the
NASDAQ Index has had two (off 18 percent in 1990 and 3 percent in 1994); the
Russell 2000 fell three times (off 20 percent in 1990, 2 percent in 1994, and 3 percent in 1998). The fund has underperformed the NASDAQ Index four times and
the Russell 2000 twice in the last 10 years.

	last 5 years		last 10 years	
worst year	5%	1997	-3%	1990
best year	72%	1999	72%	1999

In the past, Technology has done better than 20 percent of its peer group in
up markets and outperformed 50 percent of its competition in down markets.
Consistency, or predictability, of returns for Technology can be described as excellent. This fund's risk-related return is also excellent.

Management   ★★★★

There are 55 stocks in this $3.6 billion portfolio. The average technology fund
today is $1.2 billion in size. Close to 92 percent of the fund's holdings are in stocks.
The stocks in this portfolio have an average price-earnings (p/e) ratio of 55 and a

median market capitalization of $78 billion. Technology represents close to 75 percent of the fund's holdings, followed by industrial cyclicals (5 percent) and services (4 percent). The portfolio's equity holdings can be categorized as large-cap and growth-oriented issues. The fund has a correlation of just roughly 50 percent to the S & P 500 (versus 45 percent for technology funds in general).

Peter Anastos and Gerald Malone have managed this fund for the past nine years. The comanagers are particularly interested in a company's management and strategy along with current market penetration. By utilizing fundamental analysis, the fund's major sectors include semiconductors, computer hardware, software, services, and communications equipment and services. There are 156 funds besides Technology within the Alliance Capital family. Overall, the fund family's risk-adjusted performance can be described as very good.

Tax Minimization   ★★★★★
During the past five years, a $10,000 initial investment grew to $54,060 after taxes, assuming a 39.6 percent income tax bracket (state and federal combined) and a capital gains rate of 28 percent. This means that investors in this fund were able to preserve 97 percent of their total returns. Compared to other equity funds, this fund's tax savings are considered to be excellent.

Expenses   ★★★★
Technology's expense ratio is 1.6 percent; it has also averaged 1.6 percent annually over the past three calendar years. The average expense ratio for the 150 funds in this category is 1.7 percent. This fund's turnover rate over the past year has been 55 percent, while its peer group average has been 245 percent.

Summary
Alliance Technology A performs very well in every category. There are a number of technology funds that have performed better, but this portfolio's risk level is acceptable to most investors. Tax minimization has been fantastic and so has predictability of returns. One of the keys to this kind of sector investing is being able to stay in it for the long haul. With risk management like this, shareholders are likely to stay the course.

Profile

minimum initial investment $250	*IRA accounts available* .... yes
subsequent minimum investment ... $50	*IRA minimum investment* $250
available in all 50 states. .... yes	*date of inception*. .... March 1982
telephone exchanges. .... yes	*dividend/income paid* .... annually
number of funds in family 157	*largest sector weighting* ... technology

Firsthand Technology Value
101 Park Center Plaza, Suite 1300
San Jose, CA 95113
888-884-2675
www.firsthandfunds.com

total return	★★★★★
risk reduction	★★
management	★★★
tax minimization	★★★★★
expense control	★★★
symbol TVFQX	18 points
up-market performance	excellent
down-market performance	poor
predictability of returns	excellent

Total Return   ★★★★★
Over the past five years, Firsthand Technology Value has taken $10,000 and turned it into $129,890 ($59,300 over three years). This translates into an annualized return of 67 percent over the past five years and 81 percent over the past three years. Over the past five years , this fund has outperformed 99 percent of all mutual funds; within its general category it has done better than 99 percent of its peers. Technology funds have averaged 44 percent annually over these same five years (all periods ending March 31, 2000).

Risk/Volatility   ★★
Over the past five years, Firsthand has been safer than just 10 percent of all technology funds. Since its inception, the fund has had no negative years, while the NASDAQ Index has had two (off 18 percent in 1990 and 3 percent in 1994); the Russell 2000 fell three times (off 20 percent in 1990, 2 percent in 1994, and 3 percent in 1998). The fund has underperformed the NASDAQ Index twice and the Russell 2000 once since the fund's inception.

	last 5 years		since inception	
worst year	6%	1997	6%	1997
best year	190%	1999	190%	1999

In the past, Firsthand has done better than 99 percent of its peer group in up markets and outperformed just 10 percent of its competition in down markets. Consistency, or predictability, of returns for Firsthand can be described as excellent. This fund's risk-related return is also excellent.

Management   ★★★
There are 70 stocks in this $1.9 billion portfolio. The average technology fund today is $1.2 billion in size. Close to 88 percent of the fund's holdings are in stocks. The stocks in this portfolio have an average price-earnings (p/e) ratio of 46 and a median market capitalization of $20 billion. Technology represents close to 80 percent of

the fund's holdings, followed by health care (12 percent) and industrial cyclicals (3 percent). The portfolio's equity holdings can be categorized as mid-cap and growth-oriented issues. The fund has a correlation of roughly 30 percent to the S & P 500 (versus 45 percent for technology funds in general).

Kevin Landis has managed this fund for the past seven years. The fund is classified as "nondiversified" and may invest up to half its assets in just two stocks; the remaining balance must be spread out among at least 10 other issues. Management concentrates on semiconductor and networking companies as well as medical-tech and drug-research-and-development equities. High earnings growth is the fund's mantra. There are four funds besides Technology Value within the Firsthand family.

Tax Minimization   ★★★★★
During the past five years, a $10,000 initial investment grew to $123,400 after taxes, assuming a 39.6 percent income tax bracket (state and federal combined) and a capital gains rate of 28 percent. This means that investors in this fund were able to preserve 95 percent of their total returns. Compared to other equity funds, this fund's tax savings are considered to be excellent.

Expenses   ★★★
Firsthand's expense ratio is 1.9 percent; it has also averaged 1.9 percent annually over the past three calendar years. The average expense ratio for the 150 funds in this category is 1.7 percent. This fund's turnover rate over the past year has been 40 percent, while its peer group average has been 245 percent.

Summary
Firsthand Technology Value ranks as the number one performing fund in its category over the past three and five years. Returns have been simply spectacular. The portfolio's returns have been surprisingly spectacular, and so have results during bull markets. As might be expected with this kind of fund, down-market returns have been disappointing, but this is a reflection of the category and not management. Tax efficiency is also to be highly commended.

Profile
minimum initial investment $10,000
subsequent minimum investment . . . $50
available in all 50 states. . . . . yes
telephone exchanges. . . . . yes
number of funds in family 5

IRA accounts available . . . . yes
IRA minimum investment $2,000
date of inception . . . . May 1994
dividend/income paid . . . . annually
largest sector weighting . . . technology

John Hancock Global Technology A

101 Huntington Avenue
Boston, MA 02199
800-225-5291
www.jhancock.com

total return	★★★★
risk reduction	★★★
management	★★★★
tax minimization	★★★★★
expense control	★★★★★
symbol NTTFX	21 points
up-market performance	very good
down-market performance	good
predictability of returns	excellent

Total Return   ★★★★

Over the past five years, John Hancock Global Technology A has taken $10,000 and turned it into $66,340 ($48,270 over three years and $127,610 over the past 10 years). This translates into an annualized return of 46 percent over the past five years, 69 percent over the past three years, and 29 percent for the decade. Over the past five years, this fund has outperformed 99 percent of all mutual funds; within its general category it has done better than 66 percent of its peers. Technology funds have averaged 44 percent annually over these same five years (all periods ending March 31, 2000).

Risk/Volatility   ★★★

Over the past five years, Global Technology has been safer than just 10 percent of all technology funds. Over the past decade, the fund has had one negative year, while the NASDAQ Index has had two (off 18 percent in 1990 and 3 percent in 1994); the Russell 2000 fell three times (off 20 percent in 1990, 2 percent in 1994, and 3 percent in 1998). The fund has underperformed the NASDAQ Index five times and the Russell 2000 four times in the last 10 years.

	last 5 years		last 10 years	
worst year	7%	1997	-18%	1990
best year	132%	1999	132%	1999

In the past, Global Technology has done better than 65 percent of its peer group in up markets and outperformed 60 percent of its competition in down markets. Consistency, or predictability, of returns for Global Technology can be described as excellent. This fund's risk-related return is also excellent.

Management   ★★★★

There are 110 stocks in this $1.2 billion portfolio. The average technology fund today is $1.2 billion in size. Close to 85 percent of the fund's holdings are in stocks. The stocks in this portfolio have an average price-earnings (p/e) ratio of 47 and a median market capitalization of $55 billion. Technology represents close to 75 percent of the fund's holdings, followed by industrial cyclicals (6 percent) and services (2 percent). The portfolio's equity holdings can be categorized as large-cap and growth-oriented issues. The fund has a correlation of just roughly 45 percent to the S & P 500 (versus 45 percent for technology funds in general).

Barry Gordon and Marc Klee have managed this fund for the past 13 years. A huge portion of management's holdings are in technology issues that deal with development or operations. The comanagers look for stocks selling at or below 75 percent of their true value. At times, management will load up heavily on overseas issues. There are 60 funds besides Global Technology within the John Hancock family. Overall, the fund family's risk-adjusted performance can be described as good.

Tax Minimization   ★★★★★
During the past five years, a $10,000 initial investment grew to $63,685 after taxes, assuming a 39.6 percent income tax bracket (state and federal combined) and a capital gains rate of 28 percent. This means that investors in this fund were able to preserve 96 percent of their total returns. Compared to other equity funds, this fund's tax savings are considered to be excellent.

Expenses   ★★★★★
Global Technology's expense ratio is 1.4 percent; it has also averaged 1.4 percent annually over the past three calendar years. The average expense ratio for the 150 funds in this category is 1.7 percent. This fund's turnover rate over the past year has been 60 percent, while its peer group average has been 245 percent.

Summary
John Hancock Global Technology A is the second best performer in its category, but with less risk. Expense control and tax efficiency are marvelous. Management is to be commended for running such a great fund. Consistency in returns has been remarkable, and the fund has even done a good job during down markets.

Profile

minimum initial investment $1,000	IRA accounts available . . . . yes
subsequent minimum investment $1	IRA minimum investment $250
available in all 50 states. . . . . yes	date of inception. . . . . Jan. 1983
telephone exchanges. . . . . yes	dividend/income paid . . . . annually
number of funds in family 61	largest sector weighting . . . technology

T. Rowe Price Science & Technology
100 East Pratt Street
Baltimore, MD 21202
800-638-5660
www.troweprice.com\

total return	★★★
risk reduction	★★★★
management	★★★★
tax minimization	★★★★
expense control	★★★★★
symbol PRSCX	20 points
up-market performance	good
down-market performance	fair
predictability of returns	excellent

Total Return   ★★★
Over the past five years, T. Rowe Price Science & Technology has taken $10,000 and turned it into $51,890 ($37,960 over three years and $148,840 over the past 10 years). This translates into an annualized return of 39 percent over the past five years, 56 percent over the past three years, and 31 percent for the decade. Over the past five years, this fund has outperformed 99 percent of all mutual funds; within its general category it has done better than 40 percent of its peers. Technology funds have averaged 44 percent annually over these same five years (all periods ending March 31, 2000).

Risk/Volatility   ★★★★
Over the past five years, Science & Technology has been safer than just 10 percent of all technology funds. Over the past decade, the fund has had one negative year, while the NASDAQ Index has had two (off 18 percent in 1990 and 3 percent in 1994); the Russell 2000 fell three times (off 20 percent in 1990, 2 percent in 1994, and 3 percent in 1998). The fund has underperformed the NASDAQ Index and the Russell 2000 twice in the last 10 years.

	last 5 years		last 10 years	
worst year	2%	1998	-1%	1990
best year	101%	1999	101%	1999

In the past, Science & Technology has done better than 50 percent of its peer group in up markets and outperformed 35 percent of its competition in down markets. Consistency, or predictability, of returns for Science & Technology can be described as excellent. This fund's risk-related return is also excellent.

Management   ★★★★
There are 50 stocks in this $16.2 billion portfolio. The average technology fund today is $1.2 billion in size. Close to 96 percent of the fund's holdings are in stocks. The stocks in this portfolio have an average price-earnings (p/e) ratio of 58 and a

median market capitalization of $107 billion. Technology represents close to 85 percent of the fund's holdings, followed by industrial cyclicals (3 percent) and utilities (3 percent). The portfolio's equity holdings can be categorized as large-cap and growth-oriented issues. The fund has a correlation of just roughly 55 percent to the S & P 500 (versus 45 percent for technology funds in general).

Charles Morris has managed this fund for the past 10 years. Management is not restricted by market capitalization, seeking out broad themes that will outdistance individual company business cycles. There are 63 funds besides Science & Technology within the T. Rowe Price family. Overall, the fund family's risk-adjusted performance can be described as good.

Tax Minimization   ★★★
During the past five years, a $10,000 initial investment grew to $46,180 after taxes, assuming a 39.6 percent income tax bracket (state and federal combined) and a capital gains rate of 28 percent. This means that investors in this fund were able to preserve 89 percent of their total returns. Compared to other equity funds, this fund's tax savings are considered to be very good.

Expenses   ★★★★★
Science & Technology's expense ratio is .9 percent; it has also averaged .9 percent annually over the past three calendar years. The average expense ratio for the 150 funds in this category is 1.7 percent. This fund's turnover rate over the past year has been 125 percent, while its peer group average has been 245 percent.

Summary
T. Rowe Price Science & Technology is the lowest performer in its category in the book but displays some of the best risk reduction. Despite its less than stellar sector performance, the fund has beat out 99 percent of all mutual funds. The fund is highly recommended because of its predictability of returns (something rarely found in technology) and low expenses. It is also part of a large fund family that offers plenty of other good choices as well.

Profile

minimum initial investment $2,500	*IRA accounts available* .... yes
subsequent minimum investment .. $100	*IRA minimum investment* $1,000
available in all 50 states.......... yes	*date of inception*......... Sept. 1987
telephone exchanges............. yes	*dividend/income paid* .... annually
number of funds in family 64	*largest sector weighting* ... technology

United Science & Technology A

6300 Lamar Avenue
P.O. Box 29217
Shawnee Mission, KS 66201
800-366-5465
www.waddell.com

total return	★★★★
risk reduction	★★★★★
management	★★★★★
tax minimization	★★★★★
expense control	★★★★★
symbol UNSCX	24 points
up-market performance	fair
down-market performance	very good
predictability of returns	excellent

Total Return   ★★★★

Over the past five years, United Science & Technology A has taken $10,000 and turned it into $64,100 ($48,270 over three years and $127,610 over the past 10 years). This translates into an annualized return of 45 percent over the past five years, 69 percent over the past three years, and 29 percent for the decade. Over the past five years, this fund has outperformed 99 percent of all mutual funds; within its general category it has done better than 60 percent of its peers. Technology funds have averaged 44 percent annually over these same five years (all periods ending March 31, 2000).

Risk/Volatility   ★★★★★

Over the past five years, United Science has been safer than just 10 percent of all technology funds. Over the past decade, the fund has had two negative years, while the NASDAQ Index has also had two (off 18 percent in 1990 and 3 percent in 1994); the Russell 2000 fell three times (off 20 percent in 1990, 2 percent in 1994, and 3 percent in 1998). The fund has underperformed the NASDAQ Index and the Russell 2000 four times in the last 10 years.

	last 5 years		last 10 years	
worst year	7%	1997	-4%	1992
best year	103%	1999	103%	1999

In the past, United Science has done better than 45 percent of its peer group in up markets and outperformed 75 percent of its competition in down markets. Consistency, or predictability, of returns for United Science can be described as excellent. This fund's risk-related return is also excellent.

Management   ★★★★★

There are 65 stocks in this $5 million portfolio. The average technology fund today is $5 billion in size. Close to 96 percent of the fund's holdings are in stocks. The stocks in this portfolio have an average price-earnings (p/e) ratio of 57 and a median market capitalization of $78 billion. Technology represents close to 65 percent of the fund's holdings, followed by services (8 percent) and health care stocks (8 percent). The portfolio's equity holdings can be categorized as small-cap and growth-oriented issues. The fund has a correlation of approximately 45 percent to the S & P 500 (versus 45 percent for technology funds in general).

Abel Garcia has managed this fund for the past 17 years, making him one of the most senior portfolio managers in his sector. Management looks for corporations that are likely to benefit from the use or application of scientific discoveries or developments. The fund also likes those issues likely to prosper from the general demand for technology. Garcia uses a combination of a top-down and bottom-up approach to security selection. Stocks with consistent revenues and earnings are targeted. There are 56 funds besides Science & Technology within the United family. Overall, the fund family's risk-adjusted performance can be described as very good.

Tax Minimization   ★★★★★
During the past five years, a $10,000 initial investment grew to $60,250 after taxes, assuming a 39.6 percent income tax bracket (state and federal combined) and a capital gains rate of 28 percent. This means that investors in this fund were able to preserve 94 percent of their total returns. Compared to other equity funds, this fund's tax savings are considered to be excellent.

Expenses   ★★★★★
Science & Technology's expense ratio is 0.7 percent; it has also averaged 0.6 percent annually over the past three calendar years. The average expense ratio for the 150 funds in this category is also 1.7 percent. This fund's turnover rate over the past year has been 40 percent, while its peer group average has been 245 percent.

Summary
United Science & Technology A is clearly the top scorer in its category in the book, receiving 24 out of 25 possible points. Few sector funds can claim very good bear market performance, and predictability of returns has been just great. The fund also has lower risk than any of its counterparts. Not enough good things can be said about this portfolio and its management.

Profile

minimum initial investment $500	*IRA accounts available* . . . . yes
subsequent minimum investment $1	*IRA minimum investment* $50
available in all 50 states. . . . . yes	*date of inception* . . . . May 1950
telephone exchanges . . . . no	*dividend/income paid* . . . semi-annually
number of funds in family 57	*largest sector weighting* . . . technology

Utility Stock Funds

Utility stock funds look for both growth and income, investing in common stocks of utility companies across the country. Somewhere between a third and half of these funds' total returns come from common stock dividends. Utility funds normally stay away from speculative issues, focusing instead on well-established companies with solid histories of paying good dividends. The goal of most of these funds is long-term growth.

Utility, metals, natural resources, and technology funds are the only four sector, or specialty, fund categories in this book. Funds that invest in a single industry, or sector, should be avoided by most investors for two reasons. First, you limit the fund manager's ability to find attractive stocks or bonds if he or she is only able to choose securities from one particular geographic area or industry. Second, the track record of sector funds as a whole is pretty bad. In fact, as a general category, these specialty funds represent the worst of both worlds: above-average risk and substandard returns. If you find the term "aggressive growth" unappealing, then the words "sector fund" should positively appall you.

Utility funds are the one exception. They sound safe and they are safe. In fact, over the past 10 years, this category has only experienced two down years (-9.0 percent in 1994 and -1.5 percent in 1990). Any category of stocks that somewhat relies on dividends generated automatically has a built-in safety cushion. A comparatively high dividend income means that you have to worry less about the appreciation of the underlying issues.

Four factors generally determine the profitability of a utility company: (1) how much it pays for energy, (2) the general level of interest rates, (3) its expected use of nuclear power, and (4) the political climate.

The prices of oil and gas are passed directly on to the consumer, but the utility companies are sensitive to this issue. Higher fuel prices mean that the utility industry has less latitude to increase its profit margins. Thus, higher fuel prices can mean smaller profits and/or dividends to investors.

Next to energy costs, interest expense is the industry's greatest expense. Utility companies are heavily debt-laden. Their interest costs directly affect their profitability. When rates go down and companies are able to refinance their debt, the savings can be staggering. Paying 8 percent interest on a couple of hundred million dollars worth of bonds each year is much more appealing than having to pay 10 percent on the same amount of debt. A lower-interest-rate environment translates into more money being left over for shareholders.

Depending on how you look at it, nuclear power has been an issue or problem for the United States for a few decades now. Other countries seem to have come to grips with the matter, yet we remain divided. Although new power plants have not been successfully proposed or built in this country for several years, no one knows what the future may hold. Venturing into nuclear power always seems to be much more expensive than anticipated by the utility companies and the independent experts they rely on for advice. Because of these uncertainties, mutual fund managers try to seek out utility companies that have no foreseeable plans to develop any or more nuclear power facilities. Whether this will help the nation in the long term remains to be seen, but such avoidance keeps share prices more stable and predictable.

Finally, the political climate is an important concern when calculating whether utility funds should be part of your portfolio. The Public Utilities Commission (PUC) is a political animal and can directly reflect the views of a state's government. Utility bills are something most of us are concerned with and aware of; the powers that be are more likely to be re-elected if they are able to keep rate increases to a minimum. Modest, or minimum, increases can be healthy for the utility companies; freezing rates for a couple of years is a bad sign.

One hundred funds make up the utilities category. Total market capitalization of this category is over $27 billion. Over 86 percent of a typical utility fund's portfolio is in common stocks, with the balance in bonds, convertibles, and money market instruments. The typical utilities fund has about 15 percent of its holdings in foreign stocks.

Over the past three years, utility funds have had an average compound return of 22 percent per year; the annual return for the past five years has been 19 percent. For the last 10 and 15 years, these funds have averaged just under 14 percent per year. The standard deviation for utility funds has been 17 percent over the past three years. This means that these funds have been less volatile than any other stock category except equity-income funds, which have exhibited almost identical volatility. The average annual expense ratio for this category is 1.4 percent.

Standard Deviation of the Different Stock (Equity) Categories Over the Past Three Years (Ending March 31, 2000)

Category	Standard deviation	Category	Standard deviation
Technology	63.0%	Growth	27.4%
Aggressive growth	39.2%	European	25.4%
Metals	36.0%	Foreign	24.4%
Pacific Basin	35.7%	World stock	24.0%
Small company growth	33.4%	Growth & income	20.7%
Natural resources	30.2%	Utilities	16.6%

Usually, utility stock prices closely follow the long-term bond market. If long-term interest rates go up, utility stock prices are likely to go down. Utility stocks are also vulnerable to a general stock market decline, although they are considered less risky than other types of common stock because of their dividends and the monopoly position of most utilities. Typically, utilities have fallen about two-thirds as much as other common stocks during market downturns.

Worldwide, there is a tremendous opportunity for growth in this industry. The average per-capita production of electricity in many developing countries is only one-fifth that of the United States. The electrical output per capita in the United States is 12,100 kilowatt hours, compared to 2,500 kilowatt hours for developing nations. This disparity may well be on the way out. All over the world, previously underdeveloped countries are making economic strides as they move toward free market systems.

When emerging countries become developed economically, their citizens demand higher standards of living. As a result, their requirements for electricity, water, and telephones tend to rise dramatically. Moreover, many countries are selling their utility companies to public owners, opening a new arena for investors. The net result of all of this for you, the investor, is that fund groups are beginning to offer global utility funds. This increased diversification—allowing a fund to invest in utility companies all over the world instead of just in the United States, coupled with tremendous long-term growth potential—should make this a dynamic industry group. Utility funds are a good choice for the investor who wants a hedge against inflation but is still afraid or distrustful of the stock market in general.

Beta, which measures the market-related risk of a stock, is only 0.5 percent for utility funds as a group (compared to 1.0 for the S & P 500). This means that when it comes to stock market risk, utilities have only 50 percent the risk of the Dow Jones Industrial Average (DJIA) or the S & P 500. Keep in mind, however, that there are other risks, such as rising interest rates, that also need to be considered whenever utilities are being considered.

Utility Stock Funds

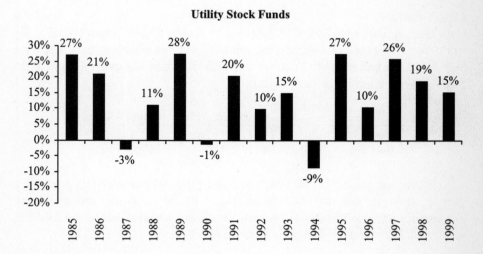

AIM Global Utilities A

11 Greenway Plaza, Suite 1919
Houston, TX 77046
800-959-4246
www.aimfunds.com

total return	★★★★★
risk reduction	★★★★★
management	★★★★★
tax minimization	★★★★★
expense control	★★★★★
symbol AUTLX	25 points
up-market performance	excellent
down-market performance	fair
predictability of returns	very good

Total Return   ★★★★★

Over the past five years, AIM Global Utilities A has taken $10,000 and turned it into $31,760 ($23,000 over three years and $44,110 over the past 10 years). This translates into an annualized return of 26 percent over the past five years, 32 percent over the past three years, and 16 percent for the decade. Over the past five years, this fund has outperformed 84 percent of all mutual funds; within its general category it has done better than 90 percent of its peers. Utility stock funds have averaged 19 percent annually over these same five years (all periods ending March 31, 2000).

Risk/Volatility   ★★★★★

Over the past five years, Global Utilities has been safer than 95 percent of all utility stock funds. Over the past decade, the fund has had two negative years, while the S & P 500 has had one (off 3 percent in 1990). The fund has underperformed the S & P 500 six times in the last 10 years.

	last 5 years		last 10 years	
worst year	14%	1996	-12%	1994
best year	34%	1999	34%	1999

In the past, Global Utilities has done better than 90 percent of its peer group in up markets and outperformed 30 percent of its competition in down markets. Consistency, or predictability, of returns for Global Utilities can be described as very good. This fund's risk-related return is excellent.

Management   ★★★★★

There are 100 stocks in this $300 million portfolio. The average utility stock fund today is $280 million in size. Close to 85 percent of the fund's holdings are in stocks. The stocks in this portfolio have an average price-earnings (p/e) ratio of 33 and a median market capitalization of $44 billion. Technology represents close to 45 percent of the fund's holdings, followed by utilities (16 percent) and nondurables

(5 percent). The portfolio's equity holdings can be categorized as large-cap and growth-oriented issues. The fund has a correlation of approximately 40 percent to the S & P 500 (versus 60 percent for utility funds in general).

A team has managed this fund for the past five years. Management invests a least two-thirds of its assets in companies that provide communications, electricity, water, natural gas, or sanitation services to the public. The prospectus allows the fund to be up to 85 percent in foreign issues. The fund currently favors telecommunications companies. There are 152 funds besides Global Utilities within the AIM family. Overall, the fund family's risk-adjusted performance can be described as very good.

Tax Minimization ★★★★★
During the past five years, a $10,000 initial investment grew to $29,220 after taxes, assuming a 39.6 percent income tax bracket (state and federal combined) and a capital gains rate of 28 percent. This means that investors in this fund were able to preserve 92 percent of their total returns. Compared to other equity funds, this fund's tax savings are considered to be excellent.

Expenses ★★★★★
Global Utilities' expense ratio is 1.1 percent; it has also averaged 1.1 percent annually over the past three calendar years. The average expense ratio for the 100 funds in this category is 1.4 percent. This fund's turnover rate over the past year has been 35 percent, while its peer group average has been 110 percent.

Summary
AIM Global Utilities A has been the number-one performer in its category for the past three years and number two for the past five years. The fund's level of risk has been quite low, making this fund's risk-adjusted returns nothing short of amazing. Tax efficiency has also been superb. This is also one of just a handful of funds in the book that receives a perfect, 25 out of 25, score.

Profile

minimum initial investment $500	*IRA accounts available* . . . . yes
subsequent minimum investment . . . $50	*IRA minimum investment* $250
available in all 50 states. . . . . yes	*date of inception* . . . . Jan. 1988
telephone exchanges. . . . . yes	*dividend/income paid*. . . . . monthly
number of funds in family 153	*largest sector weighting*. . . . . . services

AXP Utilities Income A

IDS Tower 10
Minneapolis, MN 55440
800-328-8300
www.americanexpress.com

total return	★★★
risk reduction	★★★★★
management	★★★★
tax minimization	★★★★
expense control	★★★★★
symbol INUTX	21 points
up-market performance	good
down-market performance	very good
predictability of returns	very good

Total Return   ★★★

Over the past five years, AXP Utilities Income A has taken $10,000 and turned it into $24,880 ($18,160 over three years and $37,070 over the past 10 years). This translates into an annualized return of 20 percent over the past five years, 22 percent over the past three years, and 14 percent for the decade. Over the past five years, this fund has outperformed 76 percent of all mutual funds; within its general category it has done better than 65 percent of its peers. Utility stock funds have averaged 19 percent annually over these same five years (all periods ending March 31, 2000).

Risk/Volatility   ★★★★★

Over the past five years, AXP Utilities has been safer than 80 percent of all utility stock funds. Over the past decade, the fund has had two negative years, while the S & P 500 has had one (off 3 percent in 1990). The fund has underperformed the S & P 500 seven times in the last 10 years.

	last 5 years		last 10 years	
worst year	9%	1999	-7%	1994
best year	29%	1997	29%	1997

In the past, AXP Utilities has done better than 60 percent of its peer group in up markets and outperformed 70 percent of its competition in down markets. Consistency, or predictability, of returns for AXP Utilities can be described as very good. This fund's risk-related return is good.

Management   ★★★★

There are 80 stocks in this $2.2 billion portfolio. The average utility stock fund today is $280 million in size. Close to 90 percent of the fund's holdings are in stocks. The stocks in this portfolio have an average price-earnings (p/e) ratio of 26 and a median market capitalization of $57 billion. Technology represents close to 40 percent of the fund's holdings, followed by utilities (35 percent) and retail trade

(3 percent). The portfolio's equity holdings can be categorized as large-cap and value-oriented issues. The fund has a correlation of close to 50 percent to the S & P 500 (versus 60 percent for utility funds in general).

Bern Fleming has managed this fund for the past six years. Management is most interested in large-cap, well-established domestic and foreign companies. The fund is most interested in companies that trade at low price-to-book and low p/e multiples. In a new world of industry deregulation, Fleming is also concerned with the likelihood of a company's current and future competitive strategy. There are 71 funds besides Utilities Income within the American Express Financial family. Overall, the fund family's risk-adjusted performance can be described as good.

Tax Minimization ★★★★
During the past five years, a $10,000 initial investment grew to $20,900 after taxes, assuming a 39.6 percent income tax bracket (state and federal combined) and a capital gains rate of 28 percent. This means that investors in this fund were able to preserve 84 percent of their total returns. Compared to other equity funds, this fund's tax savings are considered to be very good.

Expenses ★★★★★
Utilities' expense ratio is .9 percent; it has also averaged .9 percent annually over the past three calendar years. The average expense ratio for the 100 funds in this category is 1.4 percent. This fund's turnover rate over the past year has been 85 percent, while its peer group average has been 110 percent.

Summary
AXP Utilities Income A has turned in good results while exposing investors to some of the lowest risk possible. Tax minimization has been just great, while control over costs has been quite impressive. Even though this is considered to be a utilities fund, it has managed to outperform roughly three-fourths of all mutual funds.

Profile

minimum initial investment $2,000	*IRA accounts available* . . . . no
subsequent minimum investment . . $100	*IRA minimum investment* . . . . n/a
available in all 50 states. . . . . yes	*date of inception* . . . . Aug. 1988
telephone exchanges. . . . . yes	*dividend/income paid* . . . . quarterly
number of funds in family 72	*largest sector weighting* . . . . . . services

Liberty-Colonial Global Utilities A

One Financial Center
Boston, MA 02111
800-426-3750
www.libertyfunds.com

total return	★★★
risk reduction	★★★★
management	★★★
tax minimization	★★★★
expense control	★★★★
symbol CGUAX	18 points
up-market performance	very good
down-market performance	poor
predictability of returns	good

Total Return   ★★★
Over the past five years, Liberty-Colonial Global Utilities A has taken $10,000 and turned it into $24,880 ($19,070 over three years). This translates into an annualized return of 20 percent over the past five years and 24 percent over the past three years. Over the past five years, this fund has outperformed 76 percent of all mutual funds; within its general category it has done better than 65 percent of its peers. Utility stock funds have averaged 19 percent annually over these same five years (all periods ending March 31, 2000).

Risk/Volatility   ★★★★
Over the past five years, Liberty-Colonial Global Utilities has been safer than 45 percent of all utility stock funds. Since its inception, the fund has had one negative year, while the S & P 500 has also had one (off 3 percent in 1990). The fund has underperformed the S & P 500 five times since the fund's inception.

	last 5 years		since inception	
worst year	13%	1996	-7%	1994
best year	27%	1999	27%	1999

In the past, Liberty-Colonial Global Utilities has done better than 70 percent of its peer group in up markets and outperformed just 10 percent of its competition in down markets. Consistency, or predictability, of returns for Liberty-Colonial Global Utilities can be described as good. This fund's risk-related return is very good.

Management   ★★★
There are 40 stocks in this $180 million portfolio. The average utility stock fund today is $280 million in size. Close to 90 percent of the fund's holdings are in stocks. The stocks in this portfolio have an average price-earnings (p/e) ratio of 33 and a median market capitalization of $17 billion. The portfolio's equity holdings can be categorized as large-cap and value-oriented issues.

Phone services stocks represent 30 percent of the fund's holdings, followed by 28 percent in electric utilities and 10 percent in phone equipment companies. The fund has a correlation of 70 percent to the S & P 500 (versus 60 percent for utility funds in general).

Ophelia Barsketis and Deborah Jansen have managed this fund for the past seven years. Management invests in domestic as well as foreign issues; roughly 40 percent of the holdings are in overseas operations. There are 83 funds besides Global Utilities within the Liberty-Colonial family. Overall, the fund family's risk-adjusted performance can be described as good.

Tax Minimization ★★★★
During the past five years, a $10,000 initial investment grew to $22,150 after taxes, assuming a 39.6 percent income tax bracket (state and federal combined) and a capital gains rate of 28 percent. This means that investors in this fund were able to preserve 89 percent of their total returns. Compared to other equity funds, this fund's tax savings are considered to be very good.

Expenses ★★★★
Liberty-Colonial Global Utilities A's expense ratio is 1.3 percent; it has also averaged 1.3 percent annually over the past three calendar years. The average expense ratio for the 100 funds in this category is 1.4 percent. This fund's turnover rate over the past year has been 45 percent, while its peer group average has been 110 percent.

Summary
Liberty-Colonial Global Utilities A is consistently good or very good in every single category. Bear market performance has not been good in the past, but this will most likely change due to management's current lack of exposure in emerging markets. The fund has outperformed close to two-thirds of its peer group. Tax efficiency has also been quite nice.

Profile
minimum initial investment $1,000	*IRA accounts available* . . . . yes
subsequent minimum investment . . . $50	*IRA minimum investment* $25
available in all 50 states. . . . . yes	*date of inception* . . . . Oct. 1991
telephone exchanges. . . . . yes	*dividend/income paid.* . . . . monthly
number of funds in family 84	*largest sector weighting* . . . . . . services

MFS Utilities A

P.O. Box 2281
Boston, MA 02107
800-637-2929
www.mfs.com

total return	★★★★★
risk reduction	★★★★★
management	★★★★★
tax minimization	★★★★
expense control	★★★
symbol MMUFX	22 points
up-market performance	very good
down-market performance	good
predictability of returns	excellent

Total Return ★★★★★

Over the past five years, MFS Utilities A has taken $10,000 and turned it into $34,360 ($22,480 over three years). This translates into an annualized return of 28 percent over the past five years and 31 percent over the past three years. Over the past five years, this fund has outperformed 90 percent of all mutual funds; within its general category it has done better than 98 percent of its peers. Utility stock funds have averaged 19 percent annually over these same five years (all periods ending March 31, 2000).

Risk/Volatility ★★★★★

Over the past five years, MFS Utilities has been safer than 99 percent of all utility stock funds. Since its inception, the fund has had one negative year, while the S & P 500 has also had one (off 3 percent in 1990). The fund has underperformed the S & P 500 five times since the fund's inception.

	last 5 years		since inception	
worst year	18%	1998	-5%	1994
best year	33%	1995	33%	1995

In the past, MFS Utilities has done better than 75 percent of its peer group in up markets and outperformed 45 percent of its competition in down markets. Consistency, or predictability, of returns for MFS Utilities can be described as excellent. This fund's risk-related return is also excellent.

Management ★★★★★

There are 95 stocks in this $700 million portfolio. The average utility stock fund today is $280 million in size. Close to 80 percent of the fund's holdings are in stocks. The stocks in this portfolio have an average price-earnings (p/e) ratio of 24 and a median market capitalization of $29 billion. Utility stocks represents close to 40 percent of the fund's holdings, followed by technology (24 percent) and nondurables (3 percent). The portfolio's equity holdings can be categorized as large-cap and value-oriented issues. The fund has a correlation of roughly 50 percent to the S & P 500 (versus 60 percent for utility funds in general).

Maura Shaughnessy has managed this fund for the past nine years. The great majority of the time at least two-thirds of the holdings are in domestic as well as foreign companies that either produce, transmit, sell, or distribute energy and/or water. Management is also allowed to participate in telecommunications service and equipment providers. Frequently, approximately one-fifth of the holdings will be in BBB-rated bonds. There are 137 funds besides Utilities within the MFS family. Overall, the fund family's risk-adjusted performance can be described as good.

Tax Minimization ★★★
During the past five years, a $10,000 initial investment grew to $28,175 after taxes, assuming a 39.6 percent income tax bracket (state and federal combined) and a capital gains rate of 28 percent. This means that investors in this fund were able to preserve 82 percent of their total returns. Compared to other equity funds, this fund's tax savings are considered to be very good.

Expenses ★★★
MFS Utilities' expense ratio is 1.1 percent; it has also averaged 1.1 percent annually over the past three calendar years. The average expense ratio for the 100 funds in this category is 1.4 percent. This fund's turnover rate over the past year has been 130 percent, while its peer group average has been 110 percent.

Summary
MFS Utilities A is the number-one performer in its category over the past five years. Returns, as well as risk reduction, have been spectacular. This is one of the few "utility" funds that actually has a big exposure to traditional utility companies—a high percentage of this category should be renamed "technology/utility" funds. The portfolio ties for first place as the lowest risk offering in its category for the book.

Profile

minimum initial investment $1,000	*IRA accounts available* . . . . yes
subsequent minimum investment . . . $50	*IRA minimum investment* $250
available in all 50 states. . . . . yes	*date of inception* . . . . Jan. 1992
telephone exchanges. . . . . yes	*dividend/income paid*. . . . . monthly
number of funds in family 138	*largest sector weighting*. . . . . . services

MSDW Global Utilities B

Two World Trade Center, 72nd Floor
New York, NY 10048
800-869-3863
www.deanwitter.com

total return	★★★★
risk reduction	★★★★★
management	★★★★
tax minimization	★★★★★
expense control	★★★
symbol GUTBX	21 points
up-market performance	very good
down-market performance	poor
predictability of returns	very good

Total Return   ★★★★

Over the past five years, MSDW Global Utilities B has taken $10,000 and turned it into $28,150 ($21,970 over three years). This translates into an annualized return of 23 percent over the past five years and 30 percent over the past three years. Over the past five years, this fund has outperformed 80 percent of all mutual funds; within its general category it has done better than 85 percent of its peers. Utility stock funds have averaged 19 percent annually over these same five years (all periods ending March 31, 2000).

Risk/Volatility   ★★★★★

Over the past five years, Global Utilities has been safer than 50 percent of all utility stock funds. Since its inception, the fund has had no negative years, while the S & P 500 has had one (off 3 percent in 1990). The fund has underperformed the S & P 500 three times since the fund's inception.

	last 5 years		since inception	
worst year	13%	1996	13%	1996
best year	38%	1998	38%	1998

In the past, Global Utilities has done better than 75 percent of its peer group in up markets and outperformed 20 percent of its competition in down markets. Consistency, or predictability, of returns for Global Utilities can be described as very good. This fund's risk-related return is excellent.

Management   ★★★★

There are 100 stocks in this $1 billion portfolio. The average utility stock fund today is $280 million in size. Close to 95 percent of the fund's holdings are in stocks. The stocks in this portfolio have an average price-earnings (p/e) ratio of 30 and a median market capitalization of $41 billion. Technology stocks represents close to one-third of the fund's holdings, followed by utilities (28 percent) and retail trade (2 percent). The portfolio's equity holdings can be categorized as large-cap and value-oriented issues. The fund has a correlation of roughly 60 percent to the S & P 500 (versus 60 percent for utility funds in general).

Edward Gaylor has managed this fund for the past seven years. Management invests at least two-thirds of its fund's holdings in foreign and domestic utility companies, which is defined as those that during the most recent 12 months derived at least half of its gross revenues from the utilities industry. Manager Gaylor is always on the lookout for undervalued stocks, wherever the search may take him. On a country level, he is concerned with interest-rate trends, political factors, and currency valuation. There are 252 funds besides Global Utilities within the Morgan Stanley Dean Witter family. Overall, the fund family's risk-adjusted performance can be described as good.

Tax Minimization ★★★★★
During the past five years, a $10,000 initial investment grew to $25,620 after taxes, assuming a 39.6 percent income tax bracket (state and federal combined) and a capital gains rate of 28 percent. This means that investors in this fund were able to preserve 91 percent of their total returns. Compared to other equity funds, this fund's tax savings are considered to be excellent.

Expenses ★★★
Global Utilities' expense ratio is 1.7 percent; it has averaged 1.8 percent annually over the past three calendar years. The average expense ratio for the 100 funds in this category is 1.4 percent. This fund's turnover rate over the past year has been 40 percent, while its peer group average has been 110 percent.

Summary
MSDW Global Utilities B receives very high marks across the spectrum. Bear market performance has not been great, but that has more to do with the utility and technology sectors than with fund management. Tax minimization is particularly good—a difficult accomplishment when you consider the industry group. Risk-adjusted returns have been great.

Profile
minimum initial investment $1,000	*IRA accounts available* . . . . yes
subsequent minimum investment . . $100	*IRA minimum investment* $1,000
available in all 50 states. . . . . yes	*date of inception* . . . . Jun. 1994
telephone exchanges. . . . . yes	*dividend/income paid* . . . . quarterly
number of funds in family 253	*largest sector weighting*. . . . . . services

World Bond Funds

Global, or world, funds invest in securities issued all over the world, including the United States. A global bond fund usually invests in bonds issued by stable governments from a handful of countries. These funds try to avoid purchasing foreign government debt instruments from politically or economically unstable nations. Foreign, also known as international, bond funds invest in debt instruments from countries other than the United States.

International funds purchase securities issued in a foreign currency, such as the Japanese yen or the British pound. Prospective investors need to be aware of the potential changes in the value of the foreign currency relative to the U.S. dollar. As an example, if you were to invest in U.K. pound-denominated bonds with a yield of 15 percent and the British currency appreciated 12 percent against the U.S. dollar, your total return for the year would be 27 percent. If the British pound declined by 20 percent against the U.S. dollar, your total return would be –5 percent (15 percent yield minus 20 percent).

Since foreign markets do not necessarily move in tandem with U.S. markets, each country represents varying investment opportunities at different times. According to Salomon Brothers, the current value of the world bond market is estimated to be over $24 trillion. About 40 percent of this bond marketplace is made up of U.S. bonds; Japan ranks a distant second.

Assessing the economic environment to evaluate its effects on interest rates and bond values requires an understanding of two important factors—inflation and supply. During inflationary periods, when there is too much money chasing too few goods, government tightening of the money supply helps create a balance between an economy's cash resources and its available goods. Money supply refers to the amount of cash made available for spending, borrowing, or investing. Controlled by the central banks of each nation, it is a primary tool used to manage inflation, interest rates, and economic growth.

A prudent tightening of the money supply can help bring on disinflation—decelerated loan demand, reduced durable goods orders, and falling prices. During disinflationary times, interest rates also fall, strengthening the underlying value of existing bonds. While such factors ultimately contribute to a healthier economy, they also mean lower yields for government bond investors. A trend toward disinflation currently exists in markets around the world. The worldwide growth in money supply is at its lowest level in 20 years.

As the United States and other governments implement policies designed to reduce inflation, interest rates are stabilizing. This disinflation can be disquieting to the individual who specifically invests for high monthly income. In reality, falling interest rates mean higher bond values, and investors seeking long-term growth or high total returns can therefore benefit from declining rates. Inflation, which drives interest rates higher, is the true enemy of bond investors. It diminishes bond values and, in addition, erodes the buying power of the interest income investors receive.

Income-seeking investors need to find economies where inflation is coming under control, yet where interest rates are still high enough to provide favorable bond yields. An investor who has only U.S. bonds is not taking advantage of such opportunities. If global disinflationary trends continue, those who remain invested only in the United States can lose out on opportunities for high income and total return elsewhere. The gradually decreasing yields on U.S. bonds compel the investor who seeks high income to think globally.

While not all bond markets will peak at the same level, they do tend to follow patterns. Targeting those countries where interest rates are at peak levels and infla-tion is falling not only results in higher income but also creates significant poten-tial for capital appreciation as rates ultimately decline and bond prices increase.

Each year since 1984, at least three government bond markets have provided yields higher than those available in the United States. With over 60 percent of the world's bonds found outside the United States, investors must look beyond U.S. bor-ders to find bonds offering yields and total returns that meet their investment objectives.

According to Lehman Brothers, over the past three years, international bonds have underperformed U.S. bonds by an average of 3.2 percent per year; the figure drops to 0.2 percent over the last five years. Over the past 10 years, the figure edges up to an average of 1.6 percent per year and then falls down to just 1 percent per year over the past 15 years (all periods ending March 31, 2000).

Even with high income as the primary goal (these funds have a typical yield of roughly 6.3 percent annually), investors must consider credit and market risk. By investing primarily in mutual funds that purchase government-guaranteed bonds from the world's most creditworthy nations, you can get an extra measure of credit safety for payment of interest and repayment of principal. By diversifying across multiple markets, fund managers can significantly reduce market risk as well. Diversification is a proven technique for controlling market risk.

The long-term success of a global bond manager depends on expertise in assessing economic trends from country to country, as well as protecting the U.S. valuation of foreign holdings. The most effective way to protect the U.S. dollar value of international holdings is through active currency management. Although its effects over a 10-year period are nominal at best, currency fluctuations can sub-stantially help returns over a 1-, 3-, or 5-year period.

In the simplest terms, effective currency management provides exposure to bond markets worldwide, while reducing the effects of adverse currency changes that can lower bond values. If a portfolio manager anticipates that the U.S. dollar will strengthen, he or she can lock in a currency exchange rate to protect the fund against a decline in the value of its foreign holdings. (A strong dollar means that other cur-rencies are declining in value.) This strategy is commonly referred to as hedging the exposure of the portfolio. If, on the other hand, the manager expects the U.S. dollar to weaken, the fund can stay unhedged to allow it to benefit from the increasing value of foreign currencies.

Investing in global bonds gives you the potential for capital appreciation during periods of declining interest rates. An inverse relationship exists between bond values and interest rates. When interest rates fall, as is the case in most bond markets in the world today, existing bond values climb. Conversely, as interest rates rise, the value of existing bonds declines (they are less desirable since "new" bonds have a higher current yield).

Over the past three and five years, global bond funds have had an average compound return of 3.5 and 7.0 percent per year respectively; the annual returns for the past 10 and 15 years have been 6.5 and 10.2 percent, respectively. The standard deviation for global bond funds has been 9 percent over the past three years. This means that these funds have been less volatile than any equity fund but more volatile than government bond funds (standard deviation of 3 percent). Just 240 funds make up the global bond category. Total market capitalization of this category is approximately $21 billion.

Global bond funds, particularly those with high concentrations in foreign issues, are an excellent risk-reduction tool that should be utilized by a wide range of investors.

World Bond Funds

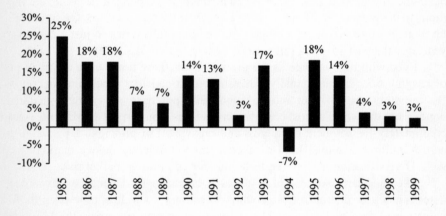

Alliance Global Dollar Government A

P.O. Box 1520
Secaucus, NJ 07096
800-227-4618
www.alliancecapital.com

total return	★★★★
risk reduction	★
management	★★★
current income	★★★★★
expense control	★★★★
symbol AGDAX	17 points
up-market performance	excellent
down-market performance	poor
predictability of returns	fair

Total Return   ★★★★

Over the past five years, Alliance Global Dollar Government A has taken $10,000 and turned it into $24,880 ($11,910 over three years). This translates into an annualized return of 20 percent over the past five years and 6 percent over the past three years. Over the past five years, this fund has outperformed 55 percent of all mutual funds; within its general category it has done better than 75 percent of its peers. World bond funds have averaged 7 percent annually over these same five years (all periods ending March 31, 2000).

During the past five years, a $10,000 initial investment became $8,460 after taxes, assuming a 39.6 percent income tax bracket (state and federal combined) and a capital gains rate of 28 percent. This means that investors in this fund were able to preserve 34 percent of their total returns. Compared to other fixed-income funds, this fund's tax savings are considered to be fair.

Risk/Volatility   ★

Over the past five years, Global Dollar has been safer than just 15 percent of all world bond funds. Since its inception, the fund has had one negative year, while the Lehman Brothers Aggregate Bond Index has had two (off 3 percent in 1994 and 1 percent in 1999); the Salomon Brothers World Government Bond Index fell three times (off 3 percent in 1989, 4 percent in 1997, and 4 percent in 1999). The fund has underperformed the Lehman Brothers Aggregate Bond Index and the Salomon Brothers World Government Bond Index once since the fund's inception.

	last 5 years		since inception	
worst year	-22%	1998	-22%	1998
best year	39%	1996	39%	1996

In the past, Global Dollar has done better than 99 percent of its peer group in up markets and outperformed just 10 percent of its competition in down markets. Consistency, or predictability, of returns for Global Dollar can be described as fair. This fund's risk-related return is very good.

Management   ★★★

There are 45 fixed-income securities in this $220 million portfolio. The average world bond fund today is $90 million in size. Close to 97 percent of the fund's holdings are in bonds. The average maturity of the bonds in this account is 13 years; the weighted coupon rate averages 9.8 percent. The portfolio's fixed-income holdings can be categorized as long-term, low-quality debt. The fund's country exposure is as follows: 20 percent in Argentina, 20 percent in Brazil, 10 percent in Mexico, 5 percent in Columbia, and 5 percent in Ecuador.

Wayne Lyski has managed this fund for the past seven years. Management looks at both macroeconomic and politics when determining the fund's country weightings. The fund can invest a substantial portion of its assets in Brady bonds. There are 156 funds besides Global Dollar within the Alliance Capital family. Overall, the fund family's risk-adjusted performance can be described as very good.

Current Income   ★★★★★

Over the past year, Global Dollar had a 12-month yield of 11.1 percent. During this same 12-month period, the typical world bond fund had a yield that averaged 6.9 percent.

Expenses   ★★★★

Global Dollar's expense ratio is 1.6 percent; it has averaged 1.5 percent annually over the past three calendar years. The average expense ratio for the 250 funds in this category is 1.5 percent. This fund's turnover rate over the past year has been 175 percent, while its peer group average has been 225 percent.

Summary

Alliance Global Dollar Government A rates as the second-best performer in its category for the book. The fund has fairly high risk and has not done a good job during market downturns. This portfolio is an excellent choice for the investor interested in portfolio diversification and the highest possible current income

Profile

minimum initial investment $250	*IRA accounts available* . . . . yes
subsequent minimum investment . . . $50	*IRA minimum investment* $250
available in all 50 states . . . . yes	*date of inception* . . . . Feb. 1994
telephone exchanges. . . . . yes	*dividend/income paid*. . . . . monthly
number of funds in family 157	*average credit quality* . . . . B

Alliance North American Government Income B
P.O. Box 1520
Secaucus, NJ 07096
800-227-4618
www.alliancecapital.com

total return	★★★★
risk reduction	★★★★★
management	★★★★
current income	★★★★★
expense control	★★★
symbol ANABX	21 points
up-market performance	excellent
down-market performance	poor
predictability of returns	excellent

Total Return ★★★★

Over the past five years, Alliance North American Government Income B has taken $10,000 and turned it into $23,860 ($14,050 over three years). This translates into an annualized return of 19 percent over the past five years and 12 percent over the past three years. Over the past five years, this fund has outperformed 55 percent of all mutual funds; within its general category it has done better than 94 percent of its peers. World bond funds have averaged 7 percent annually over these same five years (all periods ending March 31, 2000).

During the past five years, a $10,000 initial investment grew to $12,170 after taxes, assuming a 39.6 percent income tax bracket (state and federal combined) and a capital gains rate of 28 percent. This means that investors in this fund were able to preserve 51 percent of their total returns. Compared to other fixed-income funds, this fund's tax savings are considered to be very good.

Risk/Volatility ★★★★★

Since its inception, the fund has had one negative year, while the Lehman Brothers Aggregate Bond Index has had two (off 3 percent in 1994 and 1 percent in 1999); the Salomon Brothers World Government Bond Index fell three times (off 3 percent in 1989, 4 percent in 1997, and 4 percent in 1999). The fund has underperformed the Lehman Brothers Aggregate Bond Index and the Salomon Brothers World Government Bond Index twice since the fund's inception.

	last 5 years		since inception	
worst year	6%	1998	-31%	1994
best year	30%	1995	30%	1995

In the past, Government Income has done better than 95 percent of its peer group in up markets and outperformed 20 percent of its competition in down markets. Consistency, or predictability, of returns for Government Income can be described as excellent. This fund's risk-related return is also excellent.

Management   ★★★★

There are 30 fixed-income securities in this $2 billion portfolio. The average world bond fund today is $90 million in size. Close to 80 percent of the fund's holdings are in bonds. The average maturity of the bonds in this account is nine years; the weighted coupon rate averages 7.1 percent. The portfolio's fixed-income holdings can be categorized as intermediate-term, high-quality debt. The fund's country exposure is as follows: 40 percent in domestic bonds, 25 percent in Argentina, 25 percent in Mexico, and approximately 10 percent in Canada.

Wayne Lyski has managed this fund for the past nine years. Due to its high exposure in Argentina government issues, the fund is classified as "nondiversified." Management has designed the fund so that it can take advantage of the 1992 North American trade bloc. Close to half of the portfolio is in emerging markets debt. There are 156 funds besides Government Income within the Alliance Capital family. Overall, the fund family's risk-adjusted performance can be described as very good.

Current Income   ★★★★★

Over the past year, Government Income had a 12-month yield of 10.8 percent. During this same 12-month period, the typical world bond fund had a yield that averaged 6.9 percent.

Expenses   ★★★

Government Income's expense ratio is 2.1 percent; it has also averaged 2.1 percent annually over the past three calendar years. The average expense ratio for the 250 funds in this category is 1.5 percent. This fund's turnover rate over the past year has been 175 percent, while its peer group average has been 225 percent.

Summary

Alliance North American Government Income B is for the international investor who likes current income. On a total return basis, the fund has been able to outperform 94 percent of its category while being more risk conscious than any other world bond fund in the book. This is a great fund to own during good economic periods. It is just one of several Alliance offerings that investors should strongly consider.

Profile

minimum initial investment $250	*IRA accounts available* .... yes
subsequent minimum investment ... $50	*IRA minimum investment* $250
available in all 50 states .... yes	*date of inception* .... March 1992
telephone exchanges............. yes	*dividend/income paid*........ monthly
number of funds in family 157	*average credit quality*........... AA

Fidelity New Markets Income

82 Devonshire Street
Boston, MA 02109
800-544-8888
www.fidelity.com

total return	★★★★★
risk reduction	★★
management	★★★★
current income	★★★
expense control	★★★
symbol FNMIX	17 points
up-market performance	excellent
down-market performance	good
predictability of returns	good

Total Return   ★★★★★

Over the past five years, Fidelity New Markets Income has taken $10,000 and turned it into $25,940 ($12,950 over three years). This translates into an annualized return of 21 percent over the past five years and 9 percent over the past three years. Over the past five years, this fund has outperformed 56 percent of all mutual funds; within its general category it has done better than 80 percent of its peers. World bond funds have averaged 7 percent annually over these same five years (all periods ending March 31, 2000).

During the past five years, a $10,000 initial investment grew to $15,300 after taxes, assuming a 39.6 percent income tax bracket (state and federal combined) and a capital gains rate of 28 percent. This means that investors in this fund were able to preserve 59 percent of their total returns. Compared to other fixed-income funds, this fund's tax savings are considered to be excellent.

Risk/Volatility   ★★

Over the past five years, New Markets has been safer than 45 percent of all world bond funds. Since its inception, the fund has had two negative years, while the Lehman Brothers Aggregate Bond Index has also had two (off 3 percent in 1994 and 1 percent in 1999); the Salomon Brothers World Government Bond Index fell three times (off 3 percent in 1989, 4 percent in 1997, and 4 percent in 1999). The fund has underperformed the Lehman Brothers Aggregate Bond Index and the Salomon Brothers World Government Bond Index three times since the fund's inception.

	last 5 years		since inception	
worst year	-24%	1998	-24%	1998
best year	41%	1996	41%	1996

In the past, New Markets has done better than 85 percent of its peer group in up markets and outperformed 50 percent of its competition in down markets. Consistency, or predictability, of returns for New Markets can be described as good. This fund's risk-related return is very good.

Management ★★★★

There are 60 fixed-income securities in this $220 million portfolio. The average world bond fund today is $90 million in size. Close to 80 percent of the fund's holdings are in bonds. The average maturity of the bonds in this account is 20 years; the weighted coupon rate averages 7.8 percent. The portfolio's fixed-income holdings can be categorized as long-term and low quality debt. The fund's country exposure is as follows: 20 percent in Mexico, 20 percent in Argentina, 15 percent in Brazil, and 10 percent in Venezuela.

John Carlson has managed this fund for the past five years. At least two-thirds of the portfolio will always be in emerging markets debt instruments. The fund is classified as "nondiversified." Management does not bet heavily on interest rates or a single country. Instead, the portfolio is very risk conscious—a smart move considering the potentially explosive nature of emerging markets. There are 141 funds besides New Markets within the Fidelity family. Overall, the fund family's risk-adjusted performance can be described as good.

Current Income ★★★

Over the past year, New Markets had a 12-month yield of 8.6 percent. During this same 12-month period, the typical world bond fund had a yield that averaged 6.9 percent.

Expenses ★★★

Fidelity New Markets Income's expense ratio is 1.1 percent; it has also averaged 1.1 percent annually over the past three calendar years. The average expense ratio for the 250 funds in this category is 1.5 percent. This fund's turnover rate over the past year has been 480 percent, while its peer group average has been 225 percent.

Summary

Fidelity New Markets Income is by far the number-one performer in its category for the past five years. The portfolio has also been safer than close to half of its peer group. Tax efficiency has been superb. This fund, like almost all other offerings in the category, is designed for the more aggressive investor who is looking for diversification.

Profile

minimum initial investment $2,500	*IRA accounts available* . . . . yes
subsequent minimum investment . . $250	*IRA minimum investment* $500
available in all 50 states . . . . yes	*date of inception* . . . . May 1993
telephone exchanges . . . . yes	*dividend/income paid* . . . . monthly
number of funds in family 142	*average credit quality* . . . . n/a

T. Rowe Price Emerging Markets Bond
100 East Pratt Street
Baltimore, MD 21202
800-638-5660
www.troweprice.com

total return	★★★
risk reduction	★★★★
management	★★★
current income	★★★★
expense control	★★★★★
symbol PREMX	19 points
up-market performance	good
down-market performance	good
predictability of returns	fair

Total Return ★★★
Over the past five years, T. Rowe Price Emerging Markets Bond has taken $10,000 and turned it into $21,920 ($11,910 over three years). This translates into an annualized return of 17 percent over the past five years and 6 percent over the past three years. World bond funds have averaged 7 percent annually over these same five years (all periods ending March 31, 2000).

Risk/Volatility ★★★★
Over the past five years, Emerging Markets Bond has been safer than 99 percent of all world bond funds. Since its inception, the fund has had one negative year, while the Lehman Brothers Aggregate Bond Index has had two (off 3 percent in 1994 and 1 percent in 1999); the Salomon Brothers World Government Bond Index fell three times (off 3 percent in 1989, 4 percent in 1997, and 4 percent in 1999). The fund has underperformed the Lehman Brothers Aggregate Bond Index and the Salomon Brothers World Government Bond Index once since the fund's inception.

	last 5 years		since inception	
worst year	-23%	1998	-23%	1998
best year	37%	1996	37%	1996

In the past, Emerging Markets Bond has done better than 55 percent of its peer group in up markets and outperformed 45 percent of its competition in down markets. Consistency, or predictability, of returns for Emerging Markets Bond can be described as fair. This fund's risk-related return is very good.

Management ★★★
There are 70 fixed-income securities in this $170 million portfolio. The average world bond fund today is $90 million in size. Close to 95 percent of the fund's holdings are in bonds. The average maturity of the bonds in this account is 14 years; the weighted coupon rate averages 7.7 percent. The portfolio's fixed-income holdings can be categorized as long-term, low-quality debt. The fund's country

exposure is as follows: 20 percent in Argentina, 10 percent in Brazil, 10 percent in Nigeria, 10 percent in Bulgaria, and 5 percent in Poland.

A team has managed this fund for the past seven years. Management invests at least two-thirds of its holdings in emerging markets debt instruments that are rated below investment grade. The portfolio limits risk by emphasizing diversification and by careful country selection. The managers are particularly interested in a country's political reform, adherence to IMF policies, and the likelihood that the country will bring more debt to market. There are 63 funds besides Emerging Markets Bond within the T. Rowe Price family. Overall, the fund family's risk-adjusted performance can be described as good.

Current Income   ★★★★
Over the past year, Emerging Markets Bond had a 12-month yield of 9.8 percent. During this same 12-month period, the typical world bond fund had a yield that averaged 6.9 percent.

Expenses   ★★★★★
T. Rowe Price Emerging Markets Bond's expense ratio is 1.3 percent; it has also averaged 1.3 percent annually over the past three calendar years. The average expense ratio for the 250 funds in this category is 1.5 percent. This fund's turnover rate over the past year has been 75 percent, while its peer group average has been 225 percent.

Summary
T. Rowe Price Emerging Markets Bond is able to maintain a high level of current income due to its ability to keep expenses below par and its turnover way below its category average. The fund has been safer than 99 percent of its peers. This is a recommended fund for the emerging markets investor.

Profile
minimum initial investment $2,500	*IRA accounts available* . . . . yes
subsequent minimum investment . . $100	*IRA minimum investment* $1,000
available in all 50 states . . . . yes	*date of inception* . . . . Dec. 1994
telephone exchanges . . . . yes	*dividend/income paid* . . . . monthly
number of funds in family 64	*average credit quality* . . . . BB

XII.
Summary

Aggressive Growth Funds
Alger Capital Appreciation B
Bridgeway Aggressive Growth
Citizens Emerging Growth
Franklin Small Cap Growth A
Fremont U.S. Micro-Cap
Invesco Dynamics
Pin Oak Aggressive Stock
Putnam New Opportunities A
Sit Small Cap Growth
Smith Barney Aggressive Growth A
USAA Aggressive Growth

Balanced Funds
BlackRock Balanced
Guardian Asset Allocation A
Nations Capital Income Investor A
Oppenheimer Global Growth &
   Income A
Phoenix-Engemann Balanced
   Return A
Preferred Asset Allocation
Van Kampen Harbor A
Vanguard Asset Allocation
Vanguard Tax-Managed Balanced
Wells Fargo Asset Allocation A

Corporate Bond Funds
Alleghany/Chicago Trust
FPA New Income
Fremont
Harbor
Strong Corporate

Global Equity Funds
Acorn International
American Century International
   Growth Investor Shares
IDEX JCC Global A
Janus Worldwide
Julius Baer International Equity A
Legg Mason EuropeFund-Class A
Montgomery Global Opportunities R
Oppenheimer Global A
Pilgrim International Small Cap
   Growth A
Scudder Greater Europe Growth
Smallcap World

Government Bond Funds
American Century Target Maturities
   Trust 2020
Franklin U.S. Government
   Securities Series-Class A
Principal Government Securities
   Income A
State Street Research Government
   Income A
Vanguard Long-Term U.S. Treasury

Growth Funds
AIM Summit I
Alliance Premier Growth B
Federated Growth Strategies Trust A
Harbor Capital Appreciation
Janus Enterprise
Janus Mercury
Marshall Mid-Cap Growth Y
Nicholas-Applegate Growth Equity A
Reynolds Blue Chip Growth

Spectra
Strong Growth
Van Kampen Emerging Growth A
White Oak Growth Stock

Growth and Income Funds
AIM Charter A
Citizens Index
Domini Social Equity
Dreyfus Disciplined Stock
Fidelity
Gateway
IPS Millennium
Strong Total Return
Vanguard 500 Index
Vanguard Tax-Managed Growth &
   Income

High-Yield Bond Funds
Fidelity Advisor High-Yield T
Invesco High-Yield
Lord Abbett Bond-Debenture A
MainStay Hi-Yield Corporate B
MFS High-Income A

Metals and Natural Resources Funds
Franklin Gold A
Vanguard Energy

Money Market Funds
Fidelity Advisors Stable Value
Glenmede Government Cash
Glenmede Tax-Exempt Cash
Harris Insight Government Money N
Ttrust for Credit Unions Money
   Market
Vanguard Municipal Tax-Exempt
   Money Market
Wells Fargo Money Market Trust

Municipal Bond Funds
American Century California High-
   Yield Municipal
American High-Income Municipal
   Bond

Franklin High Yield Tax-Free
   Income A
Franklin New York Tax-Free
   Income A
Scudder Managed Municipal Bonds
T. Rowe Price Tax-Free Income
Van Kampen High-Yield
   Municipal A

Technology Funds
Alliance Technology A
Firsthand Technology Value
John Hancock Global Technology A
T. Rowe Price Science &
   Technology
United Science & Technology A

Utility Stock Funds
AIM Global Utilities A
AXP Utilities Income A
Liberty-Colonial Global Utilities A
MFS Utilities A
MSDW Global Utilities B

World Bond Funds
Alliance Global Dollar
   Government A
Alliance North American
   Government Income B
Fidelity New Markets Income
T. Rowe Price Emerging Markets
   Bond

Appendix A
Glossary of Mutual Fund Terms

Advisor—The individual or organization employed by a mutual fund to give professional advice on the fund's investments and asset management practices (also called the "investment advisor").

Asked or Offering Price—The price at which a mutual fund's shares can be purchased. The asked, or offering, price means the current net asset value per share plus sales charge, if any.

BARRA Growth Index—An index of 152 large-capitalization stocks that are all part of the S & P 500; specifically those with above-average sales and earnings growth.

BARRA Value Index—An index of 363 large-capitalization stocks that are all part of the S & P 500; specifically those with above-average dividend yields and relatively low prices considering their book values.

Bid or Sell Price—The price at which a mutual fund's shares are redeemed (bought back) by the fund. The bid or redemption price usually means the current net asset value per share.

Board Certified—Designation given to someone who has become certified in insurance, estate planning, income taxes, securities, mutual funds, or financial planning. To obtain additional information about the board certified programs or to get the name of a board certified advisor in your area, call (800) 848-2029.

Bottom Up—Refers to a type of security analysis. Management that follows the bottom-up approach is more concerned with the company than with the economy in general. (For a contrasting style, see **Top Down.**)

Broker/Dealer—A firm that buys and sells mutual fund shares and other securities to the public.

Capital Gains Distributions—Payments to mutual fund shareholders of profits (long-term gains) realized on the sale of the fund's portfolio securities. These amounts are usually paid once a year.

Capital Growth—An increase in the market value of a mutual fund's securities, as reflected in the net asset value of fund shares. This is a specific long-term objective of many mutual funds.

Cash Reserves—Short-term, interest-bearing securities that can easily and quickly be converted to cash. Some funds keep cash levels at a minimum and always remain in stocks and/or bonds; other funds hold up to 25 percent or more of their assets in cash reserves (money market instruments) as either a defensive play or as a buying opportunity to be used when securities become depressed in price.

CFS—Also known as Certified Fund Specialist, this is the only designation awarded to brokers, financial planners, CPAs, insurance agents, and other investment advisors who either recommend or sell mutual funds. Fewer than 7,000 people across the country have passed this certification program. To obtain additional information about the CFS program or to get the name of a CFS in your area, call (800) 848-2029.

CPI—The Consumer Price Index (CPI) is the most commonly used yardstick for measuring the rate of inflation in the United States.

Custodian—The organization (usually a bank) that keeps custody of securities and other assets of a mutual fund.

Derivatives—A financial contract whose value is based on, or "derived," from a traditional security, such as a stock or bond. The most common examples of derivatives are futures contracts and options.

Diversification—The policy of all mutual funds to spread investments among a number of different securities in order to reduce the risk inherent in investing.

Dollar-Cost Averaging—The practice of investing equal amounts of money at regular intervals regardless of whether securities markets are moving up or down. This procedure reduces average share costs to the investor, who acquires more shares in the periods of lower securities prices and fewer shares in periods of higher prices.

EAFE—An equity index (EAFE stands for Europe, Australia, and the Far East) used to measure stock market performance outside of the United States. The EAFE is a sort of S & P 500 Index for overseas or foreign stocks. As of the middle of 1997, the EAFE was weighted as follows: 59.5% Europe, 28.8% Japan, 10.6% Pacific Rim, and 1.1% "other."

Exchange Privilege—An option enabling mutual fund shareholders to transfer their investment from one fund to another within the same fund family as their needs or objectives change. Typically, funds allow investors to use the exchange privilege several times a year for a low fee or no fee per exchange.

Expense Ratio—A figure expressed as a percentage of a fund's assets. The main element is the management fee. Administrative fees cover a fund's day-to-day operations, including printing materials, keeping records, paying staff, and renting office space. Sometimes administrative fees are included in the management fee; a number of funds list such fees separately. Roughly half of all funds charge a 12b-1 fee, which pays for a fund's distribution and advertising costs. The 12b-1 fee can be higher than the management or administrative fee.

Indexing—In contrast to the traditional approach to investing that tries to outperform market averages, index investing is a strategy that seeks to match the performance of a group of securities that form a recognized market measure, known as an index.

Investment Company—A corporation, trust, or partnership that invests pooled funds of shareholders in securities appropriate to the fund's objective. Among the benefits of investment companies, compared to direct investments, are professional management and diversification. Mutual funds (also known as open-ended and close-ended investment companies) are the most popular type of investment company.

Investment Objective—The goal that the investor and mutual fund pursue together (e.g., growth of capital or current income).

Large-Cap Stocks—Equities issued by companies with a net worth of at least $7.5 billion dollars.

Long-Term Funds—An industry designation for funds that invest primarily in securities with remaining maturities of more than one year. In this book the term means 15 years or more. Long-term funds are broadly divided into bond and income funds.

Management Fee—The amount paid by a mutual fund to the investment advisor for its services. The average annual fee industrywide is about 0.7 percent of fund assets.

"Market-Neutral" Funds—A strategy that seeks to neutralize market movements by running two portfolios simultaneously—one buys stocks that are predicted to rise, and the other invests an equal amount in a similar assortment of other stocks that are predicted to decline.

Mid-Cap Stocks—Equities issued by companies with a net worth between $1 billion and $7.5 billion dollars.

Mutual Fund—An investment company that pools money from shareholders and invests in a variety of securities, including stocks, bonds, and money market instruments. A mutual fund stands ready to buy back (redeem) its shares at their current net asset value; this value depends on the market value of the fund's portfolio securities at the time of redemption. Most mutual funds continuously offer new shares to investors.

Net Asset Value Per Share—The market worth of one share of a mutual fund. This figure is derived by taking a fund's total assets—securities, cash, and any accrued earnings—deducting liabilities, and dividing by the number of shares outstanding.

No-Load Fund—A mutual fund selling its shares at net asset value without the addition of sales charges.

Passive Management—A portfolio that tries to match the performance of a target index, such as the S & P 500.

Portfolio—A collection of securities owned by an individual or an institution (such as a mutual fund). A fund's portfolio may include a combination of stocks, bonds, and money market securities.

Portfolio Diversification—The average U.S. stock fund has about 30 percent of its assets invested in its 10 largest holdings.

Prospectus—The official booklet that describes a mutual fund, which must be furnished to all investors. It contains information required by the U.S. Securities and Exchange Commission on such subjects as the fund's investment objectives, services, and fees. A more detailed document, known as "Part B" of the prospectus or the "Statement of Additional Information," is available at no charge upon request.

Redemption Price—The amount per share (shown as the "bid" in newspaper tables) that mutual fund shareholders receive when they cash in the shares. The value of the shares depends on the market value of the fund's portfolio securities at the time. This value is the same as net asset value per share.

Reinvestment Privilege—An option available to mutual fund shareholders in which fund dividends and capital gains distributions are automatically turned back into the fund to buy new shares, without charge (meaning no sales fee or commission), thereby increasing holdings.

Russell 2000—An index that represents 2,000 small domestic companies (less than 8 percent of the U.S. equity market).

Sales Charge—An amount charged to purchase shares in many mutual funds sold by brokers or other sales agents. The maximum charge is 8.5 percent of the initial investment; the vast majority of funds now have a maximum charge of 4.75 percent or less. The charge is added to the net asset value per share when determining the offering price.

Short-Term Funds—An industry designation for funds that invest primarily in securities with maturities of less than one year; the term means five years or less in this book. Short-term funds include money market funds and certain municipal bond funds.

Small-Cap Stocks—Equities issued by companies with a net worth of less than $1 billion.

Top Down—Refers to a type of security analysis. Management that follows the top-down approach is very concerned with the general level of the economy and any fiscal policy being followed by the government.

Transfer Agent—The organization employed by a mutual fund to prepare and maintain records relating to the accounts of its shareholders. Some funds serve as their own transfer agents.

Turnover—The percentage of a fund's portfolio that is sold during the year, a percentage rate that can range from 0 to 300 percent or more. The average turnover rate for U.S. stock funds is approximately 80 percent (10 percent for domestic stock index funds).

12b-1 Fee—The distribution fee charged by some funds, named after a federal government rule. Such fees pay for marketing costs, such as advertising and dealer compensation. The fund's prospectus outlines 12b-1 fees, if applicable.

Underwriter—The organization that acts as the distributor of a mutual fund's shares to broker/dealers and investors.

Value Stocks—Stocks that most investors view as unattractive for some reason. They tend to be priced low relative to some measure of the company's worth, such as earnings, book value, or cash flow. Value stock managers try to identify companies whose prices are depressed for temporary reasons that may bounce back strongly if investor sentiment improves.

■ ■ ■

The Securities Act of 1933 requires a fund's shares to be registered with the Securities and Exchange Commission (SEC) prior to their sale. In essence, the Securities Act ensures that the fund provides potential investors with a current prospectus. This law also limits the types of advertisements that may be used by a mutual fund.

The Securities Exchange Act of 1934 regulates the purchase and sale of all types of securities, including mutual fund shares.

The Investment Advisors Act of 1940 is a body of law that regulates certain activities of the investment advisors to mutual funds.

The Investment Company Act of 1940 is a highly detailed regulatory statute applying to mutual fund companies. This act contains numerous provisions designed to prevent self-dealing by employees of the mutual fund company, as well as other conflicts of interest. It also provides for the safekeeping of fund assets and prohibits the payment of excessive fees and charges by the fund and its shareholders.

Appendix B
Who Regulates Mutual Funds?

Mutual funds are highly regulated businesses that must comply with some of the toughest laws and rules in the financial services industry. All funds are regulated by the U.S. Securities and Exchange Commission (SEC). With its extensive rule-making and enforcement authority, the SEC oversees mutual fund compliance chiefly by relying on the four major federal securities statutes mentioned in Appendix A.

Fund assets must generally be held by an independent custodian. There are strict requirements for fidelity bonding to ensure against the misappropriation of shareholder monies. In addition to federal statutes, almost every state has its own set of regulations governing mutual funds.

Although federal and state laws cannot guarantee that a fund will be profitable, they are designed to ensure that all mutual funds are operated and managed in the interests of their shareholders. Here are some specific investor protections that every fund must follow:

- Regulations concerning what may be claimed or promised about a mutual fund and its potential.
- Requirements that vital information about a fund be made readily available (such as a prospectus, the "Statement of Additional Information," also known as "Part B" of the prospectus, and annual and semiannual reports).
- Requirements that a fund operate in the interest of its shareholders, rather than any special interests of its management.
- Rules dictating diversification of the fund's portfolio over a wide range of investments to avoid too much concentration in a particular security.

Appendix C
Dollar-Cost Averaging

Investors often believe that the market will go down as soon as they get in. For these people, and anyone concerned with reducing risk, the solution is dollar-cost averaging (DCA).

Dollar-cost averaging is a simple yet effective way to reduce risk, whether you are investing in stocks or bonds. The premise behind dollar-cost averaging is that if several purchases of a fund are made over an extended period of time, the unpredictable highs and lows will average out. The investor ends up buying some shares at a comparatively low price, others at perhaps a much higher price.

DCA assumes that investors are willing to sacrifice the possibility of having bought all of their shares at the lowest price in return for knowing that they did not also buy every share at the highest price. In short, investors are willing to accept a compromise—a sort of *risk-adjusted* decision.

DCA is based on investing a fixed amount of money in a given fund at specific intervals. Typically, an investor will add a few hundred dollars at the beginning of each month into the XYZ mutual fund. DCA works best if you invest and continue to invest on an established schedule, *regardless of price fluctuations*. You will be buying more shares when the price is down than when it is up. Most investors do not mind buying shares when prices are increasing, since this means that their existing shares are also going up. When this program is followed, losses during market declines are limited, while the ability to participate in good markets is maintained.

Another advantage of DCA is that it increases the likelihood that you will follow an investment program. As with other aspects of our life, it is important to have goals. However, DCA is not something that should be universally recommended. Your risk level determines whether you should use dollar-cost averaging.

From its beginnings well over one hundred years ago, there has been an upward bias in the performance of the stock market. More often than not, the market goes up, not down. Therefore, it hardly makes sense to apply dollar-cost averaging to an investment vehicle, knowing that historically one would be paying a higher and higher price per share over time.

Studies done by the Institute of Business & Finance (800-848-2029) show that over the past 50 years, a dollar-cost averaging program produced inferior returns compared to a lump-sum investment. The institute's studies conclude the following: (1) a DCA program is a good idea for a conservative investor (the person or couple who gives more weight or importance to risk than reward); (2) for investor's whose risk level is anything but conservative, an immediate, one-time investment resulted in better returns the great majority of the time; and (3) there have certainly been periods of time when a DCA program would have benefitted even the extremely aggressive investor, but such periods have not been very common over the past half century and have been quite rare over the past 20, 15, 10, 5, and 3 years.

Example of Dollar-Cost Averaging
($1,000 invested per period)

Period (1)	Cost per share (2)	Number of shares bought with $1,000 (3)	Total shares owned (4)	Total amount invested (5)	Current value of shares (2) x (4) (6)	Net gain or loss (percentage) (6) x (5) (7)
1	$100	10.0	10.0	$1,000	$1,000	0
2	$80	12.5	22.5	$2,000	$1,800	−10.0%
3	$70	14.3	36.8	$3,000	$2,576	−14.1%
4	$60	16.7	53.5	$4,000	$3,210	−19.7%
5	$50	20.0	73.5	$5,000	$3,675	−26.5%
6	$70	14.3	87.8	$6,000	$6,146	+2.4%
7	$80	12.5	100.3	$7,000	$8,024	+14.6%
8	$100	10.0	110.3	$8,000	$11,030	+37.9%

Appendix D
Systematic Withdrawal Plan

A systematic withdrawal plan (SWP) allows you to have a check for a specified amount sent monthly or quarterly to you, or anyone you designate, from your mutual fund account. There is no charge for this service.

This method of getting monthly checks is ideal for the income-oriented investor. It is also a risk reduction technique—a kind of dollar-cost averaging in reverse. A set amount is sent to you each month. In order to send you a check for a set amount, shares of one or more of your mutual funds must be sold, which, in turn, will most likely trigger a taxable event, but only for those shares redeemed.

When the market is low, the number of mutual fund shares being liquidated will be higher than when the market is high because the fund's price per share will be lower. If you need $500 a month and the fund's price is $25.00 per share, 20 shares must be liquidated; if the price per share is $20.00 per share, 25 shares must be sold.

Shown below is an example of a SWP from the Investment Company of America (ICA), a conservative growth and income fund featured in previous editions of this book. The example assumes an initial investment of $100,000 in the fund at its inception, the beginning of 1934. A greater or smaller dollar amount could be used. The example shows what happens to the investor's principal over a 66-year period (January 1, 1934 through May 31, 2000). It assumes that $10,000 is withdrawn from the fund at the end of the first year. At the end of the first year, the $10,000 withdrawal is increased by 4 percent each year thereafter to offset the effects of inflation, which averaged less than 4 percent during this 67-year period. This means that the withdrawal for the second year was $10,400 ($10,000 multiplied by 1.04), for the third year $10,816 ($10,400 multiplied by 1.04), and so on.

Compare this example to what would have happened if the money had been placed in an average fixed-income account at a bank. The $100,000 depositor who took out only $9,000 each year would be in a far different situation. His (or her) original $100,000 was fully depleted by the end of 1948. All the principal and interest payments could not keep up with an annual withdrawal of $9,000.

The difference between ICA and the savings account is over $13 million. The savings account had a total return of $26,300 (plus distribution of the original $100,000 principal); the ICA account had a total return of $13,760,000 ($3,078,000 distributed over 67 years plus a remaining principal, or account balance, of $10,682,000). This difference becomes even more disturbing when you consider that the bank depositor's withdrawals were not increasing each year to offset the effects of inflation. The interest rates used in this example came from the *U.S. Savings & Loan League Fact Book*.

SWP from The Investment Company of America (ICA)
initial investment: $100,000
annual withdrawals of: $10,000 (10%)
the first check is sent: 12/31/34
withdrawals annually increased by: 4%

date	amount withdrawn	value of remaining shares
12/31/34	$10,000	$109,000
12/31/35	$10,400	$185,000
12/31/40	$12,700	$153,000
12/31/45	$15,400	$247,000
12/31/50	$18,700	$212,000
12/31/55	$22,800	$374,000
12/31/60	$27,700	$465,000
12/31/65	$33,700	$679,000
12/31/70	$41,000	$742,000
12/31/75	$50,000	$669,000
12/31/80	$60,700	$1,007,000
12/31/85	$73,900	$1,790,000
12/31/86	$76,900	$2,104,000
12/31/87	$79,900	$2,136,000
12/31/88	$83,100	$2,336,000
12/31/89	$86,500	$2,936,000
12/31/90	$89,900	$2,865,000
12/31/91	$93,500	$3,525,000
12/31/92	$86,500	$3,673,000
12/31/93	$101,200	$3,997,000
12/31/94	$105,200	$3,897,000
12/31/95	$109,400	$4,981,000
12/31/96	$113,780	$5,830,000
12/31/97	$118,330	$7,448,000
12/31/98	$123,060	$9,026,000
12/31/99	$127,987	$10,386,000
5/31/2000	————	$10,682,000

If the ICA systematic withdrawal plan were 8 percent annually instead of 10 percent (but still increased by 4 percent each year to offset the effects of inflation), the investor would have ended up with remaining shares worth $105.5 million, plus withdrawals that totaled $2.46 million.

Next time some broker or banker tells you that you should be buying bonds or CDs for current income, tell them about a systematic withdrawal plan (SWP), a program designed to maximize your income and offset something the CD, T-bill, and bond advocates never mention: inflation.

Appendix E
Load or No-Load—Which is Right for You?

As the amount of information available on mutual funds continues to grow almost exponentially, the load versus no-load debate has intensified. What makes the issue difficult to evaluate is the continued absence of neutrality on either side. Before you learn the real truth, let us first examine who is advocating what, what their biases are, and how each side argues its point.

A number of publications, including *Money, Forbes, Fortune, Kiplinger Personal Investor*, and *Business Week*, favor the no-load camp. Although these publications appear neutral, they are not. First, each one derives the overwhelming majority of its mutual fund advertisements from funds that charge no commission. Second, all of these publications are trying to increase readership; they are in the business of selling copy, not information. A good way to increase or maintain a healthy circulation is by having their readership rely on them for advice—instead of going to a broker or investment advisor.

On the other side is the financial services industry, whose most vocal load supporters include the brokerage, banking, and insurance industries. That's not much of a surprise. These groups are also biased. Like the publication that only makes money by getting you to purchase a copy or having an editorial board whose policy favors no-load funds, much of the financial services community supports a sales charge because that is how they are compensated.

No-load proponents argue that a fund that charges any kind of commission or ongoing marketing fee (which is known as a 12b-1 charge) inherently cannot be as good as a similar investment that has no entry or exit fee or ongoing 12b-1 charge. On its surface, this argument appears logical. After all, if one investor starts off with a dollar invested and the other starts off with somewhere between 99 and 92 cents (commissions range from 1 to 8.5 percent; most are in the 3 to 5 percent range), all other things being equal, the person who has all of his money working for him will do better than someone who has an initial deduction. The press and the no-load funds say that there is no reason to pay a commission because you can do as well or better than the broker or advisor whose job it is to provide you with suggestions and guidance.

The commission-oriented community says you should pay a sales charge because you get what you pay for—good advice and ongoing service. After all, brokers, financial planners, banks that include mutual fund desks, and insurance agents are all highly trained professionals who know things you do not. Moreover, they study the markets on a continuous basis, ensuring that they have more information than any weekend investor. In short, they ask, do you want someone managing your money who has experience and works full-time in this area, or someone such as yourself who has no formal training and whose time and resources are limited?

There is no clear-cut solution. Valid points are raised by both sides. To gain more insight into what course of action (or type of fund) is best for you, let us take a neutral approach. I believe I can give you valid reasons why both kinds of funds make sense, because I have no hidden agenda. True, I am a licensed broker and branch manager of a national securities firm; however, it is also true that the great majority of my compensation is based on a fee for service, meaning that clients who invest solely in no-load funds pay me an annual management fee.

First, you should never pay a commission to someone who knows no more about investing than you do. There is no value added in such a situation, except perhaps during uncertain or negative periods in the market. (This point will be discussed later.) After all, if your broker's advice and mutual fund experience are based solely on the same financial publications you have access to, you are not getting your money's worth by paying a sales charge. I raise this point first because the financial services industry is filled with a tremendous number of inexperienced and ignorant brokers. These people may make a lot of money, but this is usually the result of their connections (they know a lot of people) or marketing skills (they know how to get new business)—neither of which have anything to do with your money.

Brokerage firms, banks, and insurance companies hire stockbrokers based on their sales ability, not their knowledge or analytical ability. The financial analysts at the home office are the ones involved in research and managing money. The fact that your broker has a couple of dozen years of experience in the securities industry or is a vice president may actually be hazardous to your financial health. Extensive experience could mean that the advisor is less inclined to learn about new products or studies because he already has an established client base. Brokers obtain titles such as "vice president" because they outsell their peers. Contests (awards, trips, prizes, and enhanced payouts) are based on how much is sold, period. There has never been an instance of a brokerage firm, bank, or insurance company giving an award to someone based on knowledge or how well a client's account performed.

Second, if your investment time horizon is less than a couple of years, it is a mistake to pay anything more than a nominal fee, something in the 1 percent range. Even though the advice you are receiving may be great, it is hard to justify a 3 to 5 percent commission over the short haul. Sales charges in this range can only be rationalized if they can be amortized over a number of years. Thus, worthwhile advice becomes a bargain if you stay with the investment, or within the same family of mutual funds, for at least three years.

Third, if you are purchasing a fund that charges a fee, find out what you are getting for your money. Question the advisor; find out about his or her training, experience, education, and designations. Equally important, get a clear understanding as to what you will be receiving on an ongoing basis. What kind of continuing education does the broker engage in (attending conferences, reading books, seeking a designation, and so forth)? Finally, make sure your advisor or broker tells you how your investments will be monitored. It is important to know how often you will be contacted and how a buy, hold, or sell decision will be made.

So far, it looks as if I've been pretty tough on my fellow brokers. Well, believe me, I'm even harder on about 99 percent of those do-it-yourself investors. I have been in this business for close to twenty years, and I can tell you that I have rarely met an investor who was better off on his or her own. Here's why.

First, it is extremely difficult to be objective about your own investments. Decisions based on what you have read from a newsletter or magazine or what you learned at a seminar are often a response to current news, such as trade relations with Japan, the value of the U.S. dollar, the state of the economy, or the direction of interest rates. This kind of knee-jerk reaction has proven to be wrong in most cases.

Mind you, out of fairness to those who manage their own investments, amateurs aren't the only ones who make investment errors. As an example, the majority of the major brokerage firms gave a sell signal just before the war in the Persian Gulf. It turned out that this would have been about the perfect time to buy. E.F. Hutton was forced to merge with another brokerage firm because they incorrectly predicted the direction of interest rates (and lost tens of millions of dollars in their own portfolio).

The mutual fund industry itself deserves a healthy part of the blame, as evidenced by their timing of new funds. Take my advice: When you see a number of new mutual funds coming out with the same timely theme (government plus or optioned-enhanced bond funds in the mid-80s, Eastern European funds after German reunification, health care funds a few years ago, derivatives and hedge funds last year), run for cover. By the time these funds come out, the party is about to end. Investors who got into these funds often do well for a number of months but soon face devastating declines.

Your favorite financial publications are also to blame. Their advice is based on a herd instinct—What do our readers think? Instead of providing leadership, they simply reinforce what is most likely incorrect information. For example, for over a year after the 1987 stock market crash, the most popular of these mainstream publications, *Money*, had cover stories that recommended (and extolled the virtues of) safe investments. For almost a year and a half after the crash, this magazine was giving out bad advice. When something goes on sale (stocks, in this case) you should be a buyer, not a seller. Since *Money* routinely surveys (or polls) their readers for feature articles, such behavior (the herd instinct) is understandable but not forgivable.

Besides the lack of objectivity and the constant bombardment of what I call "daily noise" (what the market is doing at the moment, comments from the financial gurus, etc.), there is also the question of your competence. Presumably, you and I could figure out how to fix our own plumbing, sew our own clothes, fix the car when it breaks down, or avoid paying a lawyer by purchasing "do-it-yourself" books. The question then becomes whether it is worth going through the learning curve, and, even supposing we are successful, whether the task would have been better accomplished by someone else—perhaps for less money or better use of our own time. I think the answer is obvious. Each of us has our own area or areas of expertise or skill. You and I rely on others either because they know more than we do about the topic or task at hand or because having someone else help is a more efficient use of our time.

If you're going to seek the services of an investment advisor or broker, it should be because he or she knows more than you do, because he or she is more objective, or because you can make more money doing whatever you do than in taking the time to make complex investment decisions yourself. This is what makes sense. The fact that there are brokers and advisors who put their interests before yours is simply a reality that you must deal with. And the proper way to deal with these conflicts of interest or ignorant counselors is by doing your homework. Ask questions. Just as there are great plumbers, mechanics, lawyers, and doctors, so too are there exceptional investment advisors and brokers. Your job is to find them.

Eliminating load or no-load funds from your investing universe is not the answer. If you are determined never to pay a commission, then you may miss out on the next John Templeton (the Franklin Templeton family of funds), Peter Lynch (Fidelity Magellan Fund), or Jean-Marie Eveillard (SoGen Funds). You will also miss out on some of the very best mutual fund families: American Funds (large), Fidelity-Advisor (medium), and SoGen (small). A better way to proceed is to try to separate good funds from bad ones. After all, an investor is clearly far better off in a good load fund than in a bad no-load one.

The bottom line is that performance, as well as risk-adjusted returns, for load funds often exceeds the returns on no-load funds, and vice versa. The "top 10" list (or whatever number you want to use) for one period may have been dominated by funds that charge a commission, but in just a year or two the top 10 list may be heavily populated by mutual funds with no sales charge or commission.

It might seem strange to be questioning the benefits of financial planning when our society places professions like law and accountancy in such high regard. And certainly I am not suggesting that investors should consider only load funds. But with all the load-fund bashing in recent years, it is important to recognize that no-load funds are not the perfect answer for a large percentage of investors. Approaching the mutual fund industry with an us versus them mentality results in a great deal of misleading information and unfairly discredits the work of skilled financial planners and brokers.

Appendix F
U.S. Compared to Foreign Markets

Investing worldwide gives you exposure to different stages of economic market cycles—which has given international investors an advantage in the past. Foreign equities and bonds have generally offered higher levels of short-, intermediate-, and long-term growth than their domestic counterparts. Not once during the past 13 years was the U.S. stock market the world's top performer.

Top-Performing World Stock Markets:
A 13-Year Review: 1987–1999

year	1st	2nd	3rd	4th	5th
1999	Finland 153%	Malaysia 110%	Singapore 99%	Sweden 80%	Japan 62%
1998	Finland 121%	Belgium 68%	Italty 52%	Spain 50%	France 42%
1997	Portugal 47%	Switzerland 45%	Italty 36%	Denmark 35%	**USA 34%**
1996	Spain 37%	Sweden 35%	Finland 32%	Hong Kong 29%	Ireland 29%
1995	Switzerland 44%	**USA 37%**	Sweden 33%	Spain 30%	Netherlands 28%
1994	Finland 52%	Norway 24%	Japan 22%	Sweden 19%	Ireland 15%
1993	Malaysia 114%	Hong Kong 110%	Finland 101%	Singapore 62%	Ireland 60%
1992	Hong Kong 37%	Switzerland 17%	**USA 6%**	Singapore 6%	France 3%
1991	Hong Kong 43%	Australia 39%	**USA 30%**	Singapore 23%	France 16%
1990	United Kingdom 6%	Austria 5%	Hong Kong 4%	Norway (1%)	Denmark (2%)
1989	Austria 105%	Germany 49%	Norway 46%	Denmark 45%	Singapore 42%
1988	Belgium 54%	Denmark 53%	Sweden 48%	Norway 42%	France 38%
1987	Japan 43%	Spain 41%	United Kingdom 35%	Canada 14%	Denmark 13%

The U.S. stock market has ranked among the five top performers only four times in the past 13 years. During this same period, the U.S. bond market has never claimed the number one spot against other world markets.

Appendix G
The Power of Dividends

The table below shows how important common stock dividends can be. The figures assume a one-time investment of $100,000 in the S & P 500 at the beginning of 1977. The table shows that dividends have increased for 16 of the past 23 years.

Viewed from a different perspective, if you were strictly income-oriented and invested $100,000 in the S & P 500 at the beginning of 1977, you would have received a 4.3 percent return on your investment ($4,310 divided by $100,000) for the calendar year. For the 1998 calendar year, this same investment returned 19.4 percent for the year ($19,440 divided by $100,000); for 1999 the figure decreases to 18.9 percent ($18,811 divided by $100,000). These figures assume that dividends received each year were spent and not reinvested. Moreover, these numbers do not include the over 12-fold growth of capital (the original $100,000 grew to $1,383,155 without dividends) that also took place.

As a point of comparison for the figures described in the previous paragraph, consider what would have happened if the same investor had invested in a 23-year U.S. government bond in 1977. By the end of 1999, 23 years later, the original $100,000 worth of bonds would have matured and had an ending value of $100,000. Additionally, the investor would have received approximately 7 percent for each of these 23 years—a far cry from the increased dividend stream and capital appreciation the S & P 500 experienced over the same period. Perhaps more important, the bond investor could have taken his $100,000 at the beginning of 1999 and invested the money for another 20–30 years, getting a 6 percent return for each of those years (versus the S & P 500 investor who just finished receiving over 18.8 percent, based on $100,000, and presumably will be receiving even greater dividend returns for most of the next 20 years).

The reason why the dividend income stream appears to be so large, even though it was just 1.4 percent in 1999, is that the yields are based on the yearly value of the S & P 500. Starting off with a negative return in 1977 (the S & P 500 was down 11.5 percent, excluding dividends), a $100,000 investment at the beginning of 1977 grew to $1,383,155 by the end of 1999. Thus, 1.36 percent (the actual dividend yield for 1999) multiplied by $1,383,155 equals $18,811 (shown below). As a side note, if no dividends were taken out, and instead reinvested, a $100,000 investment made at the beginning of 1997 in the S & P 500 grew to $3,041,400 by the end of 1999.

Annual Dividends from $100,000 Invested in the S & P 500

Year	S & P 500 dividend
1977	$3,857
1978	$4,821
1979	$5,800
1980	$7,321
1981	$5,640
1982	$7,280
1983	$7,761
1984	$7,177
1985	$10,141
1986	$8,525
1987	$8,465
1988	$10,901
1989	$12,808
1990	$10,445
1991	$11,897
1992	$12,428
1993	$12,427
1994	$12,192
1995	$16,873
1996	$17,254
1997	$19,275
1998	$19,440
1999	$18,811

Appendix H
Growth Stocks versus Value Stocks

Throughout the different equity sections (growth, growth and income, global equity, etc.), the end of each stock fund's "Management" paragraph often mentions whether the fund manager seeks out "growth" or "value" issues. The differences and possible consequences of these two forms of equity selection are shown in the table below.

Value means that the stocks are inexpensive relative to their earnings potential. Growth refers to stocks of companies whose earnings per share are expected to grow significantly faster than the market average.

As you can see by the table, the performance of these two types of stocks can vary from year to year. On a monthly or quarterly basis, the difference is often much more significant than on an annual basis.

The table below shows performance of the S & P Barra Value Index and the S & P Barra Growth Index (dividends reinvested in both indexes). Over the past 15+ years, an investment in both growth stocks and value stocks would have been less volatile than an investment in only one equity style.

Year	Growth stocks	Value stocks
1985	33.3%	29.7%
1986	14.5%	21.7%
1987	6.5%	3.7%
1988	12.0%	21.7%
1989	36.0%	26.1%
1990	0.2%	-6.9%
1991	38.4%	22.6%
1992	5.1%	10.5%
1993	1.7%	18.6%
1994	3.1%	-0.6%
1995	38.1%	37.0%
1996	24.0%	22.0%
1997	36.5%	30.0%
1998	42.2%	14.7%
1999	52.8%	6.5%
2000 (1st qtr.)	12.6%	1.6%

Source: S & P 500 Barra Value Index and the S & P 500 Barra Growth Index.

Although growth stocks have outperformed value stocks in recent years, value has been the winner in five of the past seven decades. The figures below are average annual returns for each of the past seven decades.

decade	growth	value
1930s	1.9%	-4.6%
1940s	7.3%	17.9%
1950s	17.9%	21.8%
1960s	8.0%	12.3%
1970s	3.8%	20.8%
1980s	14.7%	20.8%
1990s	19.4%	15.3%

The table below shows the annualized returns of growth versus value funds, as categorized by Morningstar.

Total Returns through March 31, 2000

mutual fund category	3 year	5 year	10 year
large growth	35.8%	28.7%	19.7%
large value	14.0%	17.2%	14.1%
mid-cap growth	40.9%	28.5%	19.6%
mid-cap value	11.3%	14.7%	12.8%
small growth	35.2%	24.7%	19.6%
small value	8.9%	14.1%	12.2%

Appendix I
Stock Market Declines

If you are a relatively new investor, you may not have had first-hand experience with a bear market. Since corrections are a natural part of the stock market cycle, it is important to ask yourself how you would react. Would you panic or would you be patient? It is difficult to know for sure. Stock market fire drills do not really work, because it is one thing to ponder your reaction to a market meltdown—another to live through one with your financial goals at stake. However, an historical perspective may help you gain a better perspective and, more importantly, may help you remain patient.

The table below shows all of the periods when the U.S. stock market dropped 15 percent or more from 1953 through the end of 1999 (a "bear market" is defined as a drop of 20 percent or more; a "correction" is a decline of 10 percent or more). Of these 14 down markets, the worst took place during the 1973–74 recesssion, resulting in the greatest loss since the Great Depression. Surprisingly, half of the 48 percent loss that took place during the 1973–74 decline was recovered within five months after the drop.

During the 1998 calendar year, the S & P 500 dropped 15.4 percent from the end of June through the end of August. It took just four months (end of November) for the market to recover this loss and move on to yet another high.

U.S. Market Declines of 15% or More (1953–1999)

bear year	% decline	# of down months	months to recovery
1953	15%	9	6
1956–57	16%	6	5
1957	20%	3	12
1961–62	29%	6	14
1966	22%	9	6
1968–70	37%	18	22
1973–74	48%	21	64
1975	15%	2	4
1977–78	18%	14	6
1978	17%	2	10
1980	22%	2	4
1981–82	22%	13	3
1987	34%	2	23
1990	20%	3	23
1998	15%	2	5
average	23%	7	14

One possible strategy for avoiding market declines is to sit on the sidelines until the volatility passes. According to a study by the University of Michigan, this is a bad idea. An investor who was on the sidelines during the best 1 percent of all trading days from 1963 to 1999 missed 95 percent of the market's gains.

These included investors who were sidelined in 1995 by the poor showing in 1994 for both stocks and bonds as well as those stock market investors who bailed out in 1996 because the 38 percent gain in 1995 made them nervous about a downturn. Those who bailed out in 1997 because the 23 percent gain in 1996 made them nervous missed a 29 percent gain in 1998!

Being in the market when it falls is not the greatest risk most stock investors face, it is being out of the market when it soars. The best strategy is to keep investing through any market environment.

The problem is that no one rings a bell when the market hits bottom. Similarily, you do not get any advance notice that the market is turning around. Stocks tend to gain significant ground in short periods; missing out on the first, brief phase of a recovery can be costly. For example, when the stock market took off in August 1982, ending years of mediocre performance, the market jumped 42 percent in just three months. From the October low of the 1987 crash to the end of December, just two months later, stocks rebounded 22 percent. And in the four months after the October 1990 Gulf War low, with the U.S. still mired in recession, the stock market shot up more than 30 percent.

Trying to get out of the market and get back in calls for two right decisions. There is no evidence that professional investors, market timers, brokers, financial analysts, or anyone else can get these calls right with any degree of consistency. One bad market timing call can seriously handicap lifetime performance.

The question then becomes, if stock prices fall hard, should you cut your losses and play it safe? Of all the options that investors have, this one may be the worst solution and the most devastating. An investment of $10,000 in common stocks, as measured by the S & P 500, on the day before the October 1987 crash would have fallen to $7,995 in a single day. Leaving the account intact would have resulted in a whopping 693 percent gain through December 31, 1999. Taking the $7,995 and reinvesting it in U.S. Treasury bills would have resulted in a gain of just 89 percent over the same period.

Appendix J
A Reason Not to Index

Appendix D showed a systematic withdrawal program (SWP) for Investment Company of America (ICA), a growth and income portfolio from the American Funds Group, starting with its first full year through the middle of 2000. Let us now look at two more examples of a SWP, comparing results from Washington Mutual, another growth and income fund offered through the American Funds Group, with the S & P 500.

For this example, a different time frame (January 1, 1973 through May 31, 2000) will be used, showing radically different results. Like the ICA example, it is assumed that a single $100,000 investment is made and that all capital gains and dividend payments are automatically reinvested into the fund. Also, less money is taken out in this example (8 percent, or $8,000 per year).

As you can see, applying an SWP to the S & P 500 (or an index fund that matches the S & P 500) results in the investor being flat broke by December 1996 (all of the $100,000 and its resulting growth has been depleted). Yet, by using professional management like that found with Washington Mutual (abbreviated as WM below), not only are the cumulative distributions greater ($216,000 versus $188,700), so is the remaining principal ($959,160 versus zero).

Systematic Withdrawal Program Using a
Growth & Income Fund (Washington Mutual) versus the S & P 500
$100,000 Invested in Each Portfolio on January 1, 1973

date	cumulative withdrawal from WM	cumulative withdrawal from S & P 500	remaining value of Washington Mutual (WM)	remaining value of S & P 500
1/1/73	0	0	$100,000	$100,000
12/31/73	$8,000	$8,000	$79,280	$76,890
12/31/74	$16,000	$16,000	$57,460	$48,370
12/31/75	$24,000	$24,000	$74,830	$58,050
12/31/80	$64,000	$64,000	$89,980	$52,930
12/31/85	$104,000	$104,000	$170,740	$42,890
12/31/90	$144,000	$144,000	$260,020	$28,520
12/31/95	$184,000	$184,000	$503,180	$3,910
12/31/96	$192,000	$188,700	$596,530	$0
12/31/97	$200,000		$787,050	
12/31/98	$208,000		$931,140	
12/31/99	$216,000		$933,800	
5/31/2000	$216,000		$959,160	

For the S & P 500, the average annual total return for this illustration was 6.0 percent (January 1, 1973 through December 15, 1996 when the money ran out) and 18.8 percent for the last 10 years. For Washington Mutual Fund (WM), the average annual total return for this illustration was 12.5 percent (January 1, 1973 through May 31, 2000) and 14.6 percent for the last 10 years.

Two conclusions can be reached from this illustration. First, there is a benefit to professional management versus a passively managed portfolio such as the S & P 500 (which as an index fund is also considered to be a growth and income fund). Second, moderate gains or advances in some early years can make a great difference later on (compare the value of both portfolios at the end of 1974 and 1975 versus what happened in later years, such as 1980 and 1985, when the gaps become huge due to earlier gains by Washington Mutual).

Appendix K
A Benefit of Balanced Funds

Prudence can pay off. Even though stocks usually outperform bonds, there have been extensive periods of time when a balanced portfolio (30 percent to 70 percent in bonds and the balance in stocks) can be a better way to go than a pure stock portfolio (represented by the S & P 500 below)—especially when current income is needed.

The table below shows a systematic withdrawal program (SWP) for Income Fund of America (a balanced portfolio from the American Funds Group) versus a similar SWP using the S & P 500. Both withdrawal programs assume a one-time investment of $200,000 made on January 1, 1974, annual withdrawals made at the end of each year, and a first-year withdrawal of $15,000 (7.5 percent of $200,000) that is then increased by 3.5 percent for each subsequent year (in order to offset the effects of inflation). As you can see, the balanced fund comes out ahead.

Systematic Withdrawal Program
Using a Balanced Fund (IFA) and the S & P 500
$200,000 Invested in Each Portfolio on January 1, 1972

date	cumulative withdrawal from IFA	cumulative withdrawal from S & P 500	remaining value of IFA	remaining value of S & P 500
1/1/74	0	0	$200,000	$200,000
12/31/74	$15,000	$15,000	$165,240	$131,834
12/31/75	$30,525	$30,525	$208,287	$164,740
12/31/76	$46,593	$46,593	$265,307	$187,368
12/31/80	$116,691	$116,691	$248,709	$191,095
12/31/85	$219,029	$219,029	$488,588	$221,773
12/31/90	$340,574	$340,574	$632,843	$257,400
12/31/95	$484,932	$484,932	$1,067,108	$347,972
12/31/96	$516,905	$516,905	$1,197,075	$394,987
12/31/97	$549,997	$549,997	$1,428,937	$493,109
12/31/98	$584,247	$584,247	$1,529,268	$597,424
12/31/99	$619,696	$619,696	$1,501,077	$686,033
5/31/2000	————	————	$1,511,848	$665,123

For the S & P 500, the average annual total return for this illustration was 11.5 percent (Jan. 1uary 1974 through May 31, 2000) and 18.8 percent for the last 10 years. For Income Fund of America (IFA), the average annual total return for this illustration was 13.1 percent and 11.2 percent for the last 10 years.

Appendix L
Asset Categories:
Total Returns for the Last 13 Years

The table below shows the year-by-year returns for eight different asset categories. All of the returns are in U.S. dollars, expressed as percentages, and include the reinvestment of any dividends, interest, and capital gains. The boldface type indicates the best-performing category for the year (source: Micropal).

Category	'87	'88	'89	'90	'91	'92	'93	'94	'95	'96	'97	'98	'99
S & P 500	5	17	32	-3	31	8	10	1	38	23	33	29	21
Small U.S. stocks	-9	25	16	-20	46	18	19	-2	28	17	22	-3	30
Foreign stocks (EAFE)	25	28	11	-24	12	-12	33	8	11	6	2	20	27
Emerging market stocks	14	58	55	-30	18	0	68	-1	-13	8	-15	-25	74
U.S. gov't / corp. bonds	3	8	15	9	16	7	10	-3	19	4	10	10	-1
High-yield bonds	5	13	1	-10	46	16	17	-1	19	11	13	4	5
Foreign gov't bonds	35	2	-3	15	16	5	15	6	20	4	-4	18	3
U.S. T-bills	6	7	8	8	5	4	3	4	5	5	5	5	5

Appendix M
Stock Gains, Losses, and Averages

In the five calendar years ending December 1932, the S & P 500 had a cumulative loss of almost 49 percent. Although this is quite a depressing figure (particularly since similar losses took place during the 1973–74 recession), basing your stock market strategy on a couple of terrible periods is foolish.

To get a better feel for the likely range of returns you will experience, let us examine what happens when you throw out the worst 10 percent and best 10 percent of the years and then look at performance for the remaining 80 percent of the time. Here is what you would find, looking at rolling calendar year periods from 1871 through 1998 (all figures are from *Stocks for the Long Run* by Jeremy Siegel and The Institute of Business and Finance):

- for 5-year periods (124 observations) and then eliminating the 12 best and 12 worst such periods, annualized returns ranged from 0.1 percent to 18.5 percent;
- for 10-year periods (119 observations), annualized returns ranged from 2.8 percent to 15.9 percent;
- for 20-year periods (109 observations), annualized returns ranged from 5.3 percent to 13.8 percent;
- for 30-year periods (99 observations), annualized returns ranged from 6.0 percent to 11.8 percent.

Note: If you earned 5.3 percent a year for 20 years, your money would grow 181 percent. If you earned 6.0 percent a year for 30 years, you would end up with a growth of 474 percent.

Looking at returns and variability from a different perspective Jeffrey Schwartz, a senior consultant at Ibbotson, provides an even wider range of returns. According to his figures, since the end of World War II (throwing out the best 5 percent and the worst 5 percent of the years):

- 5-year returns vary from 2.5 percent to 22.7 percent a year;
- 10-year returns vary from 4.0 percent to 20.4 percent a year;
- 20-year returns vary from 6.0 percent to 15.8 percent a year.

Appendix N
The 20 Largest Mutual Funds versus Category Averages

The table below lists the 20 largest mutual funds, their size, and total return figures for the past 3, 5, and 10 years. The second set of tables shows annualized returns for different mutual fund categories (all periods ending March 31, 2000).

The 20 Largest Mutual Funds:
Total Return Figures through March 31, 2000

	assets (billions)	3 year	5 year	10 year
Fidelity Magellan Fund	$101	121%	210%	506%
Vanguard 500 Index, Inv.	99	107	226	456
ICA	53	88	181	367
Fidelity Contrafund	47	117	235	705
Janus Fund	46	178	301	640
Washington Mutual Inv.	44	55	147	314
Janus Worldwide	43	164	334	n/a
Fidelity Gro & Inc	42	83	180	455
Amer Cent: AC Ultra, Inv.	42	157	277	898
Fidelity Growth Co.	38	232	391	875
Europacific Growth	37	102	180	368
Janus Twenty	37	285	537	1,090
New Perspective Fund	34	115	199	413
Growth Fund of America	33	185	292	593
Fidelity Blue Chip Growth	28	125	218	685
Vanguard Instl Indx; Ins	28	107	228	n/a
Putnam Voyager A	27	184	293	754
Fidelity Aggr Grow	22	319	489	n/a
Vanguard Wellington	22	41	102	233
Vanguard PRIMECAP	22	177	323	755

Mutual Fund Categories:
Annualized Return Figures through March 31, 2000

Annualized Total Return Basis

Investment Objective	1 yr	3 yr	5 yr
GENERAL STOCK FUNDS			
Large-cap growth	26.4	27.7	25.6
Large-cap value	-0.9	12.7	18.0
Mid-cap growth	61.1	32.1	24.4
Mid-cap value	4.9	9.2	13.5
Small-cap growth	57.7	27.1	21.9
Small-cap value	6.4	5.0	13.1
Multi-cap growth	46.0	30.1	26.1
Multi-cap value	-3.8	7.8	14.2
Equity-income	-6.6	7.1	13.6
S & P 500 objective	6.6	19.0	23.2
Balanced (includes bonds)	4.4	10.5	13.4
SECTOR FUNDS			
Science & technology	84.0	53.5	36.0
Health/biotechnology	67.7	23.8	24.0
Financial services	-10.1	7.5	17.6
Real estate	2.1	0.8	9.7
Telecommunications	32.4	38.9	29.4
Natural resources	15.3	2.3	9.4
WORLD			
Global	22.0	15.4	17.0
International	24.5	11.8	13.2
European region	27.0	16.1	17.6
Emerging markets	15.8	-4.1	2.9
BOND FUNDS			
High current yield	-0.7	2.6	6.4
General municipal	1.0	3.4	4.8
Intermediate inv. grade	3.4	5.0	5.4
GNMA	4.5	5.2	5.7
Corporate A-rated	2.8	4.7	5.2
General U.S. government	3.6	5.1	5.2
Intermediate municipal	2.5	3.8	4.7
Intermediate U.S. government	3.5	4.9	5.1
Corporate BBB-rated	2.3	4.3	5.6

Appendix O
Decades at a Glance (1930–1999)

The text and figures below cover the past seven decades (1930–1999). The summary information is useful in gaining an historic perspective of the market. Perhaps more importantly, it shows that despite a number of catastrophic events, the U.S. stock market has continued to trend upward.

Decade at a Glance (the 1930s)
Economic distress swept the nation after the October 1929 stock market crash. The Great Depression, which lasted from 1930 to 1936, bottomed in 1933, when one-fourth of the civilian labor force was unemployed.

Index	Average annual total return
Standard & Poor's 500 Index	-0.1%
Long-term U.S. government bonds	4.9%
U.S. Treasury bills	0.6%
	Average for the decade
Short-term interest rates	1.5%
Annual inflation rate	-2.1%
Unemployment rate	18.2%

Decade at a Glance (the 1940s)
Japan's attack on Pearl Harbor on December 7, 1941, thrust the United States into World War II and a wartime economy. In the midst of price controls and consumer goods shortages, upward trends marked the stock market from 1943 to 1946, with a vigorous bull market in 1945 as the war ended.

Index	Average annual total return
Standard & Poor's 500 Index	9.2%
Long-term U.S. government bonds	3.2%
U.S. Treasury bills	0.4%
	Average for the decade
Short-term interest rates	1.6%
Annual inflation rate	5.4%
Unemployment rate	5.2%

Decade at a Glance (the 1950s)

While Eisenhower guided America through the early years of the Cold War, the stock market made gains and by year-end 1954 stock prices had reached their highest levels since 1929. This exuberance was followed by a bear market lasting 18 months, from April 1956 through October 1957, during which the S & P 500 declined 19.4 percent.

Index	Average annual total return
Standard & Poor's 500 Index	19.4%
Long-term U.S. government bonds	0.1%
U.S. Treasury bills	1.9%
	Average for the decade
Short-term interest rates	3.2%
Annual inflation rate	2.2%
Unemployment rate	4.5%

Decade at a Glance (the 1960s)

American culture, long restrained by the sense of team spirit and conformity induced by the crises of depression, war, and the ongoing Cold War, broke loose in a multitude of swift changes. The economy was equally turbulent, and the stock market cycles recorded three bear markets. In 1963, President Kennedy submitted a federal budget with the largest deficit in history, $10 billion.

Index	Average annual total return
Standard & Poor's 500 Index	7.8%
Long-term U.S. government bonds	1.5%
U.S. Treasury bills	3.9%
	Average for the decade
Short-term interest rates	5.3%
Annual inflation rate	2.5%
Unemployment rate	4.8%

Decade at a Glance (the 1970s)

When The Organization of the Petroleum Exporting Countries (OPEC) quintupled oil prices in 1973, a deep recession hit America. The stock market plunged 45.1 percent, from January 1973 through December 1974. Unemployment reached 8.7 percent in March 1975, the highest level since 1941. In 1979, commercial banks raised their prime rates to a whopping 15.7 percent.

Index	Average annual total return
Standard & Poor's 500 Index	5.9%
Long-term U.S. government bonds	5.5%
U.S. Treasury bills	6.3%
	Average for the decade
Short-term interest rates	8.1%
Annual inflation rate	7.4%
Unemployment rate	6.2%

Decade at a Glance (the 1980s)

President Reagan signed extensive budget- and tax-cutting legislation in 1981, and sweeping tax-reform legislation in 1986. The "Black Monday" stock market crash of October 19, 1987 became the largest one-day stock market decline on record, as the Dow Jones Industrial Average fell an astounding 508.32 points.

Index	Average annual total return
Standard & Poor's 500 Index	17.6%
Long-term U.S. government bonds	12.6%
U.S. Treasury bills	8.9%
	Average for the decade
Short-term interest rates	11.8%
Annual inflation rate	5.1%
Unemployment rate	7.3%

Decade at a Glance (the 1990s)

From November 1990 through the end of 1999, stock market investors were rewarded by the longest bull market in history, which added about $7.2 trillion to households' balance sheets. The Asian economic crisis briefly shook U.S. investor confidence as the Dow Jones Industrial Average experienced the single-biggest point loss ever on October 27, 1997. The decade ended with technology stocks fueling the Nasdaq Index to its highest close ever on December 31, 1999.

Index	Average annual total return
Standard & Poor's 500 Index	18.2%
Long-term U.S. government bonds	8.8%
U.S. Treasury bills	4.9%
	Average for the decade
Short-term interest rates	8.0%
Annual inflation rate	2.9%
Unemployment rate	5.8%

Appendix P
Individual Stocks versus Mutual Funds

If you believe recent headlines in the media, you might think that mutual funds are a thing of the past and that today's investors prefer to choose individual stocks for their portfolio. However, as you will see in the table below, funds are more relevant now than they were in 1924, when MFS invented the mutual fund. Unlike individual stocks, funds provide active management with the risk-reduction benefit of diversification. Perhaps no other investment has provided a better balance of risk and return.

Did you know that:

- Over the past five years ended December 31, 1999, **31 percent** of stocks produced negative annualized total returns as compared to **less than one-half of 1 percent** of equity mutual funds
- In 1999, the standard deviation of individual stocks was **229**, while it was only **37.3** for equity mutual funds
- Historically, individual stocks have had higher annualized average returns over the 1-year period, but equity mutual funds produced higher returns over the **3-, 5-,** *and* **10-year periods** ended December 31, 1999

Individual U.S. Stocks	1 year (1999)	3 years (1997–99)	5 years (1995–99)	10 years (1990–99)
# of stocks in existence	6,242	5,323	4,122	2,397
average annualized return	42.7%	6.0%	10.3%	9.5%
median annualized return	-3.9%	2.0%	9.5%	9.3%
highest return	11,060%	476.0%	219.8%	97.0%
lowest return	-99.97%	-90.8%	-79.7%	-42.9%
standard deviation	229	37	25	14
# of stocks with negative annualized return	3,343	2,432	1,280	521
% of stocks with negative annualized return	54%	6%	31%	22%

U.S. Equity Mutual Funds	1 year (1999)	3 years (1997–99)	5 years (1995–99)	10 years (1990–99)
# of funds in existence	2,448	1,877	1,414	737
average annualized return	27.7%	20.4%	21.4%	15.0%
median annualized return	18.0%	18.5%	20.8%	14.7%
highest return	493.7%	119.4%	58.2%	37.5%
lowest return	-29.6%	-17.6%	-17.1%	-8.6%
standard deviation	37.3	12.6	7.7	4.6
# of funds with negative annualized return	311	46	5	3
% of funds with negative annualized return	13%	2.5%	0.35%	0.4%

Appendix Q
Time in the Market, Not Timing the Market

While every investor strives to buy when prices are low, a disciplined, long-term investment program in Templeton Growth Fund can produce impressive results—even when an investor's timing would appear to be terrible. The table below illustrates this point. Both halves assume an individual invested $5,000 in Templeton Growth Fund-Class A every year for the past 20 years. The left side of the table shows what would have happened if the purchases had been made when the fund hit its yearly high, while the right side shows the results of purchases made when the fund hit its yearly low.

The Worst Case: Investing Each Year at the High for Share Prices			The Best Case: Investing Each Year at the Low for Share Prices		
Date of Fund High	Cumulative Investment	Value of Account on 12/31	Date of Fund Low	Cumulative Investment	Value of Account on 12/31
11/20/80	$5,000	4,560	3/27/80	$5,000	6,650
4/27/81	10,000	8,930	9/25/81	10,000	11,770
12/31/82	15,000	14,610	8/12/82	15,000	19,470
10/10/83	20,000	24,000	1/3/83	20,000	32,180
1/9/84	25,000	29,210	6/15/84	25,000	38,380
12/31/85	30,000	42,090	1/4/85	30,000	55,240
4/21/86	35,000	55,900	1/2/86	35,000	72,790
10/5/87	40,000	61,270	12/29/87	40,000	79,870
10/21/88	45,000	80,440	1/12/88	45,000	104,670
10/4/89	50,000	103,150	1/3/89	50,000	134,240
7/18/90	55,000	97,870	11/1/90	55,000	127,160
10/1/91	60,000	133,610	1/15/91	60,000	173,650
5/29/92	65,000	143,910	11/17/92	65,000	186,030
10/18/93	70,000	196,050	1/13/93	70,000	253,300
9/16/94	75,000	202,220	12/27/94	75,000	260,270
9/21/95	80,000	247,180	1/23/95	80,000	317,800
10/18/96	85,000	303,200	1/10/96	85,000	388,960
10/7/97	90,000	356,820	12/23/97	90,000	456,880
4/15/98	95,000	352,190	10/26/98	95,000	450,640
7/15/99	100,000	464,550	2/17/99	100,000	594,297

Average Annual Rate of Return: 13.8%   *Average Annual Rate of Return: 15.5%*